The Curse Removed

The Curse Removed

A Look at Image-Based Atonement

DAN SALTER

RESOURCE *Publications* · Eugene, Oregon

THE CURSE REMOVED
A Look at Image-Based Atonement

Copyright © 2021 Dan Salter. All rights reserved. Except for brief quotations in critical publications or reviews, no part of this book may be reproduced in any manner without prior written permission from the publisher. Write: Permissions, Wipf and Stock Publishers, 199 W. 8th Ave., Suite 3, Eugene, OR 97401.

Resource Publications
An Imprint of Wipf and Stock Publishers
199 W. 8th Ave., Suite 3
Eugene, OR 97401

www.wipfandstock.com

PAPERBACK ISBN: 978-1-7252-5470-1
HARDCOVER ISBN: 978-1-7252-5469-5
EBOOK ISBN: 978-1-7252-5471-8

Unless otherwise noted, all Scripture quotations are taken from the Holman Christian Standard Bibleâ, Copyright © 1999, 2000, 2002, 2003, 2009 by Holman Bible Publishers. Used by permission. Holman Christian Standard Bibleâ, Holman CSBâ, and HCSBâ are federally registered trademarks of Holman Bible Publishers.

08/06/21

To Becky
the life of my passion

*"He leads me beside still waters.
He restores my soul."*

Psalm 23: 2b–3a, ESV

Contents

Acknowledgments ix
Abbreviations xi
Introduction xiii

PART 1 | FOUNDATION FOR RELATIONSHIP

1. Creating for Relationship — 3
2. Creation Account 1—the Physical — 13
3. Creation Account 2—the Spiritual — 22
4. The Covenant of Life — 29

PART 2 | FALL FROM PURPOSE

5. Adam & Eve's Choice — 41
6. Sin's Consequence — 50
7. Sin's Legacy — 60
8. God's Wrath — 71

PART 3 | RESTORATION PLAN FORGED

9. God's Righteousness — 81
10. Redeemer Qualifications — 90
11. Redemption & Forgiveness — 99
12. Justice & Mercy — 112

PART 4 | ATONEMENT—IMAGED & ACCOMPLISHED

13. Son of God; Son of Man — 129
14. False Ideas about Sacrifice — 138
15. The Day of the Atonement — 147
16. The Bible's Emphasis on Blood — 156

PART 5 | RESTORATION—ALREADY & BEYOND

17	The New Covenant of Life	165
18	New Covenant Living through This Age	176
19	The End of the Age & the Finishing of the Atonement	187
20	Heaven!	195

Appendix: Kinship Theology   203
Bibliography   207

Acknowledgments

Günter Salter—
My father was the consummate teacher. One great lesson I learned from him was to make sure I knew why I believed what I believed. I am grateful he did not force-feed me truth but rather led me to the buffet.

Johanna Salter—
From my mother I learned strength. The uncompromising steadiness of her love, faith, and enthusiasm gave me the security to pursue this project. Her example always challenges me to offer truth with humility and kindness.

Caren Silvester—
From playing school in the basement as kids to her editorial slashing of my nominalizations and passives, my sister has taught me English. She has also been my theology advisor, calming and clarifying my many *eureka!* moments. I don't know if I can call this work any more mine than hers. She often shook her head at my sentence structures, but her clarity in focusing my thoughts has been invaluable.

Willie Robinson—
So many mornings I'd find in my inbox another question from Willie. His faithful dissection of my Bible study summaries often challenged me to flesh out my thoughts even for my own sake.

Chris and Rachel Salter—
The confidence of my son and the dedication of his wife have often buoyed my determination (without their even knowing). They've helped shake me from doubt and weariness to keep my hope alive.

Angela Salter—

I value my daughter's support and shared vision. I appreciate her spirit which slides up so easily alongside mine and makes me smile in our dance.

Becky Salter—

To inspire literally means to breathe into, and Becky most of all breathes her life into mine, inflaming my passion. For her love and belief in me, I dedicate this book to her.

Abbreviations

CSB	Christian Standard Bible
ESV	English Standard Version
HCSB	Holman Christian Standard Bible
KJV	King James Version
KT	Kinship Theology
NASB	New American Standard Bible
NET	New English Translation
NIV	New International Version
NKJV	New King James Version
NRSV	New Revised Standard Version
NT	New Testament
OT	Old Testament
TGB	Truth, Goodness, and Beauty (God's essence)

Introduction

I'll sing aloud, that all the World may hear,
The Triumph of the buried Conquerer.
How Hell was by its Pris'ner Captive led,
And the great slayer Death slain by the Dead.

—Abraham Cowley, from "Christ's Passion"

For this reason he had to be made like them, fully human in every way,
in order that he might become a merciful and faithful high priest
in service to God, and that he might make atonement
for the sins of the people.

—Hebrews 2:17

I LOVE THE MORNINGS. Even before dawn breaks, the gradual turning of the sky's black into gray somehow makes me smile. I especially like winter mornings when I can sit wrapped in my robe in front of a warm fire, snuggled against the blustery cold just beyond the window. Coffee in hand, no place I need to go—you'd think it a wonder I ever get any work done. But it is actually on those comfortable, cozy mornings that I find myself most productive, when my body, so satisfied, allows my mind to carve and chisel in flashes that make my late-afternoon mind intensely jealous.

I dedicate many of those early hours to study and preparation for the Bible studies I teach. Looking back over my 30 to 40 years of notes, outlines, and lesson summaries, I realize I've changed positions on several interpretations I once so fiercely held. I used to be afraid of what others would think when they learned I'd changed my opinions. Would they even want to listen to a Bible teacher whose judgment of a passage may be different next year? But while doctrinal changes may be triggered by mere attraction to the new and shiny (or by the frog-in-boiling-water slide into current culture), adjustments may also occur for critically good reasons—from a deepening appreciation for and firmer grasp of the Bible's unfolding revelation.

My teaching is—as should be all biblical teaching—an offering to others for consideration. Recipients are always urged to carry the ideas home for their own deliberation whether to incorporate them into their own personal faith pursuits. That's why it is strange to me that some teachers, in dogmatic certainty, counsel others to resist even considering advancement outside their own defined ideas or those which they frame as orthodox. Also alarming are their scare tactics, pressing their points (primarily in hierarchical packs) to force the less resolute to toe the line. When speaking of the atonement, the majority view, at least for this time period of late twentieth to early twenty-first century American theology, is the penal substitution theory.

Penal substitution is so forcefully demanded in many circles today that any other view is labeled from the mild "false hermeneutic" to the harsher "heresy." Christians of opposing ideas are therefore condemned to excommunication (church discipline and separation), based on a charge of totally misunderstanding God's way of forgiveness and acceptance. (I know this is true; I've experienced it.) I found an example of the dogmatism on OpenAirOutreach's website; the following statement is made about penal substitution atonement:

> In all of our zeal to contend for every doctrine of the Bible (as commendable as such an attitude is), we would do well to remember that only a relatively few doctrines are so vital for the purity of the gospel that, to deny them is, in essence, *to corrupt the good news of salvation* in Christ. It is only fitting that, when we see these doctrines under attack, we give the primacy of our attention to defending them. And such a doctrine is the biblical conception of the atonement; that is, the conception that the atonement involves the substitution of Christ for us, by which, having taken upon himself our sins, he willingly undergoes the righteous wrath of the Father in our place. In other words, it is vital that we contend for an account of the atonement which views it as penal (that Christ satisfied the penalty of the law, as the righteousness of the Father demanded) substitution (that he underwent this penalty in our place). Any other model of the atonement will both fail the test of biblical witness, and *leave us without an adequate plea for forgiveness and acceptance with God* (emphasis added).[1]

---

1. Pitchford, "Penal Substitution."

Now, that's a scare tactic! How could we question the penal substitution theory without being labeled as "*corrupting the gospel*"? Corrupting the gospel is denying biblical witness, denying God's plan, essentially denying God. The accusations and denunciations of such statements and such teachers are intended to thwart mere consideration of any other view of atonement. But why are the threats necessary? If the penal substitution theory offers perfect cohesive and coherent answers to all atonement questions, why would its proponents feel compelled to intimidate believers into accepting it without examination on threat of losing acceptance with God?

I believe the penal substitution theory has expansive and dangerous holes that ought to deeply trouble any Christian who embraces the Bible as his or her God-breathed path toward authoritative truth. We can't simply look past the holes because the theory seems fairly plausible and think, well, look how many people believe it!

No, we have to be more circumspect than that. The Bible warns us to pay close attention to the truths we claim—to know why we believe what we believe. Paul concludes Romans 13 with a call to wake up! He recognizes that even devoted believers can fall prey to the love-lacking, sinful influences he describes in the chapter. Paul urges us instead to walk in realization of new life: "But put on the Lord Jesus Christ, and make no plans to satisfy the fleshly desires" (Romans 13:14). How, though, do we put on Christ? And why does he tell us who are already saved to put on Christ? Didn't we already do that when we first professed? Why is Paul telling Christians, first, in 13:11 that salvation is *nearer* than when we first believed and, then, in 13:14 to *put on* Christ?

We normally associate both our salvation and putting on Christ with things accomplished at conversion. We've decided so much of our spiritual activity rests on how we get into the club that we often lose focus on what this club is all about. Is the gospel—the good news—simply about how to get in, or is it about the purpose we have once we *are* in? The gospel, Paul argues throughout Romans, is not the individual assurance that a person will not suffer in hell (although that assurance is, of course, a certain aspect of it). Rather, the gospel's primary focus is that Jesus is Lord! Jesus's work that gives him his title of Lord was God's work from the beginning: to make right that which had missed the mark. Therefore, we have to realign our thinking with God's purpose if we hope to achieve a clear foundational understanding of what the work of Christ—his atonement—really is.

The little wordplay we often encounter is mostly correct—atonement does mean *at-one*-ment, a coming together, a reconciliation. That definition is also represented in the Greek word, which we translate as "atonement." But the Hebrew gives us a bit more, offering two words primarily translated as "atone" or "atonement": *kaphur* and *kippur* (from which we get Yom Kippur, the Day of the Atonement). The meaning of both these words goes beyond simple reconciliation to include the removal of that which was causing the estrangement in the first place.

This idea, then, is what Jesus accomplished for us, as the Council of Trent (sixth session) described it:

> Whence it came to pass, that the Heavenly Father, the Father of mercies and the God of all comfort, when that blessed fullness of the time was come, sent unto men Jesus Christ, His own Son who had been, both before the Law and during the time of the Law, to many of the holy fathers announced and promised, that He might both redeem the Jews who were under the Law and that the Gentiles who followed not after justice might attain to justice and that all people might attain to justice and that all people might receive the adoption of sons. Him God had proposed as a propitiator, through faith in His blood, for our sins, and not for our sins only, but also for those of the whole world.[2]

That statement is no problem for most of us. We do understand this expression as the reason for the atonement. We (or most of us steeped in biblical Christianity) believe Jesus came to do precisely what is specified in the statement. Where we begin to confuse the issue is in describing exactly *how* the activity of Jesus accomplished this purpose. What particular activities were a part of the atonement, and how did they effect redemption so that we could "attain to justice" and "receive adoption as sons"?

The church has a history of this discussion, but it was never before at the forefront as much as it has been in the last several decades. Many early church fathers wrote that people had been held in captivity by sin. Jesus paid the ransom to redeem them from that captivity, returning them to God. Of course, we see this idea in Mark 10:45, describing Jesus as the one who came to give his life a *ransom* for many and in Ephesians 4:8 as Jesus "leads captivity captive." But in attempting to understand the ransom concept better, some theologians strained to complete the imagery. They thought, "If Jesus paid a ransom, to whom did he pay it?" Irenaeus settled on a payment to Satan, thus redeeming those caught by him in captivity. But the church did not examine this issue much; the great heresies of Arianism, Apollinarism, Sabellianism, and Docetism were occupying most of its investigative efforts.

Around AD 1000, a Benedictine abbot, philosopher, and theologian took issue with the idea that Jesus paid a ransom to Satan. The ransom, Anselm argued, was instead paid to God. Anselm lived during the period

---

2. "Council of Trent."

of feudalism and therefore understood God-and-human covenant commitment in much the same way as the interaction of a feudal lord with his vassals: the vassals promised fealty to their lord in exchange for rights of life (tenant and protection). Sin, in Anselm's view, was dishonor shown by the vassals to their lord. The lord (our God) demanded satisfaction from the vassals (humanity) for the dishonor, but the vassals had no ability to rectify the dishonor except to lose their lives. God, in love through his son, became human (became a vassal) to provide that satisfaction for others and satisfy the dishonor to God. This idea, labeled the satisfaction theory of the atonement, held sway (despite some onslaught from Abelard's moral influence theory) for the next five hundred years, until the time of the Reformation.

The Reformers tweaked Anselm's satisfaction idea. While they held on to the central focus of satisfaction, they recognized that the feudal landscape had long since given way to that of the court of law. The Reformers, therefore, decided it was not God's honor but his justice that was attacked by the disobedience of lawbreaking. The scenario remained the same: the lawbreaking had to be met by a *penal* judgment to obtain satisfaction of God's wrath against the injustice done him. Still, the people could not pay without loss of life. Therefore, God in love sent his son to undergo the judgment penalty as a *substitute* for the people. God poured out his wrath on Jesus (so they say), and Jesus, undergoing the wrath and dying, thus satisfied the penal judgment, resulting in justice having been served so that humans could return to unencumbered relationship with their God.

Over the next five hundred years, this reformation idea of law-court atonement, holding elements of *penalty* (wrath of God resulting in death), *substitution* (Jesus instead of created human), and *satisfaction* (God's sense of offended justice having been made right by penalty paid) solidified into the most prevalent idea of the atonement in traditional Christianity today: the penal substitution theory. In fact, so prevalent is it today that those Christians who do not toe the penal substitution (PS) line are often charged with totally misunderstanding God's way of forgiveness and acceptance, as we saw in that statement quoted earlier found on OpenAirOutreach.com.

While I would agree that the atonement is a vital issue for Christianity, the OpenAirOutreach statement demands belief of a particular interpretation of the atonement beyond the necessary elements of Jesus as God, Jesus as redeemer, and death as necessary for relief of sin's hold.

While the major trajectory of atonement ideas over the last 2,000 years flowed from the ransom through the satisfaction to the penal substitution theory, several other theories emerged, which focused on other concepts involved in the atonement, but as standalone interpretations. For example, as briefly mentioned, Abelard taught the *moral influence* idea, emphasizing that the atonement teaches how much God loves. We are sick (not disabled) in our spiritual condition. By the example of Jesus, we are moved to accept forgiveness by seeing God's love. A similar theory, the example idea, understands the atonement as Jesus teaching—by his life of faithful obedience—how we should live.

The *mystical* view understands Jesus as overcoming the sin nature through the Holy Spirit's empowerment toward God consciousness, which in turn inspires us. The *commercial* theory, like satisfaction, sees Jesus's atonement as being of infinite honor to God. Jesus gives that expression of honor as a gift to humans. The *recapitulation* idea views Jesus, through his life, as summing up (Ephesians 1:11) all things by replacing Adam's disobedience through life by Jesus's obedience.

All these highlighted points appear to have some biblical support, but each separately does not seem to be enough to satisfy all biblical implications and, therefore, all our questions regarding how the atonement works. Another few ideas have arisen in the past one hundred years to challenge the PS theory. The *governmental* theory, begun by Hugo Grotius, a lawyer and logician (not a theologian), saw Christ punished not on behalf of humankind but rather to demonstrate God's extreme displeasure with sin in that he punished his own sinless and obedient son as a propitiation (i.e., the turning away of wrath by an offering). While this idea has many adherents among current evangelicals, it also fails to give adequate justification as to why punishing obedience gives God satisfaction with those who were disobedient. In other words, how can God justifiably attack one without sin as if guilty of another's sin? And then, how does that remove the obstacle with the original sinner?

Another currently popular idea (although originating very early along with the ransom theory) is called *Christus Victor*. The idea views the ransom, instead of as a transaction, as a rescue or liberation (along the biblical-redemption thought line). It emphasizes a dramatic battle between good and evil in which Christ on the cross wins for the good.

The *moral influence* theory has also seen revitalization through Rene Girard's *mimetic atonement*. However, Christus Victor and mimetic atonement, while standing in opposition to penal and satisfaction theories, flounder in similar difficulties although on opposite sides of the cross. One of the penal/satisfaction faults is the *how* of transferring guilt from people to the Savior—how does that happen? how can it be just? Rejecting that, the victor and mimetic ideas hold that salvation and victory are transferred from the Savior to people. But again, how? Is the atonement, then, merely giving us a good idea and rallying point? Is that what the Bible means by salvation?

Assuredly, within most of these theories, essential truths pop up at various points. However, rather than trying to sift through the theories to find those elements that may be embraced or rejected, perhaps starting from the biblical narrative and simply moving forward may be more effective in concluding how the atonement works.

When we consider the questions involved—and there are many—we may feel overwhelmed. For example, if we subscribe to the penal substitution theory, we stumble inevitably on questions such as whether Jesus actually did (as most PS proponents promote) die bearing the *guilt* of our individual sin.[3] The obvious difficulty in that case is why Jesus—the man—could be resurrected with the guilt of my sin placed on him, while I—a man—with the same guilt resting on me, could not be resurrected. In other words, what did God consider in Jesus a qualification for resurrection even though the guilt of sin rested on him, when the same guilt of sin resting on me disqualifies me from resurrection? Of course, the first point we may want to offer is that Jesus is God and is therefore able to overcome death by his power. But that answer doesn't really satisfy. God has just as much power to overcome my death as Jesus's death. Why does God use his power to resurrect Jesus but refuses to use his power to resurrect me? If guilt of sin is the only point causing the estrangement of death, and guilt of sin is present in both cases, why is there difference in result?

If we flip positions to say Jesus must not have had the guilt of sin placed on him, then what did Peter mean when he said that Jesus "bore our sins" (1 Peter 2:24)? If Jesus did not die bearing the guilt of my sin, how was it just for God to punish Jesus when Jesus had no guilt? If Jesus did not die bearing the guilt of my sin, how can I say he paid for my sins?

The questions keep flowing: what exactly occurred in Jesus's death? Was it a spiritual death or merely a physical death? If spiritual, was our one God at the time divided? If God is a Trinity and one member of that Trinity was dead, did God's essence change? If guilty of sin and no longer joined with the Father, how did Jesus fit the definition of God at the time? Did he become not God (as Luther implies)? On the other hand, if Jesus's death was only physical, how did that satisfy the penalty for sin?

---

3. R. C. Sproul said at the 2008 Together for the Gospel conference that what was pure Jesus was pure no more. God cursed and damned His Son with the hell we deserve. Luther said in his commentary, "Christ should become the greatest transgressor, of all sinners, the greatest. Is not now an innocent person and without sins; is not now the Son of God, born of the Virgin Mary; but a sinner which hath and carrieth the sin of Paul." Presbyterian theologian Francis Pieper said, "It is Scriptural to say that God did impute the guilt of man to the innocent Christ." James Boice, author, pastor, and theologian argued, Christ "violated the law—through no fault of his own–and he became technically guilty of all of the law."

These questions, whose answers are *necessary* for understanding the atonement, only scratch the surface. Yet, atonement rightly understood will indeed and nevertheless provide satisfying answers to all these questions that may at first seem puzzling. Finding those answers is our goal. We want to bring all the elements of this complicated issue to the table. We want to sort and refine and rightly interpret because the issue is critical. This topic is, after all, the very heart of our hope. We believe in life with God precisely because Jesus has accomplished our atonement!

Questions—theories—how do we choose? How do we ascertain which views best answer our questions? I believe we must start at the beginning, taking a measured approach. We should examine the biblical story, understand its intent, discover the destruction caused by sin, recognize the restoration God planned and the steps involved, and then bring all that understanding together to see God's atonement revealed. This process is the activity of theology. *Kinship theology*[4] is a systematic study based on the foundational principle that God's purpose in creation was for everlasting love relationship. But even to conclude that point, we need to take a step back to understand well who our God is. Therefore, with circumspect steps, let's begin our pursuit.

---

4. See Appendix for additional discussion of Kinship Theology.

PART 1

Foundation for Relationship

1

Creating for Relationship

Why should I call Thee Lord, Who art my God?
Why should I call Thee Friend, Who art my Love?
Or King, Who art my very Spouse above?
Or call Thy Sceptre on my heart Thy rod?
Lo, now Thy banner over me is love.

—Christina Rosetti, from "After Communion"

Who is He, this King of glory?
The Lord of Hosts, He is the King of glory.

—Psalm 24:10

I came to the funeral home the evening before the service for a boy in our church who had committed suicide. His mother and other relatives met a line of sympathizing friends that stretched through the room, out the door, and down the long corridor. As I stood waiting in line, I heard the groans welling up from deep within his mother's spirit. As I reached her and embraced her, my mind raced through Christian words of comfort. But it wasn't the time to tell her everything would be all right. It was no time to explain that God still had a plan, that God works in the world to make all things right, that his purpose would be served even in this, her tragedy. I just held her in my arms and told her I loved her.

Wouldn't God do the same? Jesus wept for those hurting at the funeral of Lazarus. And yet doesn't the Bible also tell us to put ourselves aside for the greater glory of God? Why didn't I say to her, "Give glory to God!"? Isn't that why God made us—to give him glory? Doesn't he want us in every situation and circumstance to glorify his name? The answer is yes, but in the midst of circumstances such as that funereal scene, when we're overwhelmed by the tragedies of a sin-cursed world, it may feel as though that demand might come across as a bit unsympathetic and even egotistical. Of course, we wouldn't dare voice those impressions because, well, that would be wrong. "We can't fault God," we scold ourselves. "He's all-powerful. He's our Creator. He can wipe out our puny lives with a flick of his finger." So instead of trying to understand God better—that his glory actually involves the empathetic love embrace for each other—we may presume that we *can't* understand him. "His ways are different," we mistakenly tell ourselves in a presumed hold on faith. But as to what those "different" ways are, "Well," we continue, "he's God. Whatever he does is right." Yet no matter how much determination we try to scrape together to shore up that notion, the fact remains that thinking of God in such a manner does not seem like trust at all.

God has told us how to love. He does reveal in his Word that which is good. Do we really have to resign ourselves to accepting a God who seems to act in opposition to everything he tells us about goodness? Can we really believe we have more sympathy and love embrace than does our infinite God? The answer is, as Paul would shout in his best King James English, "God forbid!" In our relationship with him, God surely does not mean for us to assume that his greater knowledge and power make him qualitatively different from what he teaches us in Scripture about truth, goodness, and beauty—about himself.

To solve the paradox of God's teaching and contradict what we perceive in his action, we must not give up our pursuit to know him in favor of unqualified acceptance. Questioning our presuppositions may, in fact, be the key to correcting our confusion. After all, isn't it just possible that our perception of God is based on our own confused assumptions? Who is this God really? We do know he has revealed himself to us in the Bible. Perhaps contemplating him along with that revelation may resolve some of the inconsistencies we often unthinkingly accept. So, then, who is this God of ours?

WHO IS GOD?

On March 24, 1988, at the University of Mississippi, J. P. Moreland, prominent Christian professor, author, and apologist, debated Kai Nielsen, then professor and head of the Department of Philosophy at the University of Calgary, on the subject "Does God Exist?" Professor Nielsen's stated position was that for someone "with a good philosophical and a good scientific education, who thinks carefully about the matter, that for such a person it is irrational to believe in God."[1] Nielsen maintained that we have no idea who God is when we talk about him. God is not physical, someone to whom you may ostensibly point. In fact, even Christians acknowledge that despite the Bible's attribution of human characteristics to God, he is actually not anthropomorphic at all. Without the ability to detect him with any of our senses, Nielsen continued, we are left not knowing who it is we are even talking about, and, thus, the concept of God itself is incoherent. He noted that even the statements we do make about God are challenging: "He is a being transcendent to the world," or "God is the maker of the heavens and the earth." Nielson argued that those concepts are so obscure and problematic, we don't even know what we are talking about when we voice them.

Of course, Professor Moreland attacked this line of reasoning by appealing to religious experience—not mere emotional response but rather numinous experience by which we may have direct apprehension of a personal being who is holy and good and upon whom we may depend for life and care. Whenever we're speaking in any sphere other than the theological, we tend to define theoretical concepts to explain their effects (for instance, when we're talking about electrons and light rays). Just because we can't see a thing itself, it does not mean we're doomed to incoherence in speaking of that thing as the cause for its effects. An understanding of God, therefore, may come from that which he has revealed to us in the world in which we live, as Paul explains in Romans 1. It is, then, not too far a logical step to understand the Bible as the message of this God who engages in revelation.

Leaving apologetics, but holding on to that point about revelation, let's explore what we can know about our God through that which he's revealed. One characteristic to which many theologians point is God's holiness. This word indicates transcendence of a sort; it describes something that is beyond or set apart from other things. In Isaiah 6:3, the angels cry out in emphatic repetition that God is holy, holy, holy. In fact, that scene prompted the Christian apologist and author R.C. Sproul to comment:

---

1. Moreland and Nielsen, *The Great Debate*, 48.

> Only once is a characteristic of God mentioned three times in succession. The Bible says that God is holy, holy, holy. Not that He is merely holy, or even holy, holy. He is holy, holy, holy. The Bible never says that God is love, love, love; or mercy, mercy, mercy; or wrath, wrath, wrath; or justice, justice, justice. It does say that He is holy, holy, holy, that the whole earth is full of His glory.[2]

Our immediate response may well echo Sproul's assessment: holiness would seem to be central and foundational to God's essence. Yet it is the very definition of holiness that argues against that conclusion. While holiness certainly describes God's transcendence in relation to us, its definition presumes a comparison. God is transcendent *to something or someone*. God's holiness shows separateness *from something or someone*. But if we're trying to discover who God is, we want to ascertain what is true of him even without someone or something else in the picture. Who is God in his transcendence? Who is God apart from creation? Who is God in his essence? If God existed before creation—before any someones and somethings were on the scene—how could holiness have characterized him? From whom or what was he separated? There was nothing! Without any *other*, terms such as "holiness" and "sovereignty," although absolutely true of God in relation to all else, lose their effect when there is absolutely nothing else. God, existent without creation, was not separate from anything. He was not transcendent when there was nothing to which to be transcendent. Holiness, then, cannot be his central quality, and we must return to the question of just who our God is.

Jesus told the woman at the well that God is spirit (John 4:24), distinguishing him from the physical. Now, our imaginations may picture spirits or ghosts as wavy, ethereal vapors that glide around like smoke. Movies, those great shapers of public perception, frequently depict ghosts as haunting houses or showing up at night in attics or basements or graveyards. But all those images limit spirits to the realm of the physical, and that, of course, may be true of spirits created for interaction with the physical: they seem bound by *location* to some place. However, the Samaritan had been asking Jesus whether God dwelled in Jerusalem or Samaria, and the point Jesus was impressing on her was that as pure spirit, beyond necessary attachment to the physical, God has no locational limitation. Jesus explained why the Jewish-Samaritan debate about where to worship God (John 4:20) was actually not a relevant concern. God is spirit, Jesus emphasized; he is non-locational; he is everywhere. The old command to worship in Jerusalem had imaged God's association with those who had relationship with

---

2. Sproul, *Holiness*, 26.

him through faith. But true worship—in the New Covenant sense—could and would occur anywhere with those with whom God desired to dwell—in other words, with those who by faith wanted relationship. That picture, Jesus went on to say, in the New Covenant reality would become a *going to God* that would no longer be a physical movement but rather a spiritual response. Furthermore, Jesus said, spiritual response is the recognition and embrace of truth—the truth of God himself.

So from Jesus's teaching, first, we realize that God is spirit. We realize his independence from creation in this quality. He is not of creation; he is not some *thing*. He is beyond or transcendent to our physical reality. Recognizing God's transcendence, therefore, is important. But we need to think of it within the confines of God's revelation to us.

In addition to his being pure spirit, God is, we learn from the Bible, infinite in knowledge, understanding, wisdom, care, mercy, and beauty. The metaphysical religious (as well as non-religious) philosophers categorized and organized these qualities as pure and infinite truth, goodness, and beauty. Church giants from Augustine and Aquinas to Barth harmonize in their praise of God as eternal truth, goodness, and beauty. Scripture certainly supports this idea. God is called true (e.g., Deuteronomy 32:4), good (e.g., Psalm 119:68), and beautiful (e.g., Psalm 27:4) in countless direct statements as well as in the narratives and poetry. We learn also that God acts in accordance with these qualities and prizes them by being faithful to them. He also looks ahead to his continued exaltation of his essential truth, goodness, and beauty in all his plans of coming glory. Thus, in his own faith and hope, he embraces his essential and inherent truth, goodness, and beauty.

WHAT'S LOVE GOT TO DO WITH IT?

God's essence is truth, goodness, and beauty. Dominating all his activity based on that essence, is his revelation; we know of our God's essence only by his active revelation. Paul opens his epistle to the Romans with that fact. He tells us that God has revealed who he is to everyone, even those who have never held a Bible or heard the good news of Jesus the Savior (Romans 1:18–20). But notice that the consequence of God's revelation is that "people are without excuse" (Romans 1:20b). Though that may sound harsh, God doesn't reveal to condemn: God intends to show his image bearers who he is so they may embrace who he is. Those rejecting the revelation are condemned because the revelation leaves them without the excuse of ignorance. Since God reveals his truth, goodness, and beauty so that we may understand and know him, we can conclude his purpose is for relationship—the benefit he intends.

The definition of love is the giving of self for the benefit of relationship. C. S. Lewis observed that "To love is to be vulnerable."[3] Jesus illustrated that definition as he explained to his disciples at the last supper, "No one has greater love than this, that someone would lay down his life for his friends" (John 15:13). John, remembering those words from that dinner, repeated them in his first letter: "This is how we have come to know love: He laid down His life for us" (1 John 3:16). It dawns on us that God's revelation of his truth, goodness, and beauty for the benefit of our relationship with him is an act of love. Put another way, God's communication of himself to us is based on his love. This realization on our part is huge and all-encompassing. What it establishes for us is that all God's communication to us—all God's revelation, all of Scripture—is the intention of God to enable us to understand him and benefit by that revelation in relationship. We know nothing of God that has not been revealed to us through and by his love. Nevertheless, the glory in love is not one-sided. Love reaches its height of enjoyment in the shared embrace of two or more persons giving of themselves in reciprocity. In other words, "love" is a relational term. Tying together the several concepts we've just gone over, we find that love relationship necessarily begins from God's selfless communication of truth, goodness, and beauty for the benefit in relationship with us, the ones he loves.

Does Scripture support this notion that love is the preeminent means by which God interacts? Yes, of course it does. Jesus himself said that all the Law rested on the commands to love God and love others (Matthew 22:40). His *new* command for the New Covenant of Life was to love (John 13:34). Truth, goodness, and beauty—the essential attributes of God—are held and communicated through faith, hope, and love, and of these, Paul tells us, the greatest is love (1 Corinthians 13:13). The Bible consistently places love at the forefront of God's interaction with us.

Hebrews also opens the door for an in-depth understanding of God as love, but it does so through the perfect imaging of Jesus. In speaking of Jesus, Hebrews 1:3a reads, "The Son is the radiance of God's glory and *the exact expression of His nature*, sustaining all things by His powerful word." God's glory is the manifestation of his worth, and the worth of God is his divine nature and eternal power—his truth, goodness, and beauty evidenced in his loving care. That worth radiated brilliantly from Jesus as the "exact expression of [God's] nature." Not only is there nothing about Jesus that didn't show God, but also there is nothing in God's nature that was not expressed

---

3. Lewis, *Four Loves*, 78.

in Jesus. No wonder Jesus told his disciples in the upper room, "The one who has seen Me has seen the Father" (John 14:9). Paul agreed: "For the entire fullness of God's nature dwells bodily in Christ" (Colossians 2:9). Pastor-theologian Greg Boyd puts it this way: "As the one and only Word of God (John 1:1), Jesus is the total content of the Father's revelation to us."[4] And we hear from author Michael Hardin: "The life of Jesus, his character, his acts, his message, his hermeneutic, his call to discipleship, corporately suggest that God is love."[5] If we want to know what God is like, the Bible tells us to study Jesus, and Jesus consistently acted in love.

Love then is *the* activity of God. He possesses, perceives, and proclaims his essence of truth, goodness, and beauty in love for the benefit of those to whom he reveals it. But our assent to this truth may still give us pause. Earlier, we had discounted holiness and sovereignty (two true characteristics of God in relation to his creation) as central to God's essence because they require comparison with creation. But doesn't love also require interaction with some other person or thing in order to be realized? As I've mentioned, "love" is a relational term. If God, by nature, loves through sharing his truth, goodness, and beauty, is the existence of his creatures necessary for him to express, reveal, and articulate himself?

Our previous principle still stands: if God created us—image bearers—because he *needed* someone else for any reason, he would be, in an absolute sense, incomplete without us. That would certainly do violence to our understanding of God as independent, needing absolutely nothing outside himself to exist infinitely secure, established, and satisfied within himself. At its core, that perfect sufficiency is what infiniteness is all about— no limitations.

That God is both independent and loving is the philosophical basis for our concept of a Trinity—Father, Son, and Holy Spirit existing as three persons in one essence. Although this concept is not expressly stated as such in Scripture, the idea of Trinity is required by this philosophical truth: God is love, and for love to exist, there must also exist some other to love. The Trinity's three-person arrangement provides for eternal love relationship. Each person of the Trinity gives of self for the others in communicating their shared essence of truth, goodness, and beauty. Who God is, then—infinite and independent—is consistent with the purpose for which he acts—love.

---

4. Boyd, *Cross Vision*, 21.
5. Hardin, "Out of the Fog," 61.

GOD'S GLORY

David wrote, "The heavens declare the glory of God" (Psalm 19:1). When we speak of the glory of God, our meaning has to refer to this understanding of who God is. John Piper, well-known Christian author and speaker, has stated that the glory of God is "the infinite worth of God made manifest."[6] I agree with his summary definition. The infinite worth of God is grounded in the infinite truth, goodness, and beauty (TGB) of his essence, and that essence is manifested in faith, hope, and love. In other words, then, regarding *God's* glory specifically, we may recast Piper's definition with these clarifications: the glory of God is his truth, goodness, and beauty (i.e., his "infinite worth") expressed (or "made manifest") in faith, hope, and love.

While these three—faith, hope, and love—all manifest God's truth, goodness, and beauty, they operate according to a progression. Faith believes TGB will occur. Hope is the motivation for activity in light of faith. But it is love that is the realized faith and hope. Love communicates God's worth for the benefit of others. This perspective, in fact, is why Scripture emphasizes love. First Corinthians 13:13 tells us that of faith, hope, and love, the greatest is love. God maintains that he proved his love in that while we were still sinners, Christ died for us (Romans 5:8). Scripture consistently presents love as the expression of God's truth, goodness, and beauty. We see love expressed in its highest form through the giving of self for the benefit of relationship: God, being infinite, and therefore of infinite love, gave of himself so that we could be redeemed. Recognizing all these elements, we can legitimately expand our definition of the glory of God: God's glory is his truth, goodness, and beauty expressed in faith hope, and love, with love as the preeminent means of that expression.

This truth holds incredible impact for both our theoretical musings on God as well as their practical implication. We will get to the theoretical importance later. But think with me for a moment of the practical implication. In that momentary struggle at the funeral I described earlier, when I embraced a fellow believer and member of covenant relationship, all I told her was that I loved her. And in her unfathomable grief, that was all she needed to hear. She drank in those words because we receive words of love more willingly and gratefully than any others. The term "love" has been stolen by the world to refer to mindless, selfish desire. But its true meaning resonates powerfully with Christians who embrace by faith and hope the gospel, which proclaims that we belong together in and through Christ with God (John 17:20–21). Radically different from the world's distortion of it,

---

6. Piper, "Rebuilding Some Basics."

our expression of love reflects and reveals our God in his purposeful communication of who he is. In this we hope; in this we breathe; in this we live. For of faith, hope, and love, the greatest of these is love.

Notice from our discussion two important points. The first is that love is central to the activity of God—actually, phrased more appropriately, love *is* the activity of God. Second, God created for relationship, the shared communication of love. These two truths indicate that though he is infinite and superior to us in every way, God designed creation for his embrace, not for unilateral activity or one-sided satisfaction. He created not for the enjoyment of sovereign command over and obedience from his creation. Love necessarily involves selfless giving. God demonstrates that truth in giving of himself for the care, promotion, and benefit of his creatures. As part of this world of caring embrace, God formed his creatures to also give of themselves. Only in so doing may we truly engage in love relationship.

GOD'S SOVEREIGNTY

Some may perhaps wonder how God could enter into love relationship when he is the infinite sovereign of all. But must God sacrifice sovereignty in order to love? The simplistic view that sovereignty can exist only by ordaining the cause and effect of all activity lacks biblical support. In Daniel 2:37, Daniel told Nebuchadnezzar, "The God of heaven has given you sovereignty, power, strength, and glory." If the simplistic idea of sovereignty is true, Daniel did not know what he was talking about. How could both God and Nebuchadnezzar ultimately ordain the cause and effect of every activity? Either Daniel misspoke or God means something different by sovereignty.

As we read through the Old Testament, we find God judging evil. But our observation of the judgment and power of God prompts the question of why there is evil at all. If God supremely rules, why was sin ever allowed to lift its ugly head? Wouldn't a sovereign, almighty God be able to thwart the actuation of evil rather than merely judge its occurrence? This idea, of course, is one of the atheist's arrows: the problem of evil.

A big part of the answer is that sovereignty isn't simply absolute will. Sovereignty is absolute control. The question presumes that God's greatest goal would be to ensure that evil never occurs. However, God apparently holds everlasting love relationship with his created image bearers as a *loftier* goal. When two otherwise good and right goals cannot both be satisfied, God prioritizes his will based on that which best fulfills the expression of his character. The existence of love trumps the absence of evil. And love is not pure love if coerced. Therefore, God allowed the possibility of evil in order to satisfy his goal of pure love relationship, the purpose for creation.

In other words, God wills according to his essence, his attributes, who he is. God prioritizes his will according to what most fully expresses his essence. Then God controls according to his priorities. This is his sovereignty. It is the sovereignty Isaiah praises in Isaiah 25:1: "Yahweh, You are my God; I will exalt You. I will praise Your name, for You have accomplished wonders, plans formed long ago with perfect faithfulness." This is a sovereignty that controls all things, including the judgment of the wicked, in order to fulfill God's priority of will based on who God is. To argue that God loses sovereignty by allowing the entrance of evil into the universe is to insist on a limited God who cannot engage in love because of a presumed need to ordain all activity. If God—because of who he is—insists on the shared embrace of love, he must exercise his sovereignty by allowing the entrance of evil without relinquishing his control to judge it.

So who is God? God is the transcendent Trinity, living according to his infinite essence of truth, goodness, and beauty expressed by his own faith, hope, and love. Consistent with his essence, He created for everlasting love relationship. And it is only by his love and care that his existing creation continues.

2

Creation Account 1—the Physical

*My heart is awed within me when I think
Of the great miracle that still goes on,
In silence, round me—the perpetual work
Of thy creation, finished, yet renewed
Forever.
Written on thy works I read
The lesson of thy own eternity.*

—WILLIAM CULLEN BRYANT, FROM "A FOREST HYMN"

In the beginning God created the heavens and the earth.

—GENESIS 1:1

NOW THAT WE RECOGNIZE who God is and have identified his purpose for creation, we need to examine the creation narratives. From them we learn we were made in God's image. God, of course, has no body of flesh like ours, so our image bearing must be something other than physical form. We discover clues of our imaging as we move through the accounts.

Few Christians puzzle over why the New Testament begins with four Gospels. We recognize quickly that each Gospel offers a unique perspective. One storyline alone is not sufficient to present what the four can do together. For example, the Gospel of John provides details of the Passion Week for almost half the entire book, and only two Gospels record the event of Christ's birth, with Matthew highlighting Joseph's view and scriptural fulfillment, while Luke concentrates on Mary and the glory of the gift. We can come to the same conclusion about the reason for two creation narratives: each provides unique perspective with the second (like the Gospel of John) revealing more of one part of the story.

The first creation account, which includes all of Genesis 1 and spills over a little into the next chapter, speaks mostly of process. Chapter 2's second account, beginning with verse 4 and continuing through the end of that chapter, focuses on relationship. Of course, the two accounts are not so dissimilar that we don't find process in the second or, importantly, relationship in the first.

EARTH'S AGE—YOUNG OR OLD?

Genesis 1 begins with God, and we see creation unfold from his perspective. Exactly how God created is, in our time, a matter of vigorous debate among believers. Should we suppose that the creative accounts of fish, birds, and animals are meant to show evolutionary progression, or do they depict direct acts? It is no longer a matter of liberal unbelief versus conservatism that draws the dividing line. Many Christians who share a faith in fundamental doctrines differ on these points of the Genesis creation process.

The question, however, has devolved into one colored by accusations of naiveté. Certainly, the bombastic dogmatism characteristic of many who hold to a more literal interpretation of the creation days does come across as simplistic. But rather than presuming that scientific maturity compels us to brush aside the traditional Christian viewpoint, we should investigate first whether our creation interpretation *requires* a reliance on science, and second whether any theological problems arise from dispensing with the young earth view.

In wondering whether reliance on science is necessary, I am not advocating a backward march into medieval darkness. Scientific advances should be welcomed and factored into our interpretive understanding. But we must determine whether that science compels us to eliminate other alternatives. Are the scientific reasons for an old earth absolutely persuasive? More seriously, do they force a change of perspective that possibly harms other more necessary doctrines?

Okay, I'll admit it. Despite the current preference among believers for a scientifically based model of origins, I still favor the young-earth model. First, I find no compelling scientific need to shift to an old-earth model. My opinion hinges on the word "compelling." I agree that a growing library of science does argue for expanses of time to allow natural process to occur. But if we presume the control of process is in the hand of God to be directed and engaged for his purposes—especially as he initially sets them in motion—we need not insist, here at the beginning, on assuming the *normal* course for those processes.

However, it is the second—the more persuasive—argument for a young earth that constrains me. We have to consider how death enters the picture and shapes events. We'll discuss death in more detail later, but for now just think about how God's purpose of relationship is so intricately involved in his creational intent that the very definition of *life* necessarily includes relationship with God. That being true, its antithesis—death—must oppose this relationship, marking non-relationship with, or separation from, God. So how can we presume that death—non-relationship with God—is a matter of creational intent? The insistence of the old-earth model is that death is part of the *normal* course of life. That indicates to me a misunderstanding of the purpose of death. In reviewing verse after verse, comparing passage after passage, we find that death is repeatedly, consistently, and absolutely presented as God's ultimate displeasure pronounced on that which does violence to his intent and purpose.

For humans, of course, death could not occur until God's image bearers (those to whom God gave dominion over physical creation) broke fellowship with him by their own sin. But equally consistent throughout Scripture is the picture of death in association with sin's consequences. From the first animal death recorded in Genesis 3 to Paul's sympathy with creation's groaning for resurrected relief in Romans 8, non-human death appears exclusively as a troubling consequence of the fall. Thus, the old-earth problem is that the view requires death—separation from God (even for animals)—*not* as consequence for sin but rather as part of the natural order in the created ideal.

Furthermore, the *appearance* of an old earth does not require an *actual* old earth. What I mean is that it may be our presumption rather than our science that is at fault. Our science regarding the earth's age reasons from information gathered (from carbon and other dating systems) based on ongoing processes. Its conclusion supports an earth much older than suggested in a flat reading of Genesis 1. However, the science requires presuming that ongoing processes must have always existed.

An earth created only six to ten thousand years ago *with the appearance of age* would register at its beginning no differently from how we view it now. And such a world is not, as some charge, odd or deceptive on God's part.

Following the traditional view, we don't think it odd or deceptive that God made Adam and Eve as fully functioning adults. If you could have walked up to Adam the moment after his creation, you would find a man who appeared fully grown, yet at that point, he had not grown at all. He simply had the appearance of age. A battery of medical tests would undoubtedly verify a person of age, and nothing would be wrong with the tests or instruments used. All the examining equipment would perform exactly as designed—to interpret based on a set of factors and processes presumed consistent. Every test considering his age would conclude he had lived for 30 years or so even though the world had not yet swung around the sun even once. Think also of the stars: though they were light years away, they could almost certainly have been seen in the night sky the first evenings after creation, and that would mean God made the light rays along with the stars themselves so that no lapse of time was necessary for Adam and Eve to watch them twinkle.

Now, should we brush the possibility of age appearance in Adam and Eve aside because it makes God appear disingenuous? Of course not. There is a purpose for the appearance of age. For the same reason, we should not think our Creator was intentionally falsifying scientific data in the rest of creation to misdirect us. These appearances of age were necessary to provide a functioning earth and universe for God's crown of creation—his image bearers. The question of which came first, the chicken or the egg, is perplexing only if we remain slavishly devoted to chronological constancy—what we consider normal. But if God created a chicken and an egg simultaneously, and then for practicality's sake set in motion the normal birth-to-life pattern, why should we presume deception as the reason for the outcome? I believe it's valid to assume that a functioning universe, including this earth, was set in motion by design for the benefit of the newly created image bearers to enjoy life and continue in its course in time to come.

I think some Christians have a tendency to lean toward evolution because nature seems so much more powerful than our human existence. But that dominance became true only after sin entered the picture. Before sin, God had his image bearers in charge (Genesis 1:26; 28). It is after the fall that the Bible shows how we became subject to nature rather than the other way around.

Disagreeing with me about the earth's age does not end our discussion. I do believe understanding how death and life are linked to relationship with God is vital to fully appreciate what relationship means. Nevertheless, our premise is that the Bible is God's Word—God-breathed. If we agree on that, whether we understand the creation week in the short or long term should not divide us regarding other truths that emerge from the accounts.

THE FIRST ACCOUNT

Genesis 1's creation account reveals a process that supports a shift of emphasis from mere history to purpose. And that shift hints that God's intention was never about chronology in the first place. Instead of mere sequence, God's point in delineating the 1-2-3 order of creation days appears to teach a grander theological structure. With relationship as God's primary concern in forming his image bearers, his teaching about relationship has to hold a high position for their development. That relational instruction begins with Genesis 1's described process.

Verse 2 presents the new creation—a mass with two distinct problems (or lacking two attributes): the creation is formless, and the creation is empty. In other words, no domains—that is, specific environments—exist in which occupants can function, and no occupants exist to function within any domains. Those problems are identified in only that one verse, but the solutions of God fill the rest of the chapter. Employing a six-day literary format, Moses demonstrates how God formed and filled the new creation with the domains of (1) light and dark, (2) sky and sea, and (3) land and vegetation. He also placed in the domains corresponding occupants: (1) sun, moon, and stars, (2) birds and fish, and (3) animals and humans.

First Creation Account Formation

	PROBLEM: Formless SOLUTION: Formed	PROBLEM: Empty SOLUTION: Filled	
	DOMAINS:	OCCUPANTS:	
Day 1	light, dark	sun, moon, and stars	Day 4
Day 2	sky, sea	birds, fish	Day 5
Day 3	land, vegetation	animals, humans	Day 6

Recognizing literary form and artistry to supply theological truth does not attack the Bible's truthfulness or authority. Of course, some writers become wildly imaginative in their figurative interpretations, torturing doctrinal cohesiveness. But shielding against that excess does not require pitching camp at the pendulum's opposite extreme. Literalism simply for the sake of literalism is just as detrimental as symbolism simply for the sake of symbolism. Interpretation demands work. Solid connection with foundation (all the way back to God's purpose for creation), consistency with God's overall plan, integrity of doctrine, and an interweaving with the whole of the passage must all coalesce.

Viewing the six days of Genesis 1 as a literary framework by which God forms and fills aligns with our interpretive guidelines. We find subtle gems of coordination scattered throughout the passage. One shining example demonstrates the link from Day 1 to Day 4. In Genesis 1:4, we read, "God separated the light from the darkness." Here in Day 1, we may wonder just how God accomplished that division. Reading on, we see how Day 4 provides the answer. Genesis 1:18 describes the purpose of Day 4's sun, moon, and stars as "to separate the light from the darkness," giving us matching phrasing in the Hebrew of what God did (verse 4) with how he did it (verse 18). If we focus on mere literal chronology of days, we miss the connection between these verses.

My insistence that chronology and duration are not really at play in Genesis 1 does not alter my previous position of earth's young age. In fact, although not intended to reflect a historical account of the day-to-day creation process, Genesis 1's creative activity still did, I would surmise, take about a week. Too much biblical emphasis on the Sabbath exists to dismiss a one-week creative duration out of hand. But, as a reminder, my young-earth opinion doesn't rest on the depiction of creation as a seven-day procedure. While some people may see adopting a literary framework (rather than a chronological one) for Genesis 1 as support for their old-earth theories, my previous objection still holds: God's expressed link between sin curse and death—for both humans and the rest of physical creation's processes—forces me to accept a less than 10,000-year age for the earth despite my less-than-literal insistence on the six days.

THE SEVENTH DAY SABBATH

When God completed the forming and filling, he rested. The process, of course, was not so strenuous that God needed a break. The resting, too, is part of the literary framework. A specified *sabbath* (Hebrew for *cease* or *rest*) signified the Creating Ruler's functional change from development to operational control. Here's how John Walton, author and Old Testament Professor at Wheaton College, explains it:

> In the ancient world, deities rested in temples, and temples were built specifically so deities would rest in them. This rest was not primarily descriptive of relaxation or sleep.... More importantly, it expresses how the temples served as the control room of the cosmic domain in the god's jurisdiction. When gods rested

in the temple, they assumed rule over their ordered cosmic domains from their command centers. In the case of Yahweh, his domain is the entire cosmos. This rule is intended to bring stability and smooth functioning to the ordered cosmos.

Day seven is the most important day in the account. Without day seven, the other days do not have meaning. God has ordered the cosmos so that it is ready to serve as sacred space in which he takes up his residence to rule over it, preserving its stability and order by his presence.[1]

In designating the seventh day as the one in which he began operational control, God demonstrated what he had pronounced: his creation was *very good*, and it was the place where his presence would rest as creation's lord. Adding that detail to our previous table produces this result:

First Creation Account Formation (Revision)

	PROBLEM: Formless SOLUTION: Formed	PROBLEM: Empty SOLUTION: Filled	
	Day 7 Rest for God, Creator/Ruler		
	DOMAINS:	OCCUPANTS:	
Day 1	light, dark	sun, moon, and stars	Day 4
Day 2	sky, sea	birds, fish	Day 5
Day 3	land, vegetation	animals, humans	Day 6

Our chart now shows the relationship of God to his physical creation. He rules as Lord over all. However, something about this setup does not seem to flow from the creation purpose discussed in our last chapter. The chart shows, first, an equal footing for humans with the rest of creation as common subjects to God. Second, we had concluded that God created for everlasting love relationship, but the master-servant construct of the chart above shows humans as mere subjected occupants. We need another adjustment to recognize at least the human-to-physical-creation relationship portrayed toward the end of Genesis 1.

The only name for God used in Genesis 1 is *Elohim*. *Elohim* means "mighty one, powerful one, supreme one." It is a fitting name for God as the text recounts how he creates from nothing, forms and fills, and rests in supreme control as creation's commander. However, when we get to verse

---

1. Bishop, *Origins*, 111–12.

26, we discover a change in the narrative form: God permits us to listen in as the Lord of all speaks to himself. The change in perspective emphasizes that what is about to happen is not outside God's control, something that just naturally occurs. Rather, the function of the human, in creation's design, was—from the very beginning—the deliberate will and purpose of *Elohim*. To heighten the intended effect, I will replace the word *God* with its Hebrew meaning, *the mighty one,* in quoting a portion of this verse: "Then *the mighty one* said, 'Let Us make man in Our image, according to Our likeness. They will rule. . . .'" Okay, stop right there. Read that portion again and reflect. The mighty one —> creates someone like him —> who will rule. Who is God? He is the supreme commander over this creation he made. Who is the human to be? One like God who will rule. The wording indicates the relationship humans are to have with the rest of physical creation; it is to be the same as God's: ruler to subject.

What is intriguing, however, is that humans are part of physical creation as well. Was God confused in assigning one part of physical creation to rule over another? He, of course, was not. Remember that we are to understand image bearers based on the one whose image they are bearing. God as Spirit ruled over physical creation. God appointed as rulers not merely animals, creatures of physical creation, but humans—persons whose construct included spirits who imaged God as well. So humans in their spirits were assigned authority (dominion) over physical creation—even over the physical creation that was part of themselves: their own bodies.

Once again, then, we need to modify the chart. Merely listing humans in the Day 6 row along with animals fails to show God's ruling intention for them. While humans as physical beings share space with the animals on the Day 6 row, humans as spiritual beings share the Day 7 Sabbath slot in ruling with their Creator over the physical.

First Creation Account Formation (2nd Revision)

	PROBLEM: Formless SOLUTION: Formed	PROBLEM: Empty SOLUTION: Filled	
	DAY 7 Rest for God, Creator/Ruler, and human spirits, appointed rulers		
	DOMAINS:	OCCUPANTS:	
Day 1	light, dark	sun, moon, and stars	Day 4
Day 2	sky, sea	birds, fish	Day 5
Day 3	land, vegetation	animals, human	Day 6

Humans sharing rule over the physical realm is precisely why Jesus responded to the Pharisees as he did in Mark 2. The Pharisees rebuked Jesus for allowing his disciples to pluck and eat grain on the Sabbath as they passed through the fields. But Jesus tells those Pharisees they've misunderstood the purpose for the Sabbath. God did not mean it as a law to control, to subjugate them. The Sabbath demonstrates human control over creation: "The Sabbath was made for man and not man for the Sabbath" (Mark 2:27).

The positioning of the human spirit relative to physical creation is a crucial first step in understanding the significance of humans in the Creator's image.

3

Creation Account 2—the Spiritual

Celestial King! Oh let thy presence pass
Before my spirit, and an image fair
Shall meet that look of mercy from on high,
As the reflected image in a glass.

—Henry Wadsworth Longfellow, from "The Image of God"

So God created man in His own image;
He created him in the image of God;
He created them male and female.

—Genesis 1:27

HOW DO WE BEAR HIS IMAGE?

Genesis 1:26–31 emphasizes that God intended humans to be like him:

> Then God said, 'Let Us make man in Our image, according to Our likeness. They will rule the fish of the sea, the birds of the sky, the livestock, all the earth, and the creatures that crawl on the earth.'
> So God created man in His own image;
> He created him in the image of God;
> He created them male and female.

CREATION ACCOUNT 2—THE SPIRITUAL 23

God blessed them, and God said to them, 'Be fruitful, multiply, fill the earth, and subdue it. Rule the fish of the sea, the birds of the sky, and every creature that crawls on the earth.' God also said, 'Look, I have given you every seed-bearing plant on the surface of the entire earth, and every tree whose fruit contains seed. This food will be for you, for all the wildlife of the earth, for every bird of the sky, and for every creature that crawls on the earth—everything having the breath of life in it. I have given every green plant for food.' And it was so. God saw all that He had made, and it was very good. Evening came, and then morning: the sixth day.

I have often tried to imagine how a decision-making session would progress among the Trinity. Considering that each Person has infinite access to their shared infinite essence, the discussion could not possibly take very long. There could be no chance for one Person to bring up a pro or con the others hadn't already thought of. With equal and absolute goodness, beauty, and truth, the Persons would reach a unanimous decision before dialogue could even begin. Things, then, would proceed much as we just read in Genesis 1:26–27.

God presents himself acting as plural though deciding as one—a brilliant example of the Trinity in form and function from the outset of Scripture. Here is no mere use of the majestic plural—that is, a plural pronoun referring to a single self that monarchs employ to assert a superiority in rank. Addressing others is not in view here. God treats us instead to an inside look at God speaking to himself—as one person to another. The verse firmly depicts the unity of the Trinity in operation, and that impression is for a purpose—an instructive purpose. God presents his three-in-one unity in order to draw attention to its reflection in the multiple-in-one image he is about to create: "He created *him* in the image of God; He created *them* male and female." Although formed as his one creation, God regards them as two, and those two were meant to subdue and rule the one physical creation.

What exactly is the image of God that humanity bears? The answer is intricate. In the previous chapter, we noticed an image-bearing of rule. Here we see that the rule is not tied to either maleness or femaleness. Both the male and the female are made in the image of God to rule physical creation. Any attempt to rip apart that unity in this creation account does violence to the context. We can no more connect subduing and ruling to male-only imagery than we could understand the image itself as including only males. The context asserts that both bearing image and functionally ruling are assigned to both individuals (who happen to be male and female).

That these two humans specifically image God distinguishes them from everything else "having the breath of life in [them]" (1:30). We must pay special attention to those image qualities pointed out in the narratives because these narratives are theologically purposed. They are not given merely to satisfy curiosity. (Moses skips way too much history for us to assume that.) Rather, they're meant to inform us about God and relationship in these accounts; specifically, we learn who we are (what our image-bearing qualities are) because of who *he* is. Since we are purposed for relationship, God necessarily would have to create us as relational creatures.

Now, we know God possesses attributes of transcendence (e.g., eternality, infiniteness, immutability). We also know that God possesses attributes of condescension (e.g., love, justice, goodness), each to a degree of absolute transcendence. For example, not only is God just, but he is also infinitely just. Not only is he good, but he is also immutably good. And volumes have been written about these attributes.

But rather than reciting these facts simply to categorize all we know and appreciate about God, I want us to see an image-bearing point that should impress us. Consider that no other creatures besides us can know or even imagine these truths about God. So while God, in his essence, surely is truth, goodness, and beauty, and all God's condescending attributes flow from these three qualities, the first wave of wonder for us is that we can actually *know* God is truth, goodness, and beauty. We can know what truth is. We can sense what is good and what is bad. We can appreciate beauty in its appearance around us. What a loss to us (and how unlike God we would be) if we could not recognize and understand his essence. We wouldn't be able to relate with or intentionally reflect God were we not able to recognize his essential qualities. Our attributes as image bearers, therefore, begin with our ability to comprehend who God is in his truth, goodness, and beauty.

COMPREHENDING GOD

Of course, everything issues from God. Everything we know of and see and live among proceeded from his hand. As God reveals and as we learn, we gain context of both the universe and life itself. In other words, we learn truth from God both from practical application and in conceptual relation. We've been given the image-bearing quality of a *conceptual intelligence*.

As we read the Genesis 1 creation account, we realize the consummate perfection of creation in macro and micro detail, and we respond with a sense of satisfaction. God pronounced each day of creation not merely done, but good. As he made his image bearers on that sixth day, he pronounced the creation very good—a degree of goodness indicating a scale of judgment by which he measured his satisfaction. We learn goodness from God; we've been given the image-bearing quality of a *conscious morality*.

God's creation functioned not only in practicality, but also in artistry. God's Eden presented to Adam's and Eve's senses sounds, smells, and sights that delighted as well as nourished. God told us that he "caused to grow out of the ground every tree *pleasing in appearance* and good for food" (Genesis 2:8–9, emphasis added). We learn beauty from God; we've been given the image-bearing quality of a *critical aesthetic*.

CONCURRING AS WE COMPREHEND

Through conceptual intelligence, conscious morality, and a critical aesthetic, we comprehend truth, goodness, and beauty. Of course, that does not mean we always receive and incorporate in our lives those qualities as they are purely and perfectly revealed. Sometimes we accept, but at other times, we reject. God wills according to his perfect intelligence, moral being, and sense of aesthetic. But *we* believe and will and hope in response to our limited and not-so-perfect intelligence, morality, and aesthetic. Thus, those image-bearing qualities of *comprehension* flow into our image-bearing qualities of *concurrence*—the ability to respond to what God reveals. We can respond in appreciation or rejection. So we've been given the image-bearing quality of a *concluding faith*—a private judgment on what we comprehend, which allows us to embrace it or reject it in favor of another imagined idea of truth, goodness, and beauty.

Through the progression of creation, the command to fill the earth and subdue it, the preservation of life through food provided, and the anticipation of rest, God shows how he has built into our existence a forward-looking view that stems from, in, and toward relationship with him. That forward look is our image-bearing quality of a *continuing hope*. This hope holds tightly to the comprehended truth, goodness, and beauty in which we have placed our faith, and then enables us to pursue them through the course of our lives to our desired goal.

COMMUNICATING WHAT WE COMPREHEND

Finally, once we *comprehend* revelation and *concur* with it, we can *communicate* it to others. In the very act of our creation and through God's interaction with us, God reveals to us his truth, goodness, and beauty. The intention of each of us toward the benefit of others is the heart of the multiple-in-one concept of love. Love foregoes selfish interest for the benefit of the whole. This love activity is God's example, and it is also God's directive. We mirror him by our love. Thus, we've been given the knowledge and experience of the image-bearing quality of *communal love.*

In these six qualities, all presented in the creation accounts (and repeated countless times throughout Scripture), we image God. The first three—conceptual intelligence, conscious morality, and critical aesthetic—we use to understand or grasp the truth-goodness-beauty essence of God, which is why we collectively call them qualities of *comprehension.* The next two—concluding faith and continuing hope—are our approval or commendation of that comprehended understanding, so we name them qualities of *concurrence.* The sixth and last image-bearing quality—communal love—is the clear expression of the comprehended and concurred concepts. This quality is that of *communication.* These image-bearing elements form the necessary bedrock on which we can recognize what the narratives (especially in Genesis 2) teach us of relationship.

The following chart presents the six qualities of our imaging in relation to essence and existence.

Notice from the chart the labeling of the essence and existence of God and how humans image them. Remember that God is multiple in existence (persons) yet one in essence (infinite truth, goodness, and beauty). God designed us as his image bearers in precisely the same manner—one in essence yet multiple in persons. But our one essence, of course, cannot be the same as God's—infinite truth, goodness, and beauty (TGB). That TGB is who God is, and although we are image bearers, we are not God. We may reflect the TGB of God, but that is his essence alone. Our one human essence is physicality, the physicality of all creation—this universe of matter and energy that seems at times, exclusive to our bodies yet never is completely so. We share this physical essence using such elements as the air we breathe and the water we drink, which constantly move in and out and around us all. Energy and mass remain constant in the universe, but not so within each of us where it adds, subtracts, and exchanges. So this physical nature is a shared essence, conjoining our independent spirits as we interact with each other.

THE PATH OF GLORY

Our essence is our physicality, but our individual spirits, intended for relationship, must base that relationship on God's essence, not ours. All relationship is based on his essence because his TGB essence holds the fundamental elements of relationship. We comprehend *his* truth through our individual conceptual intelligence. We understand *his* goodness through the conscious morality he has given us. We recognize *his* beauty through our critical aesthetic. Once those are comprehended, we (again, our persons—our spirits) may concur with them by concluding so in faith and continuing to hold that conclusion in hope. Those qualities were all designed to enable us to receive and embrace that which God reveals of himself. But also, in our persons, we are able to communicate that TGB (just as God does) in communal love—a giving of ourselves to others, both God and other persons.

The faded large arrows in the chart depict this idea of God's essence as extending through his Persons and then proceeding in revelation to our essence and our persons. This picture is the relational reality God has designed for us. It is based on who God is—his essence—and conducted through the revelation given by God. That revelation is what Paul, in Romans 1:20, insisted was apparent to everyone: he affirmed that God's divine nature (his TGB) and his eternal power (the love expression of his care) are revealed to all.

We can see this design for love relationship in Genesis 2. It is not explicitly stated but rather provided through both the real and the metaphorical activity inherent in the Covenant of Life, which we will discuss a little more in our next chapter.

The multiple-in-one construct of God (which is imaged in us) is a necessity of being. I have identified God's essence and existence as separate parts, but that distinction should not lead us to think of them as separate entities—as if God is a four-in-one construct of Father, Son, and Spirit, plus Essence. The essence of God is not a person as are Father, Son, and

Spirit. His essence holds no separate conscious existence of mind and will. But the persons of God—his existence (the Ones who do have minds and wills)—depend on their shared single essence to function. That one essence empowers the persons but depends on them as well for expression.

What is true of God is true of us as image bearers: we are not each two beings of body and spirit but rather one being necessarily existing in combination. Just as God is not God only in person but in the essence of infinite TGB, which he depends on and draws from, so also we are not beings only in person (spirit) but also in the physical essence that necessarily completes us.

In the first creation account, we read, "Then God said, 'Let Us make man in Our image, according to Our likeness. They will rule the fish of the sea, the birds of the sky, the livestock, all the earth, and the creatures that crawl on the earth.' So God created man in His own image; He created him in the image of God; He created them male and female" (Genesis 1:26–27). We often pass quickly over these two verses because we know there is greater detail coming in Genesis 2: the creation of male and female mentioned together in chapter 1 will be more fully explained in chapter 2's progression of creation. Yet unless we pay close attention right here in chapter 1, we may assume a little too much as we march ahead.

A difficulty of language here may cause us confusion. The *man*—the *adam*—of the first statement in Genesis 1:26 is not meant to indicate the male. The word is reflective of the generic *man* or, better, *human* or *humankind*. Additionally, the word *man* is translated from the Hebrew *adam*, which we normally assign as the name for the first male. But if we continue to associate this word with the generic *human*, I think the detail of these creation passages will have more significant effect on our thinking. For that reason, instead of simply using the translation *man*, I am going to specify a lower-cased and italicized *adam* in this portion, before the text begins to use "Adam" as the proper name of the separated first male.

The Hebrew language is also instructive when referring to God. The first creation account (Genesis 1) is intent on displaying God's power in creation. As already mentioned, God here is called *Elohim*, which means God of power. In power he created the heavens and earth, flung the stars into space, and gathered oceans within their boundaries. In power God created humans in his image and placed them on the land to rule. But as the second creation account begins in Genesis 2, verse 4, God's name changes. There we read "Lord God," which is translated from *Yahweh Elohim*. *Yahweh* indicates existence or being. So God now presents himself as the God of power and being. This name expansion, of course, relates to the activity of the passage. The focus of Genesis 2 shifts from the creative power of God to the image of the *adam*, the *being* created.

4

The Covenant of Life

And thou didst meet thy child,
Not in some hidden shrine,
But in the freedom of the garden wild,
And take his hand in thine,—
There all day long in Paradise he walked,
And in the cool of evening with thee talked.

—Henry Van Dyke, from "God of the Open Air"

The Lord God planted a garden in Eden, in the east,
and there He placed the man He had formed.
The Lord God caused to grow out of the ground every tree
pleasing in appearance and good for food,
including the tree of life in the middle of the garden,
as well as the tree of the knowledge of good and evil.

—Genesis 2:8–9

THE PLACE OF GOD'S PLEASURE

In the formation of his image bearers, God introduces principles of relational development. In the first creation account, we learn of relationship between the image bearers and the rest of creation: the man and woman, in spirit, were to enjoy perfect dominion over physical creation. In the second account, we learn about two other relationships. The first is between the image bearers and God. That lesson comes through the picture of the garden: "The Lord God planted a garden in Eden, in the east, and there He placed the man He had formed" (2:8). If we think of the name Eden as merely something to call the garden, we'll miss the point.

Today names tend not to carry the significance they did in the ancient world. I was named Daniel, not because my parents hoped for a son whose character proclaimed, "God is his judge." They simply liked the name. Two of my grandchildren are named Bjorn and Judah—one a Scandinavian name and the other Jewish, though their heritage is neither. However, in those early biblical times, names often served to characterize. Even the names of places became known for what they represented. Sodom, a word whose root meant "scorched" or "burning," relates to the frequent sulfuric fires around that city. The name Enoch means "dedicated." Cain gave his first son that name and then built a city, calling the city after his son, or *dedicating* it to him.

We cannot, then, simply read past the name Eden without pausing to consider its significance. Eden means "pleasure." We realize, then, that God placed Adam and Eve in the Garden of His Pleasure. Having been created perfectly without sin, Adam and Eve had opportunity to realize the purpose for creation—to enjoy God in perfect love relationship. Thus, two relationship blessings are now evident: perfect dominion over the rest of creation and opportunity for perfect relationship with God. But the text moves us along to a third relationship—image bearers in relation to each other.

CREATING MALE AND FEMALE

As the second creation narrative continues, God points out something that he, of course, had known before time began: the *adam*, this image bearer of God, could not fully realize his imaging without exercising one of its qualities—communal, or relational, love. God knew the *adam* was unfulfilled while alone (or solitary). Recall that the verb *love* means to give of self for the benefit of relationship. If there is no other, love is impossible. Even after all the "good" pronouncements on his creation, God declared it *not good* that the *adam* remain a solitary being with an unfulfilled opportunity for extending love in human-to-human relationship. God had all along planned multiples of the *adam* so that the imaging quality of love could be realized, and he used the *adam*'s recognition of solitariness as a teaching moment—an opportunity to propel this *adam* one more step along the journey toward comprehending truth, goodness, and beauty.

For this lesson, God paraded all the animals before the *adam* to name, and the *adam* no doubt thought of names descriptive of each type of creature. God designed this task of describing the creatures so the *adam* would learn that among all the creatures, not a single other was similar to the *adam*. Not one had the God-image of all those relationship-building elements, and therefore, the *adam* could find none with whom to share satisfaction of spirit. As the last animal passes by, the *adam* appears to have learned the lesson: "but for the man no helper was found as his complement" (Genesis 2:20b).

The lesson accomplished, God put the *adam* to sleep and from a side (or actually, "taking a side") God extracted and fashioned that part into another—a female. Importantly, God did not simply mold some more dirt, as he did to make the *adam* originally. The significance is that not only would this being bear the image of God as well, but also that she would bear *the same* image as the original *adam*. Let's pay close attention to this creative act. God could not have shown this sameness—this oneness—in image bearing and co-dependence if he had simply created two separate humans, albeit both at once. The staggered creation and the specific development plan of taking one from the other *emphasizes* the oneness of the image—the unity of being and worth shared by this first couple. It was in using a side of the *adam*—essentially dividing the first being—that God created this woman who was *like* the *adam* and *not like* the rest of creation.

Upon waking, the *adam*—now, the male—recognized this other one as from his original oneness. He perceived she was not different from him as were the rest of the creatures, but rather she shared his relational qualities. It was this realization of sameness—of oneness—that caused him to cry out, "This one, *at last,* is bone of *my* bone, and flesh of *my* flesh." She was not like the rest of creation that he would rule. *She was like him!* And here we see the intent of God's first description back in Genesis 1:26: "*They* will rule the fish of the sea, the birds of the sky, the livestock, all the earth, and the creatures that crawl on the earth." *They* would. Together, these two in one, in the image of God—*they*—would rule together just as God, the Three in One, rules together.

Notice that the *adam* is not identified in regard to sex until after God extracts the female, leaving the male. When he wakes and declares the glory of God's work, Adam says, "This one will be called 'woman,' for she was taken from man'" (Genesis 2:23b). This time, the Hebrew for *man* is not *adam*—generic human—but rather *ish*—male. The word *woman* is the Hebrew *ishshah*—female. What is the significance of the text's only now mentioning two distinct sexes? The answer is to demonstrate not only a separation but also the rejoining of the two sexes into a unity of feeling and purpose—a oneness reflected in their physical beings. The very next verse in the passage points specifically to this reunification: "That is why a man leaves his father and mother and bonds with his wife, and they become one flesh" (Genesis 2:24). Of course, this first male and first female did not have parents, but the verse establishes the principle for the generations to come. The verse begins "That is why." In other words, the awe-inspiring unity of verse 23, realized by the male (*ish*) and the female (*ishshah*) of the *adam*, but also by husbands and wives of succeeding generations, is the reason for the conclusion of verse 24: the relational bond of husbands and wives differs from other human relationships, even the close connection between parent and child. It is a bond that returns these two, made from one, *back into one*, a oneness implied by the sexual entwining of bodies. The synergy of sex with one inside the other is meant to emphasize this point—this image—of unity, of two becoming one in imaging their God. They are two in one; they reflect the Three in One.

The marriage relationship, in fact, pictures the multiple-in-one actuality of *all* humankind. Humans are individual persons (spirits), and there are many of us. However, we all share one physical essence—the matter/energy combination of the universe. This amalgamation of physical and spiritual elements as the one essence and multiple existence of humankind contributes to how we image God.

The relational benefit, then, was the third and final major relationship presented to the *adam*—these first two humans in the Garden of God's Pleasure. They, even as one, had enjoyed perfect dominion over the rest of creation and had opportunity for perfect relationship with God. Now, as two, they were also able to enjoy perfect relationship with each other. Let's note that in the establishment of relationships in this creation ideal, God has not even hinted at any hierarchy of authority between the man and the woman. One was not given charge, rule, or responsibility over the other based on gender or creational order. The idea of a hierarchical structure roots squarely on fabricated eisegesis. Rather, throughout the passage, God has emphasized the unity in creation, image, and purpose that he endowed to his crown of creation—the man and the woman, his image bearers. The design revealed by God for the imaging purpose of desire, satisfaction, and contentment is wrapped in pure love relationship.

And this design for relationship sheds light on how God intended to interact with his image bearers. As we can trace throughout Scripture, relational intent emerges through covenant.

COVENANTING WITH HIS IMAGE BEARERS

What is a covenant? O. Palmer Robertson begins his book *The Christ of the Covenants* saying: "Asking for a definition of 'covenant' is something like asking for a definition of 'mother.'"[1] And indeed it is. We can define "mother" with scientific certainty, yet when Jesus mourned over Jerusalem—"How often I wanted to gather your children together, as a hen gathers her chicks under her wings, yet you were not willing!" (Matthew 23:37b)—his lament had nothing to do with the biological description of a mother but everything to do with a mother's heart. Just so do we find covenant intent in God's designed relationship with us.

Robertson finally settles on a definition for covenant as "a bond of blood sovereignly administered."[2] While he provides many good insights regarding covenants throughout his book, I think he fails here to escape what he was trying to avoid in his initial argument against so many other unsatisfying *covenant* definitions. His disappointment had been that the definitions referenced elements that didn't always appear in the Bible's covenant scenes. Yet in a comparison of Robertson's definition with Scripture, we find biblical covenants that are not inaugurated with blood. Isaac's covenant with the Philistine Abimelech was inaugurated with a meal, not blood (Genesis 26). And the very covenant we wish to discuss at this point—God's first covenant with Adam and Eve—pictures no blood.

Additionally, the inclusion of "sovereignly administered" in the definition is faulty because not all the Bible's covenants had God as a party or direct administrator (such as the one in Genesis 26). Some might object by maintaining that God is always involved in and administrating over human affairs, but then why the necessity to include that proviso in the definition? Must we define farming as "the practice of agriculture sovereignly administered"? Similarly, we probably don't need to include divine administration in our definition of covenant.

By process of elimination, we have reduced Robertson's definition to "a bond," and that's almost enough. We might add only the dimension of relationship. A covenant is a bond of persons for relationship. And that's the emphasis we see in scriptural covenants.

Our definition also makes it possible to understand as covenants certain agreements among the Persons of the Trinity. For example, we discussed in chapter 1 God's purpose in creating image bearers: for everlasting love relationship. We can call that decision, or purposing, a covenant of the

---

1. Robertson, *Covenants*, 3.
2. Robertson, *Covenants*, 4.

Trinity, labeling it God's Covenant of Creative Purpose. It was an agreement of the Persons of our God regarding relationship.

We also understand from Scripture another Trinitarian covenant. Again from chapter 1, we concluded that God's one essence is his truth, goodness, and beauty (TGB). His Persons of Father, Son, and Spirit always and unchangeably act based on that essence of TGB. Therefore, we can determine their agreement to act in relationship eternally and immutably based on their essence of TGB to be a covenant. Put another way, God's *Covenant of Operational Essence* is to always and unchangeably act based on his essence of TGB. These Trinitarian covenants both fulfill our definition of covenant and serve as foundational principles for all we see God do as revealed in Scripture.

God, because of who he is as TGB, and we image bearers, because of our covenant obligation to reflect his TGB, necessarily relate on the basis of God's essence in a greater-than-and-lesser-than association. But that doesn't mean our relationship with God is simply that of master and subject. Yes, God seeks to impart growth in us, and for that reason, the relationship certainly includes a teacher-to-pupil dynamic. But it never lets go of the love purpose at its core. God established a covenant to encourage unfettered love in his relationship with us precisely because he is rich in TGB while we are poor. He obligated himself to provide us his limitless truth, goodness, and beauty upon which love relationship must be based; our obligation as image bearers was to absolutely trust in God for that provision. Both parts of the covenant are indispensable to a genuine love relationship.

In the previous chapter I hinted of these obligations and their necessity without identifying them in covenant terms. But now let's talk about creation in this context. God gave life to his image bearers. Life is not mere animation. All existence—physical or otherwise—comes from and depends on God's sustaining hand, because only God has independent existence. Without his direct involvement, nothing else *is* or can *be*. Thus, when we speak of life, we are necessarily speaking of animation that is from and in God's purposed control. If God withdraws, life is gone; death results. Stated bluntly, life necessarily depends on relationship with God. Even more simply put, life *is* relationship with God; death is no relationship with, or separation from, God.

It is necessary, then, for God to provide for his image bearers. God demonstrates in these first chapters of Genesis how he will do that. God created a garden. What need was there for a special place when he had just created an entire world? He had reviewed his creation and had pronounced it all good! If the whole world was perfect—free from sin and fear and trouble and danger—why would Adam and Eve need to live in this particular garden?

The garden symbolized something more. Through that Garden of God's Pleasure, God demonstrated his intended provision. The text introduces Eden as replete with trees "pleasing in appearance and good for food, including the tree of life in the middle of the garden, as well as the tree of the knowledge of good and evil" (Genesis 2:9). In this description we notice beauty in the appealing plant life, goodness in sustaining care, and a hint of intellectual and relational growth in the knowledge of good and evil. God is providing beauty, goodness, and truth for his image bearers as they begin their journey to his purpose—everlasting love relationship.

PROGRESSIVE DEVELOPMENT OF RELATIONSHIP

Adam and Eve needed to follow a carefully designed path of growth to realize God's full relational blessing. All biblical revelation is progressive: it is a stepped process of gradual development. Speaking of revelation in the Old Testament period, theologian Bob Reymond comments, "This revelatory activity that accompanied and served God's redemptive activity was necessarily progressive, its progressiveness possessing an organic character, that is, a perfection at every stage."[3] Even in the perfect One, Jesus, we observe progressive understanding as he "increased in wisdom and stature, and in favor with God and with people" (Luke 2:52). It makes sense that God provides experience and instruction at a suitable pace for the learning to be absorbed well. Jesus himself was aware of that necessarily measured pace: even in the midst of his most intense period of teaching—when his chosen eleven had already been watching, learning, and growing with him for three years—he had to tell them, "I still have many things to tell you, but you can't bear them now" (John 16:12).

Learning takes time, interest, and cooperation. Therefore, God planted a garden, and through it, he provided the means for understanding goodness, beauty, and also truth. But he also planned the timetable for presenting those three categories of virtue to ensure their ideal reception by Adam and Eve. So God told them, "You are free to eat from any tree of the garden, but you must not eat from the tree of the knowledge of good and evil, for on the day you eat from it, you will certainly die" (Genesis 2: 16–17). God meant for his image bearers to trust him, to wait for his instruction of TGB, to rely on his provision instead of pushing ahead based on their own limited knowledge.

The universal desire for TGB reveals that desire is inborn, but the world's heartache and struggle also let us know we have serious trouble

---

3. Reymond, *A New Systematic Theology*, 9.

finding the TGB. The path to satisfaction must be God's. God, in his essence, is the source of TGB. God does not merely measure up to some external standard of TGB. Rather, he is TGB. What he has done in creating the world, what he has done in establishing all things and all knowledge, and what he has done in revealing his purpose testify to this. But how is it conveyed to us? How do we understand it?

In contemplating God's communication of his TGB, we uncover significant differences among theological schools of thought. The traditional covenantalism of Reformed Theology[4] usually labels the first covenant with Adam the Covenant of Works; it is also sometimes called the Covenant of Creation (e.g., O. Palmer Robertson). Whatever its name, in Reformed thought, the "focal aspect of the covenant of creation relates to the more specific responsibility of man arising from the special point of probation or testing instituted by God."[5] In other words, according to Reformed thought (as expressed by Robertson), God's purpose for commanding Adam not to eat of the tree was to test his obedience. The relationship was primarily that of master and subject. Wayne Grudem concurs: "Although the covenant that existed before the fall has been referred to by various terms (such as the Adamic Covenant, or the Covenant of Nature), the most helpful designation seems to be 'covenant of works,' since participation in the blessings of the covenant clearly depended on obedience or 'works' on the part of Adam and Eve."[6]

However, what I call Kinship Theology[7] boasts an appreciably different perspective that embraces God's purpose of love relationship. Now, Reformed Theology and Kinship Theology do not collide at this precise point in a major disjunction of fundamental doctrine. Reformed Theology does acknowledge that God is love, that God wants relationship, that God is greater than his creation, that God may impose commands on his creation, that humans do sin, and that only through God's salvific plan can humankind ever hope for renewed relationship with God. Kinship Theology is in accord with all these tenets. Nevertheless, there remains a conflict of emphasis that leads to essential differences. Kinship Theology refuses to lose sight of the basic premise of God's purpose, which is everlasting love relationship, the foundation from which God's intent and interaction arise. This perspective does not view God's commands as expressions of his authority.

---

4. I know I'm generalizing here. There are a thousand stripes of covenantalism among the Reformed. But there is a certain common focus.

5. Robertson, *Covenants*, 67.

6. Grudem, *Systematic Theology*, 517.

7. See Appendix for additional discussion of Kinship Theology.

Rather, Kinship Theology asserts that God's command not to eat of the tree was not a test of obedience but a teaching tool for continued relationship.

God expressed—that is, communicated by revelation—his TGB through the command, warning Adam and Eve against pursuing those qualities based on their own feelings. He urged them to trust him for the progressive instruction that would result in their full satisfaction. But Adam and Eve chose against God's provision, trusting in themselves.

This choice was not, as some in Reformed circles might conclude, simply a failure of obedience. This test was no test at all; the command was instead a necessary step along the relational path God had planned for his image bearers to truly know him.

So often we allow our fallen condition to distort the lens through which we view God, and one of our inaccurate conceptions of him is that he exercises authority as humans do in this sin-cursed world. But God doesn't use his power with a command-and-control mentality. When we free ourselves from this picture of him, we're able to discover how God actually was and is pursuing his relational purpose through the course of every event from the dawn of the first light to the light of restoration. God created. He created image bearers. He created for the purpose of everlasting love relationship. And in his design, he established the means whereby we could actually understand him.

That concept may sound crazy: we understand God? He is transcendent—vastly above us. He is infinite; we could never know all he knows. Yes, all that is true. But let's not put an unrealistic limit on our unbounded God. This infinite God of ours is infinitely able to communicate himself to his limited creation to the exact level and degree he deems we need (and can handle) to understand him. He does so through the things he has made that surround us. He gives knowledge of himself in his creation so that we are able to recognize that he exists and that he wants relationship. He created multiples of us for understanding our multiple-in-one, relational God. He gave us an environment so we could understand his dominion and control for his love purpose. These three relationships—us with God, us with each other, and us with, well, ourselves (the person/essence interface of spirit with the physical)—are means of teaching us about him even as we image bearers live to reflect him.

PART 2

Fall from Purpose

5

Adam & Eve's Choice

Say first, for Heav'n hides nothing from thy view
Nor the deep Tract of Hell, say first what cause
Mov'd our Grand Parents in that happy State,
Favour'd of Heav'n so highly, to fall off
From thir Creator, and transgress his Will
For one restraint, Lords of the World besides?

—John Milton, from *Paradise Lost*, I, 27-32

So she took some of its fruit and ate it;
she also gave some to her husband, who was with her, and he ate it.

—Genesis 3:6

In Genesis 3, dramatic changes rock all creation. Purpose and blessing take solid hits, as all three designed relationships for humanity seem to crumble in dark distortion. The changes occur as sin enters the world.

TARGETING EVE

The first part of the chapter recounts the origin of human sin. Here, the serpent approaches Eve rather than Adam and directs his tempting argument specifically to her. Why her? Was she less intelligent, more power hungry, less perceptive, more prideful than Adam? Or was it, perhaps, as a surface reading of 1 Timothy 2:14 would indicate, that she was simply more prone to deception?

We have to be careful not to read anything into the text at this point. Eve could have been more easily deceived than Adam, but we don't know that possibility from this account so far, and, more importantly, neither did Satan. Without sin, how would she have displayed that propensity to deception? Was Adam a chronic prankster, constantly duping Eve for sport? Wouldn't it be more likely that he, who was just learning about the world himself, displayed the same innocence and wonder that would make a deceiver like Satan see an advantage over him as well?

In fact, if the patriarchal complementarians are correct in that God made Adam as a sort of middle manager over Eve, someone to be followed and obeyed, why wouldn't Satan have approached Adam first? After all, the odds of Eve's obeying an order from her deceived commander were surely higher than the likelihood of Adam's accepting fruit from his deceived underling. Yet Satan chose to approach Eve first. I think we can find a reason without having to presume any non-textual hierarchy in Adam and Eve's relationship.

From the very beginning, we are told that God did create a difference between his image bearers. The difference, however, related to their physicality: one was male and the other female. The genders embody elements that are structurally discrete yet still striking in correspondence. For example, the reproductive organs operate in opposite yet integrative fashion. Muscle size and strength—elements favoring external labor—are generally more pronounced in males. On the other hand, God structured females—again, generally—for advantage in internal labor, e.g., childbearing. Now, we may wonder whether these external and internal differences are really distinctive. After all, while it is true that only females can bear children, exerting external or internal muscular activity is certainly not limited to one or the other sex. In addition, we can all think of some women who have greater external strength than most males we know. And there are also many men with extremely limited external strength. The point is not to characterize all of either sex in absolute terms. Nevertheless, this external structural strength is a broad-spectrum gender characteristic of males as a group. *As a general rule*, males are better suited to the external exercise of strength.

Interestingly, a corresponding chemical difference apparently accompanies this physical distinction. There is not only generally greater structural ability in one sex but also a corresponding satisfaction in exercising that ability. In other words, males tend to be more satisfied through external physical exertion than females. Likewise, females commonly derive greater satisfaction from nurturing—a correspondence to the internal strength of childbearing. Again let me stress that these differences are generalizations, but they seem to be undeniable based on our physical makeup. It makes sense that we derive gratification from activities we feel more proficient in, especially when chemical elements (largely hormonal influences) are contributing to that satisfaction. Therefore, although it's certainly true that many men not only excel as nurturers but also find great satisfaction in nurturing, it's similarly true that this gratification exists to a comparatively greater degree among women as a group. Likewise, when it comes to strenuous physical performance, the male chemical composition generally induces greater satisfaction in men.[1]

These structural and chemical differences do not imply any associated authoritative rules, boundaries, or levels. God established no hierarchy based on differences, and he lists no *leading* or *following* orders that underwrite these characteristics. Rather, the Genesis 1 and 2 passage emphasizes the two-in-one unity and satisfaction in relationship. To ignore that emphasis in order to read hierarchy into the narrative is to miss the entire point.

Returning to our question of why the serpent approached Eve rather than Adam, we may possibly infer that something about her nurturing nature could have prompted the direction of his attack. In his first question, the serpent subtly urges Eve to take umbrage at God's limiting his care—his nurturing—of Adam and Eve by putting certain food off-limits. While the attack may have worked with Adam as well, Eve's propensity to nurture may have offered the serpent a greater chance for success.

SATAN'S DECEIT

Eve was near the Tree of the Knowledge of Good and Evil. Was she near it because she was already tempted by it? curious about it? or simply strolling by? Who knows? But Satan took that opportunity to attack. In the guise of a serpent—one of physical creation's forms—Satan struck up a conversation with Eve, wondering (or acting as if he were wondering) about the tree and its fruit.

Eve seemed initially to dismiss the serpent's insinuation that it was somehow unjust for God to deny them fruit from that tree. In her answer, she concentrated on the abundance that God did provide: "We may eat

---

1. A study regarding reasons for exercise among men and women concludes that women exercise primarily for weight loss and toning, whereas men exercise for enjoyment. See "Gender Differences in Exercise Habits and Quality of Life Reports: Assessing the Moderating Effects of Reasons for Exercise" at https://www.ncbi.nlm.nih.gov/pmc/articles/PMC5033515/.

the fruit from the trees in the garden. But about the fruit of the tree in the middle of the garden, God said, 'You must not eat it or touch it, or you will die'" (Genesis 3:2–3). Her reply was a good one. She affirmed God's generous provision and offered a reason for the injunction: eating the fruit would cause death—a return to nonexistence. Her answer is now the second clue that the definition of life is relationship with God. The *adam* became a living creature with God's breath. Here Eve shows her awareness that the departure of God (death) would result from ignoring God's command—his teaching of his truth, goodness, and beauty.

In her answer, Eve added that they could not even touch the fruit. Perhaps her embellishment eventuated from a conversation between her and Adam about the best means of avoidance, or it simply indicated her recognition of the seriousness of the command. Either way, her statement shows a complete awareness that eating the fruit would endanger their relationship with God.

Satan, that "Father of Lies" (John 8:44), told her they wouldn't die. Now, what was Satan trying to do with his lie? Well, we know his ultimate goal, of course, was to get these image bearers to sin, but what did he envision as the path to that sin? Did he want Eve to turn on God, disregarding him? Many people have indeed preached that kind of narrative. But the serpent had just been described in 3:1 as the "most cunning of all the wild animals." A frontal attack—inciting Eve to switch from trust in God to disregard of him—doesn't seem to fit that "most cunning" description. Although not impossible, it seems a bit of a stretch for Eve to turn from enjoyment of the garden's pleasures to disdain for their provider simply because of a brief prod from Satan.

Rather than trying to instill in Eve a contempt for God, Satan chose to downplay the importance of the act. Eve appeared adamant about not eating a fruit that would cause death. But we should remember that her conception of death was not the same as ours. She had not yet seen any lifeless bodies. She didn't understand death from a purely physical point of view. Death to Eve had been defined as separation from God, so it was separation from God that Eve feared in eating the fruit. It was separation from God that she wanted to avoid. Therefore, Satan's "No, you will not die" was not merely an assurance that Eve would continue her breathing existence. Rather, Satan attempted to ease her mind by saying, "Don't worry, you won't be separated from God. You won't lose that Covenant of Life relationship you enjoy. This garden and everything it offers will still be here for you. God is your heavenly Father, who loves you. It's okay. *No, you will not die.*"

Satan continued his deception by next suggesting that not only would she not lose relationship with God, but she would also *be like God.* Was

Satan in effect trying to lure Eve into a replication of his own pride, which was esteeming himself as great as God and worthy of the same honor and adoration? Many expositors have decided that Eve wanted power—that is, to be powerful like God. And it's true that any self-promoting removal of trust in God does evince pride and a desire for autonomous power. But we really don't have any basis from the text for surmising Eve was that power-hungry. I think Satan was simply easing Eve's mind by reducing the gravity of the act. After all, what was Eve created to be? She and Adam were *image bearers*. What are image bearers? They are beings meant to bear the image of God—to *be like God*! So Satan here was telling Eve that by eating, she would fulfill her created purpose: she would more perfectly image God; she would *be like him*.

This attack reminds us, of course, of Satan's attack against Jesus at the beginning of Jesus's ministry. Satan's strategy there, again, was not to try to turn Jesus against the Father and get him to renounce God. Rather, Satan kept tempting Jesus to achieve God's intended goals by urging him to short-cut God's intended path to those good ends. For example, God certainly wouldn't want Jesus to starve in the desert. Jesus needed to complete his mission. He needed to save the world. So Satan urged, "Turn the stones into bread to give you strength to continue the mission God has for you!" Similarly, since the desired result was for Jesus to be King of kings, Satan offered the world if he'd only bow down. But that wasn't God's way, Jesus realized. And Jesus maintained dependence on God and God's truth, goodness, and beauty rather than try to manipulate the situation to accomplish God's work.

Eve, though, didn't think like Jesus. She found herself eased by the deception. Perhaps eating that fruit was not so big a deal as she had imagined. She'd still have relationship with God; she'd still enjoy the garden; she'd be what God wanted her to be—his image bearer.

Satan's misdirection succeeded. In reevaluating, Eve "saw that the tree was good for food and delightful to look at, and that it was desirable for obtaining wisdom" (Genesis 3:6). She recognized its truth, goodness, and beauty. But instead of seeing this richness as reflective of the God who originated it all, Eve misidentified the tree itself as the source. Thus, without consciously rejecting God, she turned from her covenant requirement of dependence on him and "took some of its fruit and ate it."

Her error was not renouncing God or purposely choosing evil over good. It was her acceptance of the serpent's nudge to center her desire on the gift rather than the Giver that led to her downfall. She saw in the fruit a faster track to relational maturity and claimed that path. But of course, in that perspective she was utterly wrong, utterly *deceived*. Whether in the creation ideal of the garden or in the swamp of our sin-cursed world, success is realized only by maintaining trust in God as the source for all care and worth.

Eve bought in to the deception (as Paul confirms in 1 Timothy 2:14), and as soon as she ate, her very first active thought—as a nurturer—was to extend the fruit to her husband. Without a word, the gesture told him, "Eat too. It is good for us."

ADAM'S DILEMMA

Adam, though, was not deceived; Paul insists as much in 1 Timothy 2. Yet without explanation in the text, Adam receives the fruit from Eve and eats as well. Why? He most probably had heard the serpent's lie; perhaps Eve had even urged, "Look, I ate, and I'm okay." But none of that clouded his thoughts; he still understood the eating to be contrary to God's command. He didn't believe his image bearing would be improved. He didn't believe he'd be able to follow God better. Significantly, he didn't believe that he would not die—that he would not lose his relationship with God. *He wasn't deceived*. So why in the world did he eat?! We learn more of Adam's motivation after God exposes his sin.

In 3:11, God asks, "Did you eat from the tree that I had commanded you not to eat from?" Adam immediately replies, "The woman You gave to be with me—she gave me some fruit from the tree, and I ate" (3:12). The usual take on Adam's response is that he tried to deflect blame as if arguing, "It's the woman's fault!" or even suggesting, "It's your fault, God, for giving her to me!" It's possible Adam's response was indeed that childish and self-justifying. However, in light of the context, let's consider what might be a more plausible explanation. After all, Adam had the maturity to withstand Satan's cunning, so why would he offer so lame an excuse to God? Notice carefully that all he said was that Eve gave the fruit to him. He didn't accuse her of overpowering him or engaging her seductive charms to draw him in. Would Adam think that he could satisfactorily exonerate himself by saying, "Well, the woman gave me the fruit, so, of course, it wasn't my fault, I had no choice but to eat it." Something more must be behind his words. Something else must be the purpose for Adam's offering Eve's sharing of the fruit as his only defense.

Remember, as Eve was extending that apple (or orange, or fig, or passion fruit—passion fruit seems to fit best!), Adam was not confused, at least not about the gravity and consequence of the sin. He knew Eve had eaten. Not being deceived, he knew Eve was in trouble. What she did would cause death, a separation from God. So at that point as she extended the fruit to him, what might his thoughts have been? Look back to Genesis 2. God said it was not good for the *adam* to be alone (2:18). No one like the human was found among all the creatures of the whole earth (2:20). When Eve finally stood in front of him, Adam was overjoyed, crying out, "This one, *at last*, is bone of my bone and flesh of my flesh!" (2:23). Adam was in love with Eve! Of course, it was not a love born of years of experienced relationship. Yet he had fallen in love, and he didn't want to lose that. Perhaps overwhelming his thoughts as that fruit was suspended between them was the fear that as soon as God arrived, Eve was going to be eternally separated—not just from God—but *from him* as well!

So Adam ate. He ate not because he was deceived or because he thought the fruit might be tasty. He ate because he didn't want to lose Eve. Notice that Adam begins his defense to God by saying not just "The woman gave me some fruit," but rather "The woman *You gave to be with me*—she gave me some fruit." Again, taken in isolation, that Eve gave him fruit is no defense. We may also be certain that God's having given the woman to him is still no defense. But rather than averting blame, Adam was trying to build an argument to justify his eating.

God had presented the principle that a man will leave his parents to be one with his wife (2:24)—a principle supporting the two-in-one unity that images the relationship of the three-in-one Trinity. Adam, his mind probably spinning through various excuses, settled on the fact that they two were one: inequity and differentiation should not exist between them. So Adam's response to God was in effect, "The woman You gave to be with me, that you wanted to be with me—this woman with whom you made me one—gave me the fruit. I ate because I wanted to remain as one. That's what you wanted, right? Doesn't that make it okay?" God, however, said no, emphasizing again another major principle implied earlier but now explicitly taught. Yes, the husband-wife relationship pictures the ideal of earthly relationships. But unless a person remains fixed on God's truth, God's goodness, and God's beauty—on relationship with God—even the husband-wife (human) relationship will fall apart.

Adam had been faced with a choice. His struggle had been whether *not to* eat and maintain his relationship with God but lose Eve, or *to* eat and lose his relationship with God but somehow hold on to his bond with Eve. In attempting to satisfy his innate desire for truth, goodness, and beauty, he tragically chose for Eve and rejected God. G. K. Beale comments, "There is no explicit vocabulary describing Adam's sin as idol worship, but the idea appears to be inextricably bound up with the transgression."[2] And further,

---

2. Beale, *Biblical Theology*, 359.

"There also seems to be an element of self-worship in that Adam decided that he knew what was better for him than God did, and that he trusted in himself, a created man, instead of in the Creator."[3]

RELATIONAL BASIS

With that sin, God brought forth his judgment. In the only verse that mentions curse on creation in God's accounting for the consequence of sin (3:17), God curses physical creation for Adam's choice to favor it over the Creator. As Paul observes in Romans 1:25, "They exchanged the truth of God for a lie and worshiped and served something created instead of the Creator."

There is still one more question with which to grapple: why did God even allow Satan to slither into the garden? The place is called Eden—pleasure—and this pleasurable place was where God was intent on teaching Adam and Eve about relationship and their Covenant of Life. So why allow the influence of evil?

We should remember that in the previous scene (the end of Genesis 2), God had just completed forming Adam and Eve fully as beings, but they had only begun their journey toward relational maturity. The first step in that journey involved God's command not to eat of the tree of the Knowledge of Good and Evil. This tree was not magical; its fruit contained no special nutrients. It was merely a tree used by God for symbolic purpose, and that purpose was to help those first humans learn to depend on him for growth in that divine basis for relationship—God's truth, goodness, and beauty. Think about its name: it was not called the Tree of the Knowledge of Evil. It was not an evil tree as if knowledge of good and evil were to be shunned by God's image bearers. Quite the opposite. God did want his people, with whom he would enjoy everlasting relationship, to understand both good and evil so that their relationship could have a rich basis from which to grow and flower into perfection. But that growth required learning by God's direction, in God's time, and recognizing him as the only source for all that truth, goodness, and beauty.

So this tree, with its dangling fruit, represented not just knowledge of good and evil, but knowledge sought after easily and selfishly. "Don't get it that way," God was warning when he issued the command not to eat. Relational growth takes time. It is not immediate perception of ideal relationship. The process is experiential, and God did not mean to create a race of blindly obeying foot soldiers. Since he created for relationship, he urged

---

3. Beale, *Biblical Theology*, 360.

Adam and Eve to trust his process to build that relationship; they were not to pursue maturity selfishly.

The serpent's entrance should not be considered an accident that occurred when God wasn't looking. The serpent's communication to Eve and Adam was an initial step allowed in God's plan for their relational learning. God would use the serpent's evil for his intended good. The only attack the serpent was allowed to conduct was in challenge of the only good-and-evil lesson given thus far: don't eat (that's good); do eat (that's evil).

6

Sin's Consequence

And there, till Christ call forth the dead,
In silence let him lie: No need to waste the foolish tear,
Or heave the windy sigh:
The man had killed the thing he loved,
And so he had to die.

—Oscar Wilde, from "The Ballad of Reading Gaol"

Because you have done this, you are cursed. . . . The ground is cursed.

—Genesis 3:14, 17

Adam and Eve estranged themselves from God when they chose to trust their own perceptions of truth, goodness, and beauty rather than rely on him. The sobering consequences of that breach impress on us the severe obstacles atonement had to overcome.

LIFE AND DEATH

God had told them not to eat of the tree, and he gave them a reason: if they did, they would certainly die (2:17). So when Adam and Eve both ate from the tree, why didn't they immediately drop dead? Did God err in his pronouncement? Was he just trying to scare them? Of course not. We've already defined *life* as relationship with God, so *death*, life's opposite, would be separation from God. At the moment they ate, Adam and Eve most certainly did die. The image bearers no longer enjoyed an intimate relationship with God. Fully realized separation in an absolute sense, however, did not occur, because God had a plan for restoration already in place. But Adam and Eve were *dead* in sin (Ephesians 2:1). The rest of Genesis 3 describes that state of death and the ultimate outcome of sin.

In chapter 4, we discussed the Covenant of Life God had established with Adam and Eve. God had placed on himself the obligation of providing them with his truth, goodness, and beauty to fulfill his purpose in creation—to enjoy everlasting love relationship with them. For their part, the image bearers had to trust God, the source of TGB, for that provision. We saw God's faithfulness to his Covenant-of-Life obligation on display in the garden: God provided "every tree pleasing in appearance and good for food, including the tree of life in the middle of the garden, as well as the tree of the knowledge of good and evil" (Genesis 2:9).

In learning of and accepting God's supply, the image bearers enjoyed life—relationship with God. But when, in Genesis 3, Adam and Eve failed to trust him, they broke covenant. They shifted their trust to the creature in multiple ways—Eve to the serpent, Adam to Eve, and both to their own wisdom. Thus, the result of breaking the covenant was the severing of the covenant relationship. Just as life in the garden imaged their Covenant-of-Life relationship, expulsion from the garden (Genesis 3:23–24) imaged the death of that relationship.

Love relationship can have no basis other than truth, goodness, and beauty. That's a necessity. Since TGB comes from God alone, love relationship ultimately rests on the very essence of God. Recall (from chapter 4) that one of the Trinitarian covenants is the Covenant of Operational Essence: God, in his Persons, always and unchangeably acts based on his essence of TGB. Even his activity of relationship with image bearers *must* be based on his TGB. For God, then, to provide TGB for Adam and Eve as well as for them to respond in dependence was no mere arbitrary choice. It *had to be so* both for God to remain faithful (righteous) in all his activity and for love relationship to actually exist. That necessity is the reason such a harsh penalty existed for failure. God did not merely feel like punishing if he could not have his way. He didn't just think up the worst thing possible to fling against his failing creation. There was simply no way for relationship to continue without its being based on his TGB.

So when Adam and Eve sinned, their relationship with God *of necessity* had to end. Note that the conflict centers on the very basis for relationship. When Adam and Eve stepped off the foundation of God's essence to climb up on *their own* (the physical/material portion of their beings), their basis for relationship with God was destroyed. A curse resulted, falling squarely on that conflict area: their own essence—physical creation.

Since the image bearers changed the basis of their relationship from God's essence to their own, the inadequate base made it impossible for God to continue relationship with them even though God is infinite love and mercy. It's not that God here imposed limits on his love. The fact is that in setting up physical creation as their idol, Adam and Eve eliminated the only basis on which love relationship could exist and thrive. With that basis gone, the love relationship itself was limited—in effect, rendered impossible.

Genesis 3 relates the tragic consequences of the fall. Particularly poignant is verse 19 in which God tells Adam and Eve that they will "return to the ground, since you were taken from it. For you are dust, and you will return to dust." How disastrous! His words depict not just a physical death with the body's being absorbed into the ground. God is speaking of the ultimate death of the person, the spirit.

Adam and Eve were image bearers of the God of the universe precisely because of the spirit/physical combination—molded earth (the physical) and breathed-in life (spirit). In verse 17, we read that the physical is now cursed. And then in verse 19, we find that their bodies will return to what they originally had been—the dust of the earth. The turn toward death was sure separation from everything Adam and Eve had been. Since their very existence depended on God's active involvement, their withdrawing from God—their turning from him—would necessarily cause that existence to cease. Their spirits would die.

But why the delay in the "return to dust"? Verse 19 intimates that life, although harder, will continue for a while "until" they return to the ground. Here is revealed the majestic love of our infinite God. Death was the necessary judgment: the curse on the image bearer's physical essence was inevitable because of its direct conflict with the relational basis of God's essence. Yet God, consistent in his infinitely compassionate love, had prepared a plan in anticipation of the need to rescue his estranged image bearers. That rescue had to involve mercy (one of his infinite attributes), justice (an infinite attribute as well), and removal of the curse on his image bearers' essence (without which relationship was impossible). That plan we call the atonement.

THE SERPENT IS SATAN?

In the temptation scene discussed in our last chapter, we assumed the serpent was Satan, even though the word *satan* doesn't appear even once in

Genesis 3. I think we can justifiably assume Satan—the Devil—was the one tempting Eve in the guise of that serpent.

Actually, the word *Satan* is never used anywhere as a proper name in Old Testament Hebrew. The word literally translated means adversary, and in 28 of 29 appearances in the Old Testament, the term is preceded by a definite article—*the* adversary (though few Bible versions translate it that way). Only one time does it lack the definite article. First Chronicles 21:1 reads, "Satan stood up against Israel and incited David to count the people" (HCSB).[1] Considering the verse on its own and especially without the article, we might think the term "satan" is being used as the Devil's name. But this verse has a parallel in 2 Samuel 24:1, which reads, "The Lord's anger burned against Israel again, and He stirred up David against them." The Hebrew, then, seems to indicate in its use of "an adversary" in one verse and "the Lord" in another that God, at that moment, was acting as Israel's adversary (which, I believe, is the reason the NET translates it as "an adversary" rather than "Satan").[2] The point I'm making is that the naming convention for Satan is not so clear as we may have supposed.

However, when we turn to the New Testament, we encounter a little more clarity. The Greek *satanas* does derive from the Aramaic and Hebrew *satan*, but translators record the proper name "Satan" for all 36 appearances. Whether the term should be a proper name or remain as the common noun "adversary" is not that important: What *is* significant is that the New Testament characterizes the evil demon in a way that permits us to so confidently link him to certain *adversarial* activity in the Old Testament.

The other New Testament name, "Devil," means accuser or slanderer, which links to *the adversary* in Job. We read of the Devil's tempting Jesus in the wilderness in a manner similar to the serpent's temptation in the garden. Jesus calls the Devil a "*murderer* from the *beginning*" and the "*father [originator] of lies*" (John 8:44), providing further connection between the Devil and the serpent, whose *lying* in the *beginning* led to *death*. The ultimate correlation is provided in Revelation 20:2, which joins all three words—serpent, Devil, and Satan: "the dragon, that ancient *serpent* who is

---

1. Only the NET among major translations (e.g., CSB, NIV, NRSV, ESV, NASB, KJV, NKJV) translates it as "an adversary" rather than as a name.

2. Attributing to Satan the incitement in one verse while to the Lord in another could also be possible. We would reconcile the paradox in the same way we reconcile Pharaoh's hardening his own heart in Exodus 9:34 with the mention of God's hardening Pharaoh's heart two verses later (Exodus 10:1). See chapter 8, section "Reacting to Sin," and chapter 18, section "Wrath of God," for discussion of how withdrawing from God affects a sinner's activity.

the *Devil* and *Satan*." This evidence supports the contention that the serpent of the garden was, in fact, Satan.

But if so, why does the text not explicitly say so? After all, in other places, Scripture tells us exactly when Satan (the *adversary*) is acting. We read that Satan instigated Job's calamities. John writes that Satan entered Judas (John 13:27), propelling him out into the night toward his betrayal. So why not specify that Satan entered the serpent? I think lack of definite identification keeps the emphasis on physical creation as the temptation rather than on Satan as the tempter. Although we may deduce with some confidence that Satan was involved, the passage directs our attention to physical creation as the basis for Adam's and Eve's decisions. Yes, the serpent beguiled Eve, but Eve chose wrongly because she thought she would be more satisfied in the physical than in God's instruction about TGB. And God wants us to see how his image bearers gave up their authority over creation (Genesis 1:26–28) to place themselves in subjection not to Satan, but to that physical creation.

CONSEQUENCES FOR ALL

The text details the sin consequences in Genesis 3:14–19, dividing them among the three characters of the story: the serpent, Eve, and Adam.

Consequences of Original Sin

Characters	Consequence
Serpent	Crawling on belly and eating dust
	Hostility with the woman and her seed
Eve	Pain in childbearing
	Discord in the marriage relationship
Adam	Pain and suffering in working the land
	Return to dust—Death

Although some of the consequences are specific to a character (e.g., pain in childbearing), most are common to more than just the individual addressed. For example, Adam's return to dust applies, of course, to Eve and the serpent as well. The discord prophesied to Eve concerning her relationship with Adam had no less an ill effect on Adam, and we also note conflict between the woman's seed and the serpent. Adam's predicted struggle in working the land doesn't mean that Eve and all women are blessed with green thumbs. These common sin consequences should direct us to an overarching purpose that differs from mere punishment doled out to individuals. These consequences present the all-encompassing tragedy of Adam's and Eve's treason.

In the Hebrew, Scripture records these consequences in metrical fashion—a kind of poem, if you will. We saw poetry in Genesis 1:27 when God spoke of the imaging of humankind—the first relational statement. We saw poetry next in Genesis 2:23 when Adam awoke to find Eve and expressed joy in their relationship. Now here in Genesis 3 as relationship breaks down, it's sadly ironic—as well as poignant—that the failure is communicated poetically.

Although on the surface the consequences appear to be segregated by character, they evince a chiastic structure that connects them. (In fact, this rhetorical pattern is fairly typical of biblical writing.) A *chiasmus* is a literary device in which ideas are placed in a pattern to provide emphasis. The pattern links the first idea with the last, the second idea with the second to last, and so on. The middle idea or ideas are often the conclusion or target to which the other phrases point. Here is what the structure looks like:

Point A^1
—Point B^1
——Point C^1
——Point C^2
—Point B^2
Point A^2

A chiasmus may have fewer or more points, but it will always be organized similarly to our example—the first and last points in parallel with subsequent parallel links as the structure progresses inward. The chiasmus derives its name from the Greek letter *chi*, which is written as "X." The logic behind the name is that the first point of the X, where we position a pen in writing it, is at the top left. As we draw, that point connects with the last point (bottom rightmost) of the letter. The second and third points are connected within that outer context (bottom left to top right). An additional feature of the chiasmus is that the points proceeding to the central idea usually follow one line of thought, while the subsequent points receding from the center follow another thought line.

So now let's insert the listing of sin's consequences in our chiastic structure to determine the emphases.

Consequence A^1: Crawling on belly and eating dust
—**Consequence B^1**: Creation essence hostile to woman and seed
——**Consequence C^1**: Pain in childbearing
——**Consequence C^2**: Discord in marriage relationship

—**Consequence B^2**: Pain and suffering in working the land
Consequence A^2: Return to dust—Death

As we view the consequences, let's keep in mind that the man and woman both withdrew trust from God, but did so for differing reasons. Eve was deceived by the serpent's lie; Adam, however, rejected God's direction with full awareness and chose instead to maintain his relationship with Eve. Therefore, God presents the consequences for their sins arranged according to those distinctions—to the serpent and Eve according to her sin and then to Eve and Adam based on his sin.

Consequence A^1 regards the serpent's deceit. We know the serpent spoke and connived because of Satan's influence. Since the name *Satan* doesn't appear, the text is implying that we should keep our focus on physical creation, of which the serpent is just a part; it was the draw of physical creation—the image bearers' essence—that seduced Eve's trust. Thus, without denying Satan's involvement (or God's reaction to him specifically), the curse on the serpent should be recognized primarily as a curse on physical creation for its having captured the imagination of the image bearer to pursue TGB apart from God.

The serpent, one representative part of creation, is told it will be at odds with other parts of creation—a breakdown in the smoothly run operation of created physical essence. And we still can recognize the creation's specific conflict with Satan, who would now, as it were, lick its dust.

The major impact, though, of these first two consequences is their destruction of relationship between the physical essence of the woman and her spirit. The result of her desire to control the source of TGB was ironically a loss of control that elicited hostility between her and her physical essence (which hostility continued also between her progeny and their physical essence). In the ongoing rupture of our spirits from the physical creation in which they are housed, we live out this curse we simply cannot overcome.

As humans, we comprise spirit and body without possibility of ever being human without both. Yet each human is in conflict between body and spirit, actually having our spirits dominated by our flesh in direct and cursed consequence from that which God originally intended—the dominion by our spirits over our bodies (Genesis 1:28). Paul illustrates that internal conflict multiple times as he speaks of our war against the flesh, especially in his plaintive cry at the end of Romans 7.

God continues presenting sin's consequences by directly addressing the woman. Remember her chemical distinction: the woman (generally and especially) derives satisfaction through her nurture. Her sin, in directing her nurturing care toward herself, however, again causes the opposite result, illustrated by her pain in childbirth. While still finding joy in childbirth and still delivering nurture, the difficulties image the breakdown in human relationship based on her sin.

Through the path of these first three consequences, we recognize Eve's fault in her sin that led to the relational destruction. In choosing to eat the fruit, she thought she could maintain relationship with God while, controlling life and judging life for others. But these consequences show with drastic force the result of relying on her own essence for TGB: conflict between spirit and body for herself and all those who would come from her.

The last of the consequences addressed to Eve pivots the emphasis from her motivation for sin to Adam's so that the three consequences, designated as C^2, B^2, and A^2, highlight his sin.

Although at first, consequence C^2 appears directed to Eve alone, it actually heralds breakdown of relationship for both the woman and the man. Eve had determined to eat the fruit because she decided it was good for her, but immediately after eating, she handed the fruit to Adam because—she decided—it was good for him as well. Speaking of this consequence, God told her that this propensity to make decisions solely on her judgment would not abate but rather become pronounced. Trusting herself, reasoning on her own what was good, she would continue to attempt to rule her husband. We find that idea in the phrasing "your desire will be for your husband" (Genesis 3:16b).

Notice that the same construction shows up in Genesis 4 when God speaks to Cain in verse 7: "But if you do not do what is right, sin is crouching at the door. *Its desire is for you.*" Cain's sin, like Eve's, was a desire to control. But in both cases, sinful desire ended up mastering them. Eve's husband and his own sin-desiring control would eclipse her sin.

For the first time, the Bible speaks of ruling control of one spouse over another. It was not inherent in the created ideal. It happens in the consequence to sin. Why does the husband dominate? It is merely a matter of physical capability. The male will rule because he is physically able to do so based on his structural distinction. We should not translate God's statement of sin's consequence into a God-ordained dictum. The created ideal was a mutual employment of each one's strengths to support the other's vulnerabilities. That's how the woman was to love the man as his help (Genesis 2:18). And that's how the man was to love the woman. But sin broke that relational ideal so that both the woman and the man sought dominance. Instead of using his abilities *for* the female, the male would use them *against* her in a sin-driven struggle for control.

A simplistic solution to this battle for control would be the designation of one partner as the authority in the relationship to whom the other must submit. But it is the desire itself for control that is the problem. The creation ideal of interactive devotion—of mutual submission—should be what mitigates the desire for control. Yet the curse means that the husband, because of his structural advantage, is able to take command in the sin-driven discord.

Consequence C^2, although directed to Eve, extends to Adam and turns our attention to his sin. Vying for control does not grow loving relationship. If relationship deteriorates, both parties feel the cursed effects. Furthermore, in this particular relationship, recall Adam's motivation for his sin. He intentionally chose for Eve against God in hopes of maintaining a harmonious relationship with her. Yet his action caused the opposite effect—the contentiousness of a control-seeking environment.

Immediately following the revelation of the conflict in spousal relationship, God tells Adam that his relationship with the land will suffer (consequence B^2). Of course, this image focuses attention again on the curse on physical creation. That which God had created for humankind to dominate would now enslave the image bearer. That slavish relationship of spirit to physical creation highlights the error of Adam's desire in his sin.

Finally, point A^2 (return to dust—death) also relates to the sin of Adam. By his choice of TGB apart from God, life (relationship with God) ended. Choosing relationship with Eve over relationship with God cursed both physical creation (the essence of Eve) and the harmony of spousal relationship (relationship of image-bearing spirits).

Notice, then, the related consequences along the chiastic structure. A^1 and A^2 both point to the bodily (physical) curse: the serpent (representing creation) will lick dust, and the human body (the essence of the image bearer) will return to dust. This curse on physical essence is something we'll examine further when we come to how God will redeem. Points B^1 and B^2 both pertain to the hostility between the cursed creation and the image-bearing persons (the woman in B^1 and the man in B^2). Finally, the central points, C^1 and C^2, present the discord among image-bearing persons because of sin. The pattern of the whole chiasmus begins with the curse of creation (A^1 and A^2), moves to conflict between that cursed creation and the image bearers (B^1 and B^2), and ultimately centers on the conflict among image bearers (C^1 and C^2).

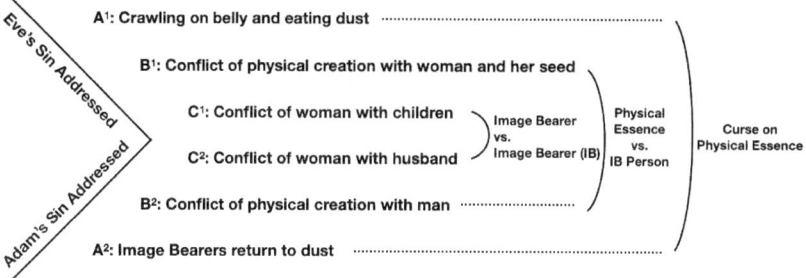

The destructive activity of the garden is repeated in example after example throughout the Bible. Adam and Eve were issued a command: don't eat—in other words, wait for God's teaching of relationship. God issued Israel, at the base of Sinai, a similar command: wait for God. The purpose in both cases was for good to come: relationship and the teaching of the Law. But Adam and Eve did not wait, and neither did the Israelites when they made the golden calf. They all made a choice for physical creation, and the result in each case was physical death.

Similarly, Paul in Romans 7 declares that because of God's revelation, he understands the imperative to do good. Yet his flesh constantly revolts against what he knows he should do. Paul ends chapter 7 crying out for separation from his physical essence—from that "body of death" (Romans 7:24). And that conflict is what leads us, in all three cases, to the atonement—our rescue from the curse of creation, which is our corrupted essence.

7

Sin's Legacy

And the last is Peter Bell,
Damned since our first parents fell,
Damned eternally to Hell—
Surely he deserves it well!

—Percy Bysshe Shelley, from "Peter Bell the Third"

Who can produce something pure from what is impure?
No one!

—Job 14:4

So far we've discussed the purpose of God in creation, how we were created, and the fall into sin that changed our course from perfect love relationship. Now we need to spend some time pondering the primary obstacle to a restored relationship: the curse of death on all human beings.

THE CHARACTER OF DEATH

In his book *The Evolution of Adam*, Peter Enns, professor of biblical studies at Eastern University in St. Davids, Pennsylvania, avers that "[t]he biblical authors tell a very different story of human origins than does science."[1] I agree. In fact, I know of no conservative theologians who would challenge

---

1. Enns, *Evolution of Adam*, ix.

that statement. Science simply cannot tell the whole story of an earth created from nothing. No one can apply the scientific method of systematic observation, measurement, and experimentation to an existence created *ex nihilo*. However, the purpose of Dr. Enns's observation is not to state the obvious but rather to support the removal of any historical significance from the Genesis account. Since Dr. Enns insists the biblical record at this point must start with science,[2] it is curious that he still holds to the particular scriptural truth of "the universal and humanly unalterable grip of both death and sin, and the work of the Savior, by the deep love and mercy of the Father, in delivering humanity from them."[3]

What makes his statements curious to me (and my purpose for bringing them up) is not to engage in a debate about evolution but rather to point out what I think is an inconsistency among most evolutionary theists in treating some parts of the biblical story differently from others. Dr. Enns justifies the miracle of the resurrection of Jesus, which is normally viewed as a scientific impossibility, while insisting that humanity's beginning could not similarly occur miraculously because science will not allow it.

Of course, Dr. Enns's views deserve more attention than these brief comments. And I don't mean to pick on him. I actually respect him as a Christian who cares deeply about questioning and thinking through matters of interest to Christians. None of us should blindly accept doctrines without grappling with the reasons that support their claims. We should all take advantage of the tools God has given us—both Scripture *and* our minds—to find consistency in God's purpose and plan. Ignoring valid investigation is not faith. Faith is our confidence in spiritual evidence despite any appearances to the contrary.[4] So while I do not always agree with Dr. Enns's conclusions, I can nevertheless appreciate his searching.

But since Dr. Enns agrees with the core of Christianity—that Jesus died for us—I think we should reflect on why our *Savior* came to deliver humanity from death and sin, even when we are contemplating the Genesis story. We humans did need saving; satisfactory relationship with God was impossible without salvation from sin and death. The question, then, is how

---

2. For example, on the same page, Dr. Enns states, "The Human Genome Project, completed in 2003, has shown beyond any reasonable scientific doubt that humans and primates share common ancestry."

3. Enns, *Evolution of Adam*, xi.

4. Dr. Enns actually says it himself: "I have found that the gospel calls us to abandon all hope in our ability to work out in our minds what the Creator is up to." He clarifies his meaning so as not to sound as if he is abandoning reason and theological discourse: "Our reasoning is limited not only by our humanity, but by our time and place in this long drama we call 'the universe.'" (Enns, "Thought about Easter.")

all of humanity arrived in this pre-salvific state of sin and death to which our human experience bears painful witness. This point separates Peter Enns and most evolutionary adherents from those who view the Genesis beginning as more immediate. In most theistic evolutionary approaches, sin and death are assumed from the start. In other words, for evolutionists, no specific act caused a fall from perfect relationship. The Edenic story of Adam and Eve merely illustrated that sin and death were natural functions of the human condition. And because sin and death existed, the evolutionary process was able to advance.

Of course, evolutionary theism encompasses many theories. Some of them regard Adam and Eve to be the literal first-conscious human characters emerging from evolutionary development. Others regard Adam and Eve as mythical characters depicting the general development of the human race, first into conscious beings, and then into selfish, sinful beings. (As I understand it, Peter Enns holds to another option that regards the mythical account of Adam and Eve as the metaphorical start of Israel—the people of God.)

I believe how we view Adam and Eve is important for our understanding of God's plan and purpose. Apart from the debated creation sequence, Genesis does directly state, and many times implies, the desire of God for relationship. God, we are told, created the world good. We read that humans—image bearers of God—were given dominion over the world. What did that look like? I think it may have looked a lot like Jesus, who, in his humanity and by his spirit, exercised dominion over physical creation by calming the seas and feeding 5000 from a few fish and loaves. But apart from Jesus, we see only a picture of the natural world dominating humans—not only by volcanos, tornados, and earthquakes but also by fleshly desires that attack our spirits.

The Bible implies that these conditions of woe were not God's intention in creation. God created for pure, unencumbered love relationship. From the relational Creator of Genesis 1 who desired image bearers, through the story of Eden's covenantal environment, to the breaking of relationship in the Fall, and all the way to a restoration, the Bible highlights *relationship*. Not only does the Genesis 3 story recount a fall from a prior non-sinful relationship with God, but the whole Bible presents that fall as the overwhelmingly dark condition of humanity against which we struggle and from which God hopes to bring about recovery. Even in his discussion of divorce—a relationship-breaking activity—Jesus tells his stunned audience that that was not God's intent *"from the beginning"* (Matthew 19:3–8). There was a beginning that did not include relationship-breaking. And so there was a beginning in which sin (missing the mark of relationship) had not yet encroached and in which death (the separation from God in broken relationship) had not yet occurred.

When the image bearers broke relationship with God, the physical world God had made for them to dominate switched roles from controlled to controller. Adam and Eve had prioritized their physical essence in their hearts; they idolized the physical rather than worshipping God. For that sin, the idol itself was cursed. The curse was not a punishment on physical creation. The curse was a necessary result of God's remaining true to his Covenant of Operational Essence. And therefore, I cannot read Genesis 1–3 in that light and still embrace an old-earth understanding of the normalcy of death.

What is more, without reading creation and the fall in the way I argued, I think we lose the emphasis the Bible places on redemption and restoration (words indicating a return to a prior state) and on the logic for what occurs in the atonement (which will be made clear in coming chapters).

In chapter 6, we discussed the consequences of Adam's and Eve's sins. Their own relationship with God was broken, but the consequence of sin did not end with them. It spread to all subsequent humanity. How exactly did—and does—that occur?

HUMAN SPIRIT ORIGIN

The question of precisely how and why we experience the effects of original sin goes all the way back to the church fathers, who debated about how souls come into existence. One of these early theologians, Origen, seemed to believe in God's new creation of each individual spirit *ex nihilo*. But another of these fathers, Tertullian, suggested something different—that our parents generate our souls just as they do our bodies. Of course, Tertullian could offer no idea of how that generation might occur. So down through the centuries, proponents of these two options have been wrestling: those who espouse generationism, or traducianism (from the Latin *tradux,* meaning branch of a vine), and those who favor creationism (the new-from-nothing individual-spirit creation).

Let's investigate these ideas using the following means:

1. Biblical statements
2. The logic of inheritance
3. The structure of the image bearer
4. The meaning of being born in sin

WHAT THE BIBLE HAS TO SAY

First, then, what does the Bible have to say? Romans 2:6 (as well as its sources in Psalm 62:12 and Proverbs 24:12) insists God will judge and repay based on our own individual works: "He will repay each one according to his works." I don't mean to argue from silence, but this verse certainly doesn't mention anything about being punished for Adam's sin. So even if we could find elsewhere a passage implying that punishment does result from guilt for Adam's sin, we would have to reconcile it with Paul's unequivocal declaration here.

Ezekiel 18 mentions God's displeasure at the Jewish proverb: "The fathers eat sour grapes, and the children's teeth are set on edge." This proverb can be interpreted to imply that the wrongdoing of fathers leads to punishment for their children. In fact, the Jews used the proverb exactly that way—to explain their terrible condition in Babylonian captivity as God's judgment resulting from the sins of their fathers. Jeremiah 31 recounts the same Jewish complaint in citing this proverb. But let's note that God is displeased with the attitude of these Jews. God insists they are suffering not for their parents' sin but rather for their own. Therefore, God tells them in Ezekiel 18:20, "The person who sins is the one who will die. A son won't suffer punishment for the father's iniquity." God appears emphatic that sin does not move from parent to child so that the child must pay the penalty.

Of course, consequences of the parents' sin do remain. If I, in a drunken stupor, kill someone in a car accident, his or her family certainly suffer for my sin. Yet I alone am guilty. Thus, consequences for parents' sins may be felt by their children, but God insists that guilt does not pass from one person to another.

In Deuteronomy 1, God is displeased that the Israelites failed to trust him for support to enter the Promised Land. For their sin, they spend the next 40 years wandering in the wilderness until they all die out. After their deaths, their children are allowed entrance. Verse 39 reads, "Your little children, whom you said would be plunder, your sons, who don't know good from evil, will enter there. I will give them the land." Not being included in the judgment on their parents demonstrates that the children did not inherit their parents' sin guilt.

One more verse in Ecclesiastes 12 is worth highlighting. In speaking of death, Solomon concludes in verse 7, "And the dust returns to the earth as it once was, and the spirit returns to God who gave it." Solomon implies here that the body and spirit do not originate from the same source. The body came from the earth, and it is thus passed on by parents to children. But God directly confers on us the spirit, and it returns to God.

THE LOGIC OF INHERITANCE

Having reviewed some Scripture, let's now think in philosophical terms. Traducianism attempts to explain how the path of guilt wound its way from Adam to us. It begins with the Bible's declaration that we were born with a fallen nature (Ephesians 2:3; Psalm 51:5). But traducians reason that it would be unjust of God to create new spirits with sinful natures. Thus, our spirits (so the logic goes) must have resulted from a preestablished, already fallen existence. In other words, the traducian supposes our corrupted spirits are inherited, just as our bodies are, from Adam through our parents.

This line of argument, however, isn't as simple as it appears. If our spirits are generated from our parents, why is only the guilt for Adam's sin passed along? Would not the logic require the passing of all the guilt from all the sins of all our parents, grandparents, great-grandparents, and beyond? How could God selectively transmit only the guilt of Adam's sin but not some other sin? By that reasoning, if Hitler were my father or grandfather, God would need to consider me just as guilty and, therefore, just as accountable for his genocidal evil. No matter that I did not actually commit his atrocities: even were I to express my sincere disgust of his actions, nothing could remove the guilt—*if* my spirit derived from my parents. Traducianism, then, must either view people as guilty for all the sins of their ancestors or believe God selectively holds us accountable for only Adam's sin while arbitrarily wiping clean the rest.

But as we've just seen from Scripture, the Bible doesn't appear to support those assumptions. The insistence of Paul, David, Solomon, Moses, and the rest that the justice of God requires accountability for only our own sin is precisely to argue against the concept of spiritual generation from prior spirits.

Creationism does not have that particular problem. Creationism posits that the newly created spirits of newly conceived individuals are without sin. Traducians may retort that it leaves the spirit with no connection to original sin. Without any obvious tie, we would have to conclude original sin has no bearing on our spirits—one of the Pelagian heresies.

Trying to resolve this puzzle has long been the struggle of scholars. Calvin ultimately attributed the difficulty to God's inscrutability: "I again ask how it is that the fall of Adam involves so many nations with their infant children in eternal death without remedy unless that it so seemed meet to God?"[5] I recoil at Calvin's almost facile imputation of this and other horrific actions to what seems "meet"—suitable, appropriate—to God, or as other translators

---

5. Calvin, *Institutes*, 630.

phrase it, "because it so *pleased* God" (emphasis added).[6] The idea is impossible; God declared in Ezekiel 18:32: "For I take no pleasure in anyone's death."

Creationism finds some support in the principle of federalism, or federal headship. Federalism views Adam not just as the actual father of our souls, but the representative of our race. Since he was our representative, when he sinned, we all became guilty. Federalism bases this idea of representation on Romans 5:12, specifically the claim that the verse teaches imputation of sin:

> Therefore, just as sin entered the world through one man, and death through sin, in this way death spread to all men, because all sinned.

Now, this verse is a chiasmus, arranged in this way:

A^1: Just as sin entered the world through one man
—B^1: and death through sin,
—B^2: in this way death spread to all men,
A^2: because all sinned.

The chiasmus, though, clarifies a point that the federalists miss. It is not that Adam sinned and then that sin is imputed to everyone else. Rather, the balance of the verse indicates that just as Adam sinned and received death, so all people sin and receive death.

The federalists also argue that the rest of Romans 5 shows Paul's contrast of our two representatives, Adam and Christ, even though the text never mentions representation. In fact, as Paul continues his discussion in chapter 6, we learn that we've died to Adam (and his cursed race) and have been made alive (reborn) in Christ. The comparison is not representational at all; it is relational.

Federalism rests on the concept that Adam is our agent in the original covenant of humankind with God; Adam's actions have consequence for all those embraced in the covenant—all humans. But federalists have randomly imposed agent rules for this covenant that don't exist for other covenants. Abraham, in covenant development with God, believed him, and it was counted to Abraham as righteousness. Yet his righteousness was not imputed to all participants in the Abrahamic covenant. The same is true for other covenants. So with that inconsistency and without direct biblical reference, it is unsatisfying to assume federal headship based on a particular interpretation of Romans 5:12, when other interpretations are not only plausible but more likely.

---

6. Calvin, "Quotes."

THE STRUCTURE OF THE IMAGE BEARER

Traducianism and federalism share one overarching problem that renders both lines of thought in regard to original sin impossible: they presume that the effect of Adam's sin transmits through our spirits, either by spirit derivation (traducianism) or imputation (federalism). But let's note what was actually *cursed* in the fall. It was not Adam and Eve's individual spirits, though they were indeed guilty of sin. Rather, the curse fell on their one shared essence—*physical* creation. How are we actually related to Adam? We are related through our bodies—our essence—*physical* creation. How, then, would the effect of sin pass from generation to generation? The passing of the curse makes sense only if passed through our essence, through *physical* creation, the only tie we actually have with Adam. Adam's sin resulted in a curse on physical creation (our essence), and subsequent human spirits are born into that corrupted physical essence and in turn are dominated by the influence of sin; thus, they require redemption to return to life (relationship) with God.

Another look at the image-bearing chart from chapter 3 will help illustrate how original sin continues its influence.

Recall that the chart shows God to be multiple-in-one by the distinction between essence and existence. In his one essence, God is TGB. All three persons of the Trinity recognize their one essence through their intelligence and moral and aesthetic senses. They show respect for that essence by holding it in faith and hope. And they use it in operation by revealing

TGB in loving care. All three of these attribute groupings (the recognition, respect, and revelation) describe how each person functions based on the one TGB essence. That is our God.

Since the persons of God function only according to their essence, God needs to base relationship in creation also on his TGB. So God created us with attributes that mirror his own and by which we can recognize and understand his essence. He gave us attributes of comprehension (conceptual intelligence to grasp his truth, conscious morality to understand his goodness, and critical aesthetic to recognize his beauty). He made us with attributes of concurrence (faith and hope) so we could conclude from our understanding and preserve the TGB in hope. And he made us also able to communicate his revealed TGB through communal love for him and for others. All these attributes of comprehension, concurrence, and communication exist in each created person—each image bearer. But all image bearers also are united in one essence, which is our physical materiality.

All God's relational interaction depends on God's activity of revealing himself. Therefore, as Paul explains in Romans 1, God reveals his invisible attributes: his divine nature (which is his essence of TGB) and his eternal power (which is his activity of loving care). He reveals this essence of TGB to and through his physical creation (Romans 1:20), which is our essence. In other words, God essentially reveals his essence (TGB) through his persons to our essence (physical creation), and we comprehend his essence by our persons—our individual spirits.

Reviewing this chart helps us see how sin has distorted things. We humans have shrouded God as revealer by our sin (as Paul describes in Romans 1). But even after dismissing God as the source of TGB, we keep searching for TGB based on our innate desire for it. Because of our sin, we look no further than our own essence—the physical creation through which God has revealed himself. Instead of acknowledging God, then, we claim ourselves and our physical world and beings as the source of TGB.

THIS BODY OF DEATH

That failure, we learned from Genesis 3, was the sin of Adam and Eve, actuated in eating the fruit. When Adam and Eve sinned, they bore—in their persons, their spirits—the full responsibility (guilt) of their evil action. They had been given dominion over creation and had been told to subdue it (Genesis 1:28). In their sin, they allowed physical creation to take the upper hand; they caused creation to be cursed and, by the curse, corrupted. Because they as individuals knelt in worship to their essence, they became enslaved to it, and it continued to influence them in corrupt and dominant rule. As generations followed, this same evil influence dominated human spirits as they were newly created. The influence of original sin, then, is through fallen physical creation. In Romans 1 through 3 (and beyond), Paul shows that we all fall to this dominating influence of our flesh, which is precisely what we're talking about when we refer to our sinful natures. Remember that God's divine nature is his essence—his TGB. Our human nature is dominated by our essence—our bodies of physical creation—and our essence is corrupted.

OVERCOMING THE CURSE

The connection of these ideas to the atonement is hopefully now clearer. God knew no one could overcome that dominance of evil influence by our flesh (Romans 3:23). So he became the rescuer. He came to enter into this corrupted flesh (Romans 8:3). But through the strength of his spirit, Jesus did not allow his flesh to dominate. He, the perfect man, trusted in God despite the pressure of his body's own corrupt temptation, and he remained sinless. He died, putting that tainted physical essence to death, and he rose again, reclaiming or redeeming his body devoid of the corruption. In this renewal of flesh, he is called the firstfruits of a restored physical creation (I Corinthians 15:20).

The consequence of Adam's sin (the curse of our physical essence) had destroyed God's creative purpose—our shared everlasting love relationship with him. Relationship with God, which had been based *on* God's essence, was always meant to take place *within* our physical essence. Thus, for relationship with God to occur, our physical essence, which had been corrupted through the curse, had to be made holy as God is holy. That idea is central to redemption.

The Bible all along asserts that our physical essence is the place where we meet God. The garden first illustrated that point, representing that place of relationship. Before the fall, meeting with God was in sinless pleasure. After the fall, Adam and Eve wanted to hide because of their nakedness—the unworthiness of their essence. In Genesis 3:22-23, God casts them out of the garden, the place of relationship, which now represents a cursed, corrupted, and unholy housing for love relationship.

Throughout the Old Testament, the same idea presents itself in many stories. The story of the Noahic covenant begins in Genesis 5, recounting how humankind was made in God's image for the intent of relationship. But just as Adam chose Eve over God, so did the "sons of God" choose the "daughters of men" (Genesis 6:1–2), leading the world in its downward spiral of "widespread wickedness." The rest of chapter 6 showcases God's plan for redemption, symbolized by the ark. Genesis 7 pictures the destruction of the earth (the old essence), and Genesis 8 highlights the rebirth to new essence. The story is capped in Genesis 9:1–17 as God promises never again to destroy the essence; the promise symbolizes the everlasting renewal of the believer in new essence at Christ's return.

We recognize the same idea in the Abrahamic covenant, including its three major promises: offspring (signifying our spirits), land (signifying our bodies—our essence), and blessing to the nations (signifying restored relationship).

The Mosaic covenant reveals its own perspective of the same picture. The children of Israel were imprisoned in Egypt, which images our sinful essence. Rescue through the Red Sea portrays our atonement escape. The wilderness wanderings depict our time now awaiting new essence. The passing through the Jordan represents passing to Christ's redeeming embrace, shrugging off this old, corrupt essence. And the entering into the Promised Land pictures our new bodies—new essence received at Christ's return.

Perhaps the greatest biblical metaphor for our bodies as the meeting place with God is the tabernacle/temple. The tabernacle in the wilderness, set up in the middle of the camp, was the place to meet with God. But that tabernacle had to be made holy with the sprinkling of sacrificial blood prior to the meeting.

Jesus tells the Pharisees in John 2:19 that if they destroy his body (his temple), in three days he will raise it up; his body redeemed from curse highlights the unspotted housing of relationship with God. Jesus is indeed the firstfruits of this refined, redeemed, restored physical essence, as 1 Corinthians 15:22–23 tells us.

While it is God's essence on which relationship is based, it is the image bearers' essence in which relationship takes place. That essence must be purified and holy for relationship with God. Adam's sin cursed our physical essence and made it impossible for us to have relationship with God. But God's redemption plan, with its fulfillment in the atonement, was to rescue us from this curse of sin—our corrupted physical essence—so that we could again meet with God.

8

God's Wrath

There is a time, we know not when,
A point we know not where,
That marks the destiny of men
To glory or despair.

There is a line by us unseen,
That crosses every path;
The hidden boundary between
God's patience and his wrath.

—Joseph Addison Alexander, from "The Hidden Line"

For God's wrath is revealed from heaven
against all godlessness and unrighteousness
of people who by their unrighteousness suppress the truth.

—Romans 1:18

The poem at the opening of this chapter reveals a distorted view of God. It pictures in vaguely threatening terms a God poised at some mysteriously defined line to unleash a torrent of wrath on anyone who oversteps—a God who will take only so much bad behavior and then let loose with retributive rage. That character is not our God who champions love.

Yet don't certain passages in both the Old and the New Testaments show judgment and wrath raining down on sin? There seems to be no shortage of proof texts, for whichever side of the issue you choose. John makes clear in his first epistle that "God is love!" (4:8) and "God is light, and there is *absolutely* no darkness in him!" (1:5). So how could black clouds of wrath roil in the heart of God? Yet Paul makes it clear in Romans 1:18 that it is God's wrath revealed that brings destruction on the unrighteous. Is this paradox too much of a mystery for us ever to reconcile?[1]

REACTING OUT OF CHARACTER

In his classic sermon, "Sinners in the Hands of an Angry God," Jonathan Edwards presents some truth but fails to apply it correctly. Consider this paragraph:

> The God that holds you over the pit of hell, much as one holds a spider, or some loathsome insect over the fire, abhors you, and is dreadfully provoked: his wrath towards you burns like fire; he looks upon you as worthy of nothing else, but to be cast into the fire; he is of purer eyes than to bear to have you in his sight; you are ten thousand times more abominable in his eyes, than the most hateful venomous serpent is in ours. You have offended him infinitely more than ever a stubborn rebel did his prince; and yet it is nothing but his hand that holds you from falling into the fire every moment. It is to be ascribed to nothing else, that you did not go to hell the last night; that you were suffered to awake again in this world, after you closed your eyes to sleep. And there is no other reason to be given, why you have not dropped into hell since you arose in the morning, but that God's hand has held you up. There is no other reason to be given why you have not gone to hell, since you have sat here in the house of God, provoking his pure eyes by your sinful wicked manner of attending his solemn worship. Yea, there is nothing else that is to be given as a reason why you do not this very moment drop down into hell.[2]

---

1. When I state that John's and Paul's statements on this topic are "clear," I am speaking at least partly tongue-in-cheek. After all, if the points are so *clear*, why do they result in paradox? And why do adherents of a position always claim definitive clarity for *their* side? Correct interpretation more often than not requires painstaking examination of a passage. As theologian Greg Boyd likes to say, we need to apply ourselves to find the *something else that is going on* below the surface level presented.

2. Edwards, "Sinners."

In his zeal to prompt his listeners to contemplate their eternal fate, Edwards paints a frightening image of a potentate who holds his subjects in contempt for their offenses. This overlord dangles the unsaved over a fiery pit until his loathing causes him to drop them into the torture of the fire. It is recorded that overwhelmed congregants cried out in distress. Some fainted. Others clung to their pews or church pillars in fear of slipping into hell.

Such a god violates the Bible's love description. I believe we radically misunderstand God in attributing to him the frustration common to sin-influenced humans. We read in the Bible about "propitiation" and presume that restoration must involve what we ourselves would require to satisfy a sense of injury. This view of God as an offended party who can be placated only with a debt payment prompted James Stuart Stewart, the Scottish minister and author, to write, "Its greatest merit was the serious view it took of sin. Its greatest defect was its disastrous view of God" (Stewart 2012, 216). He continued, "It cannot be too firmly emphasized that the whole idea of propitiating [satisfying] God is radically unscriptural" (Stewart 2012, 217).

The bit of truth that I suggested can be found in Edwards's rant is that God's supporting hand does indeed keep us from devastation. Humankind does hang perilously over immediate and complete destruction, and it *is* only the hand of God that prevents the fall. But God does not hold out his hand in scornful vagary. The heart of our God loves limitlessly. Thus, the solution to the paradox of John's God of love and Paul's God of wrath cannot rest on a presumption that God's heart is divided between hatred and benevolence. God loves. "God is love so all God does is loving."[3] What follows, then, is that what the Bible terms "wrath" is God's ultimate withdrawing of himself or turning himself away.

REACTING IN CHARACTER

To understand more fully this point about wrath, we need to shore up our chapter 1 conclusion that God is infinite love. Without repeating the philosophical path we walked there, let's begin by turning to the revealed God of Scripture.

While the Bible mentions God on virtually every page, these references do not hold equal weight in showing us an accurate picture of who God is. Many reasons account for the variance, but a major one is the struggle of Old Testament prophets and writers to know this God who had not yet fully revealed himself to them. What we can conclude from them and from the fully informed sensibilities of New Testament authors is that Jesus alone

---

3. McKnight, *Hum of Angels*, 86.

reveals our God perfectly. Notice how Hebrews emphasizes that truth of Christ's revelation:

> Long ago God spoke to the fathers by the prophets at different times and in different ways. In these last days, He has spoken to us by His Son. God has appointed Him heir of all things and made the universe through Him. The Son is the radiance of God's glory and the exact expression of His nature, sustaining all things by His powerful word. After making purification for sins, He sat down at the right hand of the Majesty on high. (Hebrews 1:1–3)

Christ was there at the beginning, through the prophets' initial attempts at revelation, and at the apex when redemption became reality. But particularly important is the statement in verse 3: "The Son is the radiance of God's glory and the exact expression of His nature." The emphasis is on Jesus as the *radiance* of God's glory! God's glory is the manifestation of his worth. God's worth is his divine nature and eternal power—his TGB revealed by and provided through his loving care. And that worth, or glory, *radiated* brilliantly from Christ. He was the "*exact* expression of [God's] nature." That phrase means not only that there was nothing about Jesus that didn't reveal God, but also that *there is nothing in God's nature that was not expressed in Jesus*. As we reflected in chapter 1, no wonder Jesus told his disciples in the upper room, "The one who has seen Me has seen the Father" (John 14:9). He claimed deity itself in John 8:58, telling the Pharisees, "I assure you: Before Abraham was, I am." And Paul agreed with this, declaring, "For the *entire fullness* of God's nature dwells bodily [or, dwells within the body] of Christ" (Colossians 2:9).

If we want to know what God is like, we must study the passages about Jesus. If we want to know what God is doing in the Old Testament, we must follow the principles shown in the life of Jesus. God would not do or even want to do anything not seen in Jesus because Jesus is "the *entire fullness* of God's nature." Watching Jesus at work in the Gospels and contemplating the discussions about Jesus by the other New Testament writers, we learn of the purpose and operation of the kingdom of God, which is also Christ's kingdom. Jesus operated according to and in pursuit of that kingdom and its ideals throughout his life.

At the very beginning of Jesus's ministry, right after his baptism, Jesus was led by the Spirit into the wilderness for 40 days. Satan approached Jesus toward the end of that period and tempted him with the kingdoms of the world. Jesus could have them all if he would just bow to Satan. The choice was clear—gain the kingdoms by bowing to Satan (and his worldly way of doing things) or maintain his gaze on God (and his TGB). Jesus recognized that doing things Satan's way would simply amount to a transfer of slaves—that is, humankind—from their old master to a new one; that was not God's purpose. So Jesus turned the Devil down in a decided rejection of Satan's purpose and methods—grasping for kingdoms to control as master commander. God's way of victory, in contrast, is through a love that will not and cannot coerce. It is that attitude of love, born of God's TGB, that Jesus pursued.

That pursuit, in fact, bookends his ministry. In John 18, Jesus stood before Pilate, who worried that Jesus was claiming kingship in order to lead a physical insurrection against Rome. "My kingdom is not of this world," said Jesus, specifically to let Pilate know he was not interested in a coercive control of the world's kings and governments. His kingdom was built on love, not compelled obeisance. It was an upside-down, ostensibly impossible way of doing things. But Jesus proved its power by gaining victory precisely through this "backwards," love-based means. He won the victory through the cross.

All along the Bible emphasizes this upside-down kingdom of love:

- Matthew 5:5 "The gentle are blessed, for they will inherit the earth."
- Luke 6:27–28 "Love your enemies, do what is good to those who hate you, bless those who curse you, pray for those who mistreat you."
- Romans 12:20 "If your enemy is hungry, feed him. If he is thirsty, give him something to drink."
- 1 Peter 3:8–11 ". . . seek peace and pursue it."

God's kingdom is characterized by love. God reveals that primary attribute in himself at the beginning of Genesis in pursuit of his creative purpose of everlasting love relationship. All God's communication to us is for our benefit—the very definition of love. Not only is everlasting love relationship God's *creation* purpose; it is his *restoration* purpose as well. And Jesus—who is the "exact expression" and "entire fullness" of God's nature—showed us the greatest love. He told his disciples in the upper room before his death, "No one has greater love than this, that someone would lay down his life for his friends" (John 15:13). That evening's teaching was etched in the mind of John, who passed it on as he later wrote, "This is how we have come to know love: He laid down His life for us" (1 John 3:16). God's kingdom is indeed characterized by love.

REACTING TO SIN

Sin frustrates the working of this love kingdom, because sin "misses the mark" of God's purpose of love relationship. So how does God react to sin? Is his reaction different from his other activity? Isn't it here that he reveals his wrath? To understand God's response to sin, let's review how sin began. Adam and Eve violated God's command not to eat from that tree: "You are free to eat from any tree of the garden, but you must not eat from the tree of the knowledge of good and evil, for on that day you eat from it, you will certainly die" (Genesis 2:16–17).

As we discussed, the purpose of this command was not to conduct a mere test of obedience. Aligning with the character of God and his kingdom, the command's purpose was to ensure the proper growth of love relationship. God does not coerce love. (Although I've already stated this, it bears repeating. It is a truth about love which many believers give assent to before misshaping it into a twisted notion of "sovereignty.") Although God reveals himself and his TGB, he will not force himself into the heart, mind, and life of anyone who continues to reject him. He simply can't do so, because force would end any hope of true love relationship, which is free interchange of selfless giving and receiving.

The growth of love relationship takes time. So God issued his command to refrain from eating of that particular tree—a tree of life-functioning knowledge—not because he didn't want Adam and Eve to have the insight, but rather because he wanted them to receive that education—the revelation of TGB—through their experience with him, the true source of the TGB.

But they sinned. They missed that mark—the target, the goal—of true love relationship and incurred the penalty God had forewarned them of: the end of relationship—that is, death—for both their spirits and their bodies. Although instantaneous in some respects, the penalty was not immediately complete. God had anticipated the fall and had devised a plan to overcome sin's consequences. The plan included forgiveness and redemption. It was a heart of love that moved God to offer forgiveness to repentant spirits desiring restored love relationship. And God assured us of his love by deciding that he himself would accomplish redemption for our cursed physical state, returning control of human essence to our spirits.

Notice that love promotes both parts of this plan. Regarding forgiveness, love prompts the *sinner* to return to God's relational embrace. But love also prompts the *forgiver* to both offer and embrace the forgiveness—to relinquish any claim to resentment and requital. Likewise, love prompted God in Christ to become human so he could redeem. And love prompts the sinner to consider dead his or her own cursed physical essence to welcome unity with Christ's redeemed condition (Romans 6:11). That is the Bible's teaching about restoration (Matthew 26:26; John 6:53–58; Romans 6:1–11; 8:10). Jonathan Edwards was totally wrong in his characterization of an angry God. God's motivation in holding his creatures away from the flame has always been love.

God's reaction to the sin of the repenter, then, corresponds to who God is—a God of love. But when love does not prompt the sinner toward restored relationship, how does God respond? Ultimately, with reluctance and grief, he simply lets go. He *will not* coerce. He certainly does not aim lightning bolts with measured anger at unbelievers or unceremoniously toss them into the flame. He doesn't inflict pain and suffering on those who refuse to love him. (That response would make no sense: "I love you. You don't love me back? Then I'll just have to torture you.") Rather, in the face of resolute rejection, he turns away. And when the source of *all* truth, goodness, and beauty turns away, there is *nothing* good left to be felt or experienced by the rejecting spirit. As C. S. Lewis put it, "God cannot give us happiness and peace apart from himself, because it is not there. There is no such thing."[4]

Scripture affirms this response by God. In the same chapter in which Paul warns of the wrath of God against unrighteousness (Romans 1), he describes that wrath three times, not as God's angrily inflicting evil on those who reject him, but rather as God's *giving them over*. The release is not in disgust or complaisance. Remember that God is completely revealed in Jesus, and Jesus groaned in misery when he encountered stubborn rejection: "Jerusalem, Jerusalem, who kills the prophets and stones those who are sent to her. How often I wanted to gather your children together, as a hen gathers her chicks under her wings, but you were not willing!" (Matthew 23:37).

Ultimately, God leaves our wills free to rejection. God is still working to accomplish his goal—repentance of all humans who will reunite with him. But again, he will not coerce. He interacts in the affairs of humankind, but he allows his image bearers, as free creatures, to interact in the affairs of humankind as well. A favorite question of atheists is why evil exists if there is an all-powerful, all-good God. We briefly discussed this question in chapter 1. Their conclusion—that God must be either not all powerful or not all good—is short-sighted. God's goal of true love relationship requires that he *not* coerce to force himself on free creatures. How exactly he interacts and to what extent he reveals himself to draw people to him without obstructing their free choice are matters so complex they would require us to be . . . well . . . God to figure out. But he does just that.

---

4. Lewis, *Mere Christianity*, 2001.

If God's care and concern is love, God's turning away—separating, withdrawing himself (thus withdrawing his TGB)—is his wrath. He does not strike out in evil to destroy. But when he removes his TGB, the only possible result is destruction. The whole point of existence is love relationship. If rejecters will not have it, it is no loving act to keep them in existence to live without love and to harm the love relationship of those who have turned to God. After extending every possible opportunity for love, God leaves, and his wrath—God's absence—descends in horrific, all-encompassing destruction.

PART 3

Restoration Plan Forged

9

God's Righteousness

His scepter is the rod of righteousness,
With which he bruiseth all his foes to dust.

—Edmund Spenser, from "A Hymn of Heavenly Beauty"

For I am not ashamed of the gospel,
because it is God's power for salvation to everyone who believes,
first to the Jew, and also to the Greek.
For in it God's righteousness is revealed from faith to faith,
just as it is written: The righteous will live by faith.

—Romans 1:16–17

God formed his restoration plan to rescue his fallen image bearers. But he didn't intend merely to return sinners to a behavioral standard. They had broken covenant relationship founded on his very own divine nature. God's restoring design, then, had to first ensure his own covenant faithfulness, even as he charted the path for their return.

God is righteous—a dynamic element of covenant relationship that Paul explains in Romans. But as we read the words "God's righteousness" in Romans 1:17, we tend to gloss over their significance. "Sure, God is perfect, without sin," we acknowledge. "Now, let's move on to Paul's real point about the gospel!" But the phrase "God's righteousness" has more depth than we may at first realize, and we subsequently misunderstand its function in redemption. Righteousness means faithfulness to covenant obligations. Recognizing that, we should appreciate that God has covenant responsibilities, too. Let's look at how Paul bolsters this idea in Romans.

As he opens his Romans letter, Paul insists the gospel reveals God's righteousness from faith to faith (Romans 1:17). While we instinctively agree with that assertion, we can find ourselves stumbling when trying to explain its meaning. How exactly does the gospel do that—reveal *God's* righteousness? What is it about God's faithfulness to his covenant obligations that actually produces the gospel? The introduction speaks to Paul's purpose for writing.

The Christian life of the apostle Paul (perhaps more so than the lives of any of the other eleven called-by-Jesus-himself apostles) bounded the apostolic period. Christ overwhelmed Paul on the Damascus road within a couple of years after the first Christian Pentecost, and Christ rejecters martyred him just before the AD 70 destruction of the temple. So his mission to the Gentiles fully spanned the apostolic age. More importantly, as apostle of (not merely preacher to) the Gentiles, he introduced the gospel to them, which meant introducing it to the world outside Palestine. Of course, it was Peter who preached the first sermon to a non-Jewish assembly (the household of Cornelius in Acts 10), and his preaching resulted in the salvation of the non-Jewish Cornelius. But from a historically backward perspective, we see that God purposed, through Peter's delivery, to notify the other apostles of the direction Paul would lead the gospel—to the world beyond Jerusalem. God, then, singled out Paul for the gospel's initial thrust to the Gentiles (Romans 1:1). And what better places to do so than in the cities of influence, especially Rome? So Paul intended to preach and proclaim in Rome based on his sure understanding of the Holy Spirit's direction. He began his mission to that city with this letter presaging his coming.

What exactly did Paul want to tell the Romans? Of course, he went to preach the gospel to the Gentiles (Romans 1:15); that was his mission. But if we want to comprehend his true motivation, we have to sharpen our perception of what "preaching the gospel" means. Paul's mission did not center on seeing souls saved. (I feel the stunned pause. Hang on; take a breath; I haven't renounced orthodox Christianity.) Yes, I'm sure Paul *wanted* to see souls saved. We know that from Luke's narrative and his own appeals, and Paul did in fact lead people to Christ. But his *mission*—the intention of this letter—was to explain precisely how God accomplished his victory in conquering the sin-imposed curse separating image bearers from their God.

You may wonder whether I am splitting hairs with this distinction about Paul's mission. Isn't proclaiming the gospel—how God defeated the enemy—just about the same as actually seeing souls saved? One, after all, results from the other. But if we want to understand thoroughly how God conquered, we can't just jump to the outcome. Simply cheering our rescue doesn't do justice to the good news of how God destroyed sin and death to fulfill his *righteous* promise-keeping by abolishing the curse Adam caused. The gospel, both in its entirety and in its most important element, means something much more than the relief and joy of our own personal perspectives.

I believe that as Paul started to write Romans, he had firmly in mind the concepts we have already discussed in this book, so quickly reviewing them will direct us to the righteousness of God that is Paul's main theme. Two important words center our efforts: creation and covenant. God *created* for relationship. Relationship is dependent on who God is—his essence, his truth, goodness, and beauty. For his creatures to be in relationship with him, God had to create them as image bearers to enable them to understand, assent to, and then, in relationship, share that TGB. So God made us able to comprehend, develop in faith and hope, and mimic him in love regarding TGB. Since he made us to crave TGB, and since God is their only true source, God *covenanted* with his image bearers to provide that TGB as they in turn trusted him for it. Only then could relationship between God and image bearers be completely satisfying.

Of course, sin got in the way. Those image bearers, *breaking their covenant*, chose to pursue TGB apart from God, a pursuit that ended in the severing of relationship with God. From before creation, God knew his creatures—gifted with the ability for uncoerced love but without immediate complete relational knowledge—could fail in that initial covenant. But in pre-creational resolve, God *covenanted* with himself (Trinities can do that) to redeem soon-to-fall humankind to restore his creation purpose of everlasting love relationship. In other words, before creation ever happened, God had already determined his redemption plan specifically to ensure his covenanted purpose in creating.

REDEMPTION'S NECESSITY— OVERCOMING THE CURSE

Redemption. The word rolls easily off the tongue of every Christian. Although it has become synonymous with the whole of God's restoration plan, we should accurately apply it to only a part of the plan—albeit a hugely important part, that which made the cross necessary.

Adam's sin brought the curse on creation. Adam (not deceived by Satan as Eve had been) had chosen to seek truth, goodness, and beauty from Eve—from a part of physical creation—instead of from God. Adam effectively made creation his god. He had done what Paul describes in Romans 1:21–23, 25 (my paraphrase):

> Though Adam knew God as his Creator, he did not glorify him as God (faithfully assent to his worth as TGB source) or show gratitude. Instead, his thinking became nonsense, and his senseless mind was darkened. Believing he was thinking wisely (for his own ultimate good), he became a fool by exchanging that glory of the immortal God for the image-bearing of mortal Eve. Thus, he exchanged the truth of God for a lie (of his own making) and worshiped and served the creation (humankind's physical essence) instead of the Creator, who is praised forever.

Here is the fall in all its tragic significance. Adam did not simply fail to dutifully perform his master's command. God is a forgiving God. Those who fail, repent, and pray for forgiveness genuinely receive it from God's heart of love. The Old Testament testifies to that. God can dismiss a failure as he embraces the repentant one. But Adam did more than miss the mark of simple obedience to a command. Adam chose to replace Yahweh as his god with physical creation in the form of Eve. He moved his basis for relationship from God's essence to his own, which Eve shared. Missing the target of worshipping the one true God by *righteously* depending on him, Adam caused the curse—a curse on the physical creation. Adam had claimed it as his idol as he worshipped and depended on it for satisfaction. Because of that exchange, the Bible highlights his sin, rather than Eve's, in both Old and New Testaments as the sin which constituted the fall.

In the opening chapters, I labeled physical creation as the one essence of humankind. While our bodies superficially appear to be all our own, distinct from the rest of physical creation, we know that these bodies cannot exist independently. We constantly need the common air, water, and nutrients of physical creation to pass through us to maintain our physical lives. The interchange of matter and energy continually coursing through every human draws attention to the common—the one—essence we all share. It is our spirits who are individually separate. Our multiple spirits in one physical essence are one way we image our multiple-in-one God.

When Adam sinned by putting God aside and choosing this one essence of ours as his god, he chose against faithfulness to the Covenant of Life. Remember that the Covenant of Life is a bond of relationship between God and his image bearers. It obligated God to provide his TGB in loving care, and it obligated image bearers to depend on God for that loving care.

God had given to image bearers' spirits the ruling control over their essence. In Genesis 1:26, God linked the way humans were to rule to his own ruling ways, since the image bearers were indeed to bear his image. How does God rule? He rules by applying his TGB in loving care. How, then, were the image bearers to rule? In the same way of course: by applying God's TGB in loving care for creation. Adam's choice, however, tore physical creation from God's TGB basis. In effect, Adam separated creation from God, making it his own god, devoting it to another—an unholy—purpose. The Hebrew term for what Adam did is *harem*. New Testament Greek calls it *anathema*. Thus, Adam's sin made physical creation *anathema*—a curse—because it dedicated physical creation to this unholy purpose. Genesis 3 delineates the curse, and it forms the background for Paul's discussion of release in Romans 8:20 and for John's description of its absence in Revelation 22:3.

That curse of physical creation is the great gulf that separates us from God. God cannot simply destroy cursed creation so that we can come to him as spirits without it. The definition of being human involves both spirit *and* body, not just spirit. To destroy our essence, then, would be to destroy us! Rather than destroy physical creation, God had to remove its curse.

CHRIST'S RIGHTEOUSNESS

Since our physical essence has no mind and will (they exist in the spirit), it cannot repent as the spirit can in seeking God's forgiveness. Furthermore, forgiven spirits cannot simply give their essence back to God in the same way they took it away. We no longer control our physical essence; it controls us. So far as restoration goes, we, on our own, are hopeless. God had to step in to redeem, and his plan necessitated the cross. Here's the plan: (1) Jesus took on this cursed physical essence by becoming human; (2) Jesus did not succumb to the control of his essence—that is, he never made it his god (although tempted in every way as we are [Hebrews 4:15]); (3) Jesus put that essence, his own body, to death on the cross, and by so doing fulfilled the separation-from-God curse requirement; (4) Jesus then reclaimed his bodily essence without the curse; (5) Jesus presented that redeemed essence to God for renewed, restored embrace in everlasting love relationship.

The reclamation of step 4 was possible because of the righteousness of Jesus. Remember, righteousness means faithfulness to a covenant. Jesus was faithful to the original Covenant of Life obligation for image bearers to trust God to provide TGB. Step 2 above highlights that righteousness. Because Jesus alone was faithful, he alone maintained control over physical creation. Therefore, he had the right in dominion over the flesh to take back his body from death (from separation—from the curse) to present it to God. He displayed a return to God in the only way possible, as a wholly purified being—a guiltless spirit with a body cleansed from curse.

That day on the road to Damascus, as the light blinded Saul of Tarsus, he suddenly realized the cataclysmic change Jesus had effected in the world's history. Jesus had accomplished all that the Old Testament insisted was part of God's redemptive plan. Through his death and resurrected life, Jesus, the Messiah, redeemed cursed creation. And *that* was the good news—the gospel—that the Jews had been (or should have been) waiting for based on the directed writings of Moses and all the other prophets. Sin no longer reigned; Jesus reigned. Jesus is Lord!

That phrase—*Jesus is Lord*—directly rebutted the world's helpless and hopeless state. Clueless masses had cried out, "Caesar is Lord," to a Roman world searching for TGB through its own means. The gospel countered with *Jesus is Lord*, summing up the full scope of God's redemptive plan. This gospel defined Paul's mission: Paul was to proclaim Jesus as Lord to the Gentile world. And this gospel shines as the centerpiece of his letter to the Romans.

Paul argues in Romans 1:16 and 17 that there is no shame in achieving victory through death. Physical death ends the relationship of spirit with its cursed essence, which remained separated from God. To the world, brainwashed with evil, the physical is god. The world considered crucifixion as a means to degrade a person (the spirit) by violently separating it from its god. Thus, both Romans and Jews saw shame in crucifixion; they brutally attacked the physical essence so valued by rebels and criminals and forced their spirits into exile. However, where they saw shame, Paul recognized only glory. By Christ's crucifixion, Jesus had flung aside his cursed essence and by his righteous spirit then raised that body up to embrace victorious redeemed life with God.

GOD'S RIGHTEOUSNESS REVEALED

Jesus is Lord. He became Lord by maintaining his faithfulness to his Covenant of Life commitment to God. But let's be careful not to confuse that display of Jesus's righteousness with the righteousness of God. The Covenant of Life commitments to which Jesus remained faithful were image-bearer obligations. Of course, Jesus is God, but when discussing Jesus's role in redemption, we celebrate the victory of righteousness on our side of the covenant—the side of Adam's defeat.

Nevertheless, Jesus's righteous victory also *revealed* the righteousness of God. God, of course, is always righteous—always faithful—regarding every covenant in which he is party to because he always fulfils his obligations. We discussed in chapter 4 that the Bible implies a couple of covenants we call Trinitarian—covenants in which God either makes promises to himself or operates based on who he is. God's persons will always operate according to their own one essence of truth, goodness, and beauty. We cannot even imagine, for example, God the Father acting in opposition to the Holy Spirit regarding a matter of TGB. And from Jesus's claim in John 14 of being the Way, the Truth, and the Life to Romans 8:28's insistence on all things working together for good, we know God's persons always operate intentionally in infinite TGB. If any did not, not only would the Trinitarian covenant be broken, but God would essentially cease to be God (an incomprehensible theoretical concept).

Recall that another of God's Trinitarian covenants involves the agreement among his persons to create image bearers for everlasting love relationship—his Covenant of Creative Purpose. The Bible summarizes that promise best in Titus 1:1-2: "Paul, a slave of God and an apostle of Jesus Christ, to build up the faith of God's elect and their knowledge of the truth that leads to godliness, in the hope of eternal life that *God, who cannot lie, promised before time began*. . . ." To whom did God make such a promise before time began? The only existent being was God. The Persons of the Trinity, then, must have decided this promise—this covenant.

These two Trinitarian covenants appear good and compatible. But Adam and Eve created a huge dissonance by eating that apple. Instead of there being a harmonious conjunction of the Trinitarian covenants, the entrance of sin pitted one against the other. On the one hand, God had to maintain his faithfulness in operating according to his TGB; he had to judge and separate from sin. But on the other hand, if God eternally separated from his sinful creation (essentially turning from them, leaving them to their total destruction), he would be unfaithful to his Trinitarian Covenant of Creative Purpose to create image bearers for *everlasting* love relationship.

God, of course, knew beforehand of this problem. He therefore agreed to a third Trinitarian covenant to redeem this creation, particularly his human image bearers, after the fall. Notice that this covenant, which is certainly an act of love because God always acts in love, has the added dimension of being necessary to maintain *God's righteousness*, to balance his faithfulness to both other Trinitarian covenants.

In the Covenant of Restoration, God initiated several covenants with humankind to picture the progressive development of his purpose. The four major covenants of analogy are the Noahic Covenant, the Abrahamic Covenant, the Mosaic Covenant, and the Davidic Covenant. The Noahic Covenant demonstrated that God would be true to his Trinitarian Covenant of Creative Purpose by not totally destroying creation because of sin. The Abrahamic Covenant emphasized that relationship with God is based on faith rather than force or coercion; the relationship is essentially one of love. The Mosaic Covenant, however, emphatically indicated that relationship with humans is possible only on the basis of TGB. Sin cannot be tolerated, and the Mosaic Covenant, then, became a marker to point out human inability and the need for a savior. Finally, the Davidic Covenant spoke of rule and reign. God intended image bearers to rule over physical creation, and this rule is pictured in David's reign over God's Promised Land.

No created spirit who was born into Adam's cursed flesh could perfectly fulfill all the righteous requirements of these four covenants picturing restoration. God, in his Trinitarian Covenant of Restoration, determined he would himself take on human flesh as Jesus to succeed where created humans failed. Thus, Jesus the man—the new Adam—fulfilled the human obligation in the Covenant of Life by his total dependence on God. Then putting his cursed flesh to death and reclaiming (or redeeming) it in resurrection, he provided the way for humankind to be reborn into him and into relationship with God.

So we see how both God's righteousness and Christ's righteousness fit their purposes hand-in-glove. Indeed, "God's righteousness is revealed from faith to faith." Since the biblical idea of faith is not separate from faithfulness,[1] we can express the idea of being faithful to a covenant in New Testament terms as having faith. God considers our attitude important. To be faithful and to act in faithfulness does not mean simply to perform a duty (see Isaiah 1:11–15); it means to embrace the covenant wholeheartedly as you meet its obligations.

Therefore, "God's righteousness revealed from faith to faith" starts with his own committed faith in fulfilling his own covenant obligation to care for his image bearers. God did so by redeeming them. He redeemed them through the Messiah, whose own faithfulness—showcasing love's pinnacled perfection (John 15:13)—fulfilled the old Covenant of Life obligation for humankind. Thus, this "faith to faith" idea carries us from God's initial covenant faithfulness to the faithfulness of the Messiah. And even beyond that, the umbrella of faith extends over us as we embrace the New Covenant through our belief in Jesus, God's faithful gift.

Notice that the "faith to faith" idea is supported on the back end of the verse by a quotation from Habakkuk 2:4: "The righteous will live by faith." In that passage, Habakkuk complained of the oppression of Israel by

---

1. The evidence is in the Old Testament translation of the Hebrew *emuwnah* and *aman* as *faithfulness* and *faithful* (almost nowhere translated as *faith*) and the New Testament translation of the Greek *pistis* and *pistos* as *faith* and *faithful* (never *faithfulness*).

its enemies and pleaded for God's redemptive care. God's replies refocused Habakkuk's understanding of what his care involved. First, as the world's judge, God would righteously satisfy justice in dealing with the sin of Israel. Yet, as Israel's protector, God would righteously see to their good so that "the righteous will live by faith." In other words, God would provide his TGB to those who faithfully embraced him until God displayed his faithfulness in bringing forward the Messiah.

Paul saw clearly that God made all things right in Jesus. How could shame ever be a part of the good news that God had been righteous? God fulfilled his covenant obligation through his power in bringing salvation to everyone who believes. That redemption plan excited Paul as he wrote the opening verses of Romans. "This is the gospel!" he exclaimed. This is the good news! Note that Paul didn't say the gospel *was* salvation (in 1:16). Paul said the gospel was *the power* for salvation. The gospel revealed God's righteousness (1:17) in his faithful accomplishment of all three of his Trinitarian Covenants. God is bringing the world to right through Jesus, the human covenant keeper, who in his death and resurrection became the redeeming Lord of all creation. Jesus is Lord! This is the gospel!

10

Redeemer Qualifications

She cried, "Laura," up the garden,
"Did you miss me?
Come and kiss me.
Never mind my bruises,
Hug me, kiss me, suck my juices
Squeez'd from goblin fruits for you,
Goblin pulp and goblin dew.
Eat me, drink me, love me;
Laura, make much of me;
For your sake I have braved the glen
And had to do with goblin merchant men."

—Christina Rossetti, from "Goblin Market"

"In a surge of anger I hid My face from you for a moment,
but I will have compassion on you with everlasting love,"
says the Lord your Redeemer.

—Isaiah 54:8

God paints his message of redemption across the Old Testament canvas with both story and Law. Genesis 14 recounts an outstanding example of redemption in Abraham's rescue of his nephew Lot. Abraham's and Lot's prosperity had increased to the point that the sheer number of animals and servants created difficulties for their living in close proximity. They decided to separate: Lot chose the land east of the Jordan river valley, whereas Abraham settled to the west in the land of Canaan.

The story goes on to relate how five kings of city-states, among whom Lot lived, rebelled against subjection to Chedorlaomer, another city-state king. In response, Chedorlaomer gathered his army and the armies of three other vassal kings to fight the insurgents; he prevailed in capturing their possessions and even some of the leaders. Among the spoils, he also seized Lot and his possessions.

When Abraham heard of his nephew's plight, he and his trained servants (318 men) pursued, caught, and defeated Chedorlaomer, restoring (*redeeming*) the possessions of those five kings and his nephew. The specifics of this story help to clarify the Bible's view of redemption. For example, while Abraham did rescue Lot, the text highlights Lot's and the kings' *possessions* both in the taking (14:11–12) and in the restoring (14:16, 22–23). Connecting the redemption to the possessions, rather than to the people, strikes a common chord with other Old Testament redemption stories and becomes significant as we consider Christ's redeeming work in his own atonement.

Fast forward a few hundred years. This time God writes redemption into the Law itself. When the Israelites returned from Egypt to God's promised land, they divided the land not only among the tribes but also among each tribe's family groups. The Israelites considered the land God's, so these divisions signified not so much ownership as they did control. Israelites could use the land or sell it. But even if sold, every fiftieth year (the year of Jubilee), the land reverted to the original family divisions.

The land gave them their livelihood. So if an Israelite sold his land to pay off a debt, he would be hard-pressed to make a living. There were no government food stamp programs to rely on or minimum-wage convenience store jobs in this underdeveloped, agricultural society. So although the seller may have paid off his debt with the land-sale proceeds, he and his family could still starve without any other income support. The Law's kinsman redeemer code pertained to such situations. The man could petition a close relative to redeem his land—that is, buy back control for him. The relative who bought it back (redeemed it) would then allow the man to work on his land, with an arrangement, of course, for paying off the redemption price. Therefore, even here in the Law, redemption concerned the land—the possession, the physical object—although the person whose land was being redeemed often came along with the deal.

THE RUTH METAPHOR

The kinsman redeemer appellation identified the redeemer as a close relative, a family supporter who could act on behalf of the one in trouble, danger, or need. Rules applied. The story of Ruth extensively illustrates the kinsman-redeemer concept in action. Not only does the narrative deliver insight on how redemption worked in Israel's law, but we also learn how its structure relates to God's Kinsman Redeemer for the whole world.

Ruth's story occurs during the time of the judges. In the 4000 years of Old Testament recorded history, certain major milestones loosely orient us to the stories and events. Right in the middle of that 4,000-year span, Abraham lived around 2000 BC. More precisely, Abraham was probably born closer to 2117.[1] But the actual date is not important for our story.

Dividing again in half on either side of Abraham, we find Adam's son Seth to have died in approximately 3000 BC, while on the other side, David ruled as king in approximately 1000 BC. That millennium between Abraham (2000) and David (1000) is our focus now. During the first half of that millennium, Jacob's twelve sons settled in Egypt, and after about 400 years, Moses led them out. By around 1500 BC, the Israelites were settled back in the Promised Land, having divided up the land for each tribe. But not until around 1100 did Saul become Israel's first king. We refer to that span between the return to the Promised Land (1500) and Israel's first king (1100) as the period of the judges, in which certain prophets of God acted as leaders for Israel. Since we know that Ruth was the great-grandmother of David (noted in the general genealogy at the end of the book of Ruth), we can roughly calculate that the story of Ruth takes place around 1200 BC, comfortably within that period of judges.

Israel's tribe of Judah had settled immediately to the west of the Dead Sea. The kingdom of Moab occupied the area immediately to the east of the Dead Sea. Moab's territory covered the same area in which Lot had lived and where the cities of Sodom and Gomorrah had previously existed. The Moabites descended, in fact, from Lot through his daughter (Genesis 19:36–37).

The book of Ruth records actual history, but God intends the story also to provide an extended metaphor for how Christ as Kinsman Redeemer would restore the world to relationship with God. Therefore, although the text recounts the activity of genuine, historical characters, they represent the various players in the world's overall redemptive history. But although God so coordinates the story's affairs to serve the metaphor, we should bear in mind that metaphors are seldom perfectly analogous in every detail.

---

1. Anstey, *Romance*, 7.

Within the opening few verses, we learn that a famine afflicts the land of Judah. Because of the famine, Elimelech (representing Adam) sells his land and moves his family to Moab in search of greener pastures. While we in our day would not judge that move as anything other than common sense, his decision held greater significance during the time of Ruth. God had emphasized his care in the years just previously by returning the Israelites to his Promised Land with the additional promise that he would watch over them as they trusted in him there. The leading by God in returning the Israelites to the promised land related to God's covenant with Abraham. The Bible identifies the land as "promised" precisely because it was promised to Abraham. And that covenant had highlighted the faith of Abraham (and subsequently his offspring) as key to God's attending hand. The hardship endured in wandering through the desert for 40 years happened because the Israelites had worried God would not provide. Likewise, many years later, Isaiah records their distrust of God's faithful care as Judah's King Ahaz sought protective treaties with other nations. So back in Ruth, Elimelech, also not fully trusting God, takes matters into his own hands to provide for his family apart from God.

Of course, we recognize the analogy to Adam. God had placed Adam in his own promised land—the garden—and told him to trust God for TGB. Elimelech erred in the exact manner of Adam, who chose for himself—his own pursuit of TGB—rather than trusting in God's provision. Adam's choice resulted in death—separation from God. It turns out the same for Elimelech. He left the care of God, and verse 3 immediately tells us he died.

The Genesis 5 genealogy of Adam through Seth highlights image bearing. God formed Adam in his image, Adam's son Seth bore Adam's image, and Moses continues recording image-bearing sons. But in Genesis 6, those "sons of God" find their way to the "daughters of men," turning aside from God. Just so did the sons of Elimelech turn to the daughters of Moab to find wives (Ruth 1:4). In a parallel to the result in Genesis 6, Elimelech's sons likewise died (Ruth 1:5).

Following their deaths, the action centers on Naomi, Elimelech's wife, and her two daughters-in-law, Ruth and Orpah. Naomi represents Israel, Ruth represents believing Gentiles, and Orpah represents unbelieving Gentiles. Israel knew the one true God and had covenanted with him at Mt. Sinai to be his people and priests to the world. However, Israel didn't do a very good job of it, and neither did Naomi.

Naomi had nothing to keep her in Moab. Her husband and sons were gone. She had no land or other income potential. All her relatives lived back across the Jordan. She decided to return to her tribal land, the land of her God, hoping for the best (just as Israel had followed God in leaving Egypt to return to the Promised Land). The image, of course, demonstrates dependence and trust returned to God. But as the journey commenced, Naomi urged her Moabite daughters-in-law to return to their own mothers (1:8). Sending them back represents Israel's own self-interest and rebuff of other nations. (God didn't want Israel to accept other nations to assume their pagan practices, but he did want them to be faithful to their Sinai commitment: they should have embraced others with the intention of introducing them to God. So Naomi's action illustrates how Israel had failed to be that light for God.) Naomi insisted she could not help her daughters-in-law.

Based on Naomi's urging, Orpah, who represents unbelieving Gentiles and who probably supposed her own land and gods offered more hope for her, turned back. However, Ruth clung to Naomi, indicating that she treasured their relationship. The text uses the same Hebrew word for *clung* in 1:14 as Moses did in Genesis 2:24 when describing a husband's leaving his parents to *cling* to his wife—a relational union that imitates the love of God. Ruth's declaration in 1:16–17 (often quoted in wedding ceremonies) expressed her desire to leave all else to pursue a course with Naomi, Naomi's people, and Naomi's God.

Naomi and Ruth arrived back in Naomi's native land without inheritance or immediate male help, a social and functional necessity in that sin-devolved society. Their only immediate prospect for survival came from what the Law allowed for the poor: gleaning from the fields. By the Law's instruction, land controllers harvested with only one pass through their fields while also leaving the field edges unharvested. God intended to provide for the poor who could glean food from these unharvested portions.

The beginning of Ruth 2 introduces Boaz, the Christ figure. The text immediately mentions his connection to Naomi as her relative and then repeats the connection by explaining that he is from Elimelech's family. The repetition of kinship, albeit from a slightly different perspective, emphasizes the story's imaging purpose: Christ is our relative. We learn that truth through the genealogies, the birth narratives, his title as Son of Man, and the bodily emphasis of Romans. Thus, Boaz's relationship to Naomi and Elimelech emphasizes the New Testament's insistence on the kinship of Christ because redemption requires kinship.

As Ruth gleaned in the fields of Boaz, he saw her and learned of her story before she herself told it to him. Impressed with her devotion, Boaz welcomed her, encouraging her to stay in the field. The scene reminds us of the similar attitude of Christ, who, seeing hearts of faith, welcomes those who come to him whom he "will never cast out" (John 6:37). Boaz urged Ruth to remain "with my women" (to be with God's people) because she sought to be under God's wings (that is, through faith she sought the provision of God). Boaz even invited her to the place of the reapers at mealtime to partake of roasted grain—the fruit of the harvest—just as we who follow God in faith partake of his harvest of blessing.

The grand import of this portion of the story relates to Ruth's only partial understanding of Boaz's care. Ruth began to trust Boaz for help even before she knew exactly the full extent of how he would care for her. In analogy, the Old Testament believers did not know the full extent of how God would care for them through his redemption. But they trusted him. They embraced his care. In due season, God brought them full redemption through Christ.

When Ruth reported all that Boaz had done, Naomi realized that his favorable impression of Ruth could lead to a kinsman redemption. Elimelech had sold his allotted land during the famine and had taken the money to Moab with him. Control of the land did not pass to Naomi upon Elimelech's and his sons' deaths. The purchaser would maintain control until the year of Jubilee. However, the family of Elimelech could redeem—purchase back—the land. And Naomi recognized that Boaz might be willing to do just that.

Naomi's urging Ruth to follow Boaz echoes the story of the world's redemption. God provided through Israel the way for Gentiles to come to Christ. Of course, the Ruth story is metaphor, so all the details do not align perfectly. Some important elements, however, do link to Paul's discussion in Romans 11. There Paul argues that Israel's stumbling made a way for the Gentiles to come to Christ (11:11). Though Naomi's attitude may contrast with that of the first century Jews who put Jesus to death, the overall picture of Israel's pointing Gentiles to the Redeemer remains.

Chapter 3 provides further evidence of the continued faith and devotion of Ruth. At the threshing floor while Boaz slept, Ruth uncovered his feet and lay down by him. Despite the faultfinders who read sexual tension into this scene, none actually exists. Ruth uncovered his feet to ensure he would wake. The cold would make him uncomfortable, waking him and giving him a chance to notice her. Just so, Boaz did wake up to see Ruth beside him. She asked him to spread his cloak over her, not to hide some sexual promiscuity but to shield her from the elements as well—a sign of protection that she expressly linked to a request for redemption. Boaz immediately understood the intent so that along with covering her, he promised to act (if he could) as kinsman redeemer on her behalf. The covering with care mimics Christ's care now as we await applied redemption at his coming.

While Boaz was willing to redeem, another relative of closer relation than Boaz could have exercised his right if he so chose. So before Boaz could officially take on the redemptive role, he had to discover the mind of that other closer relative. The other closer relative has no direct counterpart in

God's overall redemption plan, except that the incident does illustrate the fact that no one besides Christ qualified to be our redeemer.

The morning after Boaz promised redemption, he made his way to the city gate—the place of judgment—to determine whether he would, in fact, be able to do so. There Boaz asked the closer relative whether he wanted to redeem the land—to purchase it to bring it back into the family's and, specifically, the close relative's control. At first, that relative expressed interest. He possibly knew that Elimelech and his sons were dead, so the land would increase his income-producing property, which would offer his own children a greater inheritance.

However, what it appears he did not know of was Ruth's return from Moab. To redeem the land of a dead Israelite whose widow yet lived meant that the widow would be included with the redeemed land. In other words, the Law obligated the redeemer to marry that widow to raise up sons for the redeemed union who, although biologically fathered by the redeemer, would carry the name or line of the dead father. Thus, the redeemer (and his children) would not profit from the redeemed land but would rather pass the profits to the control of the offspring of the redemption union.

In this case, as soon as the closer relative learned that because of Ruth's existence, the land would be of no financial benefit to his own children, he changed his mind; he did not want to follow through with that arrangement; he did not want to redeem.

This passage, then, reveals three requirements qualifying the kinsman redeemer: (1) he had to be a close relative, (2) he had to be able to pay the price, and (3) he had to *want* to fulfill the obligation. A redeemer who was worthy to redeem must meet all qualifications. Only Boaz was worthy to redeem. Not only was he a close relative and financially able to purchase the land, but he also wanted to do so—he wanted Ruth as his wife; his decision was based on love.

So Boaz redeemed the land and married Ruth, and through that union they had a child, Obed. The story illustrates Christ's building his church. Chapter 4 reveals that not only was Ruth (representing believing Gentiles) blessed in the redemption, but Naomi (believing Israel) was blessed as well because the child through the Boaz-Ruth redemption union could be claimed as her grandson—son of her son. The activity pictures how Christ did not come to save Gentiles only but to redeem also the chosen of Israel, as Paul recounts in Romans 11:25–26, where he says that with the "*full number* of the Gentiles" coming into the family of God, so too would "*all* Israel" be saved.

As an interesting aside (a minor issue of analogy, but one that nevertheless showcases Jesus as the Kinsman Redeemer), the story provides a history lesson in how Boaz sealed the agreement with the other kinsman.

Chapter 4 records that, in the presence of witnesses, the kinsman took off his shoe and gave it to Boaz. The practice, in essence, pictured his vow that he would not *walk on* (or, more precisely, *try to take control of*) the land to which he had just given up his right of control. The text explains that the shoe-exchange custom thus demonstrated the relinquishing of rights. But by the time of the writing of Ruth, Israel had already changed the custom. Participants in legal agreements in Israel no longer sealed them by the witness of shoe-passing. Instead, they began to record the legal arrangements and terms on a scroll and seal and keep it as witness to ensure against any change or misunderstanding.

Remember that the story of Ruth took place in about 1200 BC. By the time of Jeremiah in the 500s, the recorded scroll sealed legal arrangements. In Jeremiah 32, the text reveals that Zedekiah, a son of Josiah, who had been appointed king by Nebuchadnezzar after the rebellion of Jehoiakim and Jehoiachin (aka Jeconiah), had also rebelled against Babylon just as his brother and nephew had. Because of the rebellion, Nebuchadnezzar again laid siege to Jerusalem. Jeremiah prophesied that Babylon would overthrow Judah, and because of the prophecy, Zedekiah had thrown Jeremiah in prison. Ignoring his own sin, Zedekiah seems to have thought it would be impossible for the God of Israel to allow Jerusalem and their promised land to be lost in captivity, because then Judah would be lost forever.

But Jeremiah corrects that errant thought. He explains that while God really would send Babylon in to defeat his people, the captivity would not be the end of Judah. God would later bring his people back; he would *redeem* them. Jeremiah gets his point across by explaining that God told him to redeem a certain land possession of one of his close relatives. Why would he do this if Babylon was to capture the land? Well, Jeremiah was to redeem it anyway and write the terms of the sale on a scroll to be kept in Jerusalem as record of the redemption. That record would stand to the day when God would bring the Jews back to the land so that the legal redemption could take effect. The sealed scroll, then, was the title deed to the property.

Revelation 5 illustrates redemption terms sealed on a scroll, which only a qualified kinsman redeemer could open. In Revelation, the only one worthy (qualified) to act as kinsman redeemer for the world is Jesus, shown by his taking the scroll from the hand of God and opening its seven seals.

Thus, the entire book of Ruth provides details about redemption and metaphorically demonstrates the redemption of the world. The story supplies the initiating event of a loss that makes redemption, the gaining back, necessary. It presents the desire and longing for redemption. And it shows the path toward redemption, highlighting the kinsman-redeemer activity. The story outlines the requirements, or qualifications, of the kinsman redeemer, one of which is his own passionate desire. The story also shows that the redemption focuses on the land, although the person involved motivates the kinsman redeemer's action. (In other words, Boaz would not have been so interested in redeeming the land had he not wanted Ruth herself.) Finally, the story ends with the glory of redemption accomplished, with its attendant relationship and benefits. So the Ruth story gives a complete picture of redemption. Or does it?

REDEMPTION—MISSED?

The story seems not to include one important element of the redemption process. Where in Ruth do we actually see redemption take place? The need is there; the desire is there; the way is made clear, but where in Ruth do we *see* the actual redeeming transaction take place? The fact is, we don't. The text does not record the actual transaction for redemption—the action accomplishing redemption. It occurs sometime in chapter 4 between verses 12 and 13, but the text does not mention a word about that transaction. Why would that be? Why would God leave the redemption itself out of the only book that provides an extended metaphor of Christ as the Kinsman Redeemer?

The text leaves the transaction out, I think, so as not to overshadow the book's main emphasis. Notice that the story also leaves out the initial transaction—the original sale by Elimelech of the land. The book tucks away both *cause* (the original sale) and *final result* (the transaction to buy back) so that the story can rather highlight what gets us from cause to final result: the *solution* of qualifying a kinsman redeemer. In the overall redemption story of humankind, that qualifying solution is also central: the qualification for Jesus to become Kinsman Redeemer by means of his sinless life, offer of death, and perfect resurrection. Remember, the application of redemption for us—the actual taking back of our corrupt bodies in incorruption—will occur at final resurrection when Christ returns.

I must emphasize one other important aspect before leaving the book of Ruth: the motivation that carries the story along. The desire for redemption that motivates Naomi and Ruth (Israel and Gentile believers) is obvious. The motivation for Boaz to become qualified and then redeem is also readily apparent. So, then, in the greater story of humanity that the book of Ruth depicts, motivation of the redeemed and redeemer should match. Repentance and faith, an inseparable duo in the reconciliation process, rise to the forefront as humankind's motivation. And forgiveness, in reciprocity, reveals God's and Christ's love desire. Thus, both redemption and forgiveness play entwining roles in the reconciliation activity of God.

11

Redemption & Forgiveness

He came to my desk with quivering lip—
The lesson was done.
"Dear Teacher, I want a new leaf," he said,
"I have spoiled this one."
I took the old leaf, stained and blotted,
And gave him a new one all unspotted,
And into his sad eyes smiled,
"Do better, now, my child."

—Carrie Shaw Rice, from "A New Leaf"

Rise up! Help us!
Redeem us because of your faithful love.

—Psalm 44:26

Consider my affliction and trouble,
and forgive all my sins.

—Psalm 25:18

The two verses introducing this chapter touch on our subjects: redemption and forgiveness. Both verses request help from God, but their common theme of rescue should not cloud how the verses significantly differ in regard to the atonement terms *redemption* and *forgiveness*.

REDEMPTION

As we saw in Ruth, redemption concentrates on the land or possessions. The Old Testament uses a couple of Hebrew words to convey the idea; both translate as *redemption,* and they essentially mean the same thing. One stresses more the idea of rescue and avenging, whereas the other conveys more the notion of deliverance and even paying the redemption price. Half the uses apply the redemption to land, animals, and other possessions, but the other half refer to people. Yet even in regard to people—when, for instance, the term relates to a redeemer's releasing slaves or avenging a group or ensuring their safety—it focuses on the rescue of physical life. The Bible consistently concentrates on the physical even as we shift to the New Testament.

In Ephesians 1:7, we read of our possessing redemption in Christ through his blood. But the verse does not make clear whether Paul here speaks of spiritual or bodily redemption. If God has already applied the redemption, certainly Paul must be referring to redemption of the spirit since our bodies, the flesh of our housed spirits, remain corrupt. But remembering that the Bible normally connects redemption with land and possessions—the physical—we should probably not conclude Paul's topic to be spirit redemption. And Paul does clarify his intent as he continues. Only a few verses later, regarding the Holy Spirit, Paul says, "He is the *down payment* of our inheritance, *for* the redemption of the possession" (1:14). The verse implies that the redemption discussed is still to come and must, therefore, be bodily redemption. Paul explains further in 4:30: "And don't grieve God's Holy Spirit. You were sealed by him for the day of redemption." Paul assures us with the terms "down payment" and "sealing" that he speaks of Jesus's return when Christ will apply the redemption he won to us—when we will receive our new, uncorrupted bodies, our refined physical essence (Romans 8:19–23; 1 Corinthians 15:50–52). Of course, while we wait for his coming, we may still sing the hymn "Since I *Have Been* Redeemed" celebrating Jesus's accomplishment of the future application, just as Ruth could take comfort in Boaz's promise even though the transaction had not yet been finalized.

FORGIVENESS

Driving redemption, however, is God's forgiveness. *Forgiveness* means to pardon or to spare. In other words, forgiveness is the cancellation of an *unpaid* debt. Elements of forgiveness appear in the Old Testament—in the time prior to Christ's atonement. Israel sang of God: "You took away Your people's guilt; You covered all their sin" (Psalm 85:2). Almost as a continuation of that thought, David cries out, "How joyful is the one whose transgression is forgiven, whose sin is covered!" (Psalm 32:1). Despite some scholars' speculation that David must have been imagining a future, post-Messiah time, David's words grab our attention precisely because he speaks of forgiveness as though it has already occurred. The Jews rejoiced in forgiveness as they sang, long before Christ came to rescue and provide the only way back to God.

Further, Leviticus 19:22 states, "The priest will make atonement on [a sinner's] behalf . . . with the ram . . . and [the sinner] will be *forgiven*." What? Don't we learn in Hebrews that "it is *impossible* for the blood of bulls and goats to take away sins" (10:4)? But even Jesus assured various persons who came to him, "Your sins are forgiven" (Matthew 9:2; Luke 7:48), though he had yet to go to the cross. It would seem from these statements that forgiveness existed before (and apart from?) Christ's atonement. But even as we begin to entertain that thought, Paul holds up a hand in 1 Corinthians 15:17 to slow us down: "And if Christ has not been raised, your faith is worthless; you are still in your sins." So what exactly is going on? Can Paul be right and those other Scripture writers and speakers—including Jesus(!)—wrong?

HOLDING TO BOTH

The complexity of sin's hold and the equal intricacy of God's restoration plan force us to think more deeply to comprehend the whole. The task is not daunting so long as we organize our efforts. Consider this chart:

GOD'S RESTORATION

MOTIVATION		Desire for love relationship		
	F	↙ ↘		**R**
	O			**E**
MEANS	**R**	Pardon or cancel	Remove obstacle	**D**
	G	unpaid debt	to relationship	**E**
	I	↓	↓	**M**
	V			**P**
APPLICATION	**E**	Release	Put curse to death;	**T**
	N	vengeance	Reclaim possession	**I**
	E	↘ ↙		**O**
	S			**N**
RESULT	**S**	Restored love relationship		

The chart structures the many elements of the process. We're not here talking about forgiveness in just a general sense but rather God's forgiveness as we move from the fall to the restoration. So the chart provides a biblical view of forgiveness from the divine perspective.

The chart depicts God's restoration as it follows two distinct paths from a common purpose toward a common goal. The most intriguing aspect of this process is its motivating force. No outside authority ever obligated God to act. No greater or even other force compelled him to, as it were, *do the right thing*. Our earlier chapters emphasized that God *is* truth, goodness, and beauty. God operates in his persons always through love. Therefore, it is his very essence and existence that provide the motivation—love born in and of himself.

Dropping down to the chart aspect labeled *Result*, we find firmly settled the goal of the process. Unlike proponents of satisfaction theories of the atonement, we cannot imagine restored pride or dignity as God's goal; rather, his objective must fulfill God's creative purpose—to realize everlasting love relationship. And because of the nature of love, his love purpose not only motivates God but also draws the estranged to him. No forced restoration mars the picture. Love relationship cannot possibly exist with those who have no desire to love. The targeted restoration goal, then, depends on both the longing by the rescuer to forgive and redeem as well as the desire by the rescued to be forgiven and redeemed.

That reciprocating desire certainly played out strongly in the story of Ruth. The redemption of land and embrace of care began with the desire in the hearts of both Boaz and Ruth. Ruth displayed her heart by coming to Boaz that night in the threshing room. Boaz demonstrated his soul's passion by pursuing redemption at the city gate. Mutual desire had to exist to result in the satisfaction of their marriage relationship.

The chart's path from motivation splits to satisfy two necessities for God's restoration: forgiveness and redemption. Following the forgiveness path, we find the means through the pardoning or canceling of an unpaid debt. In pardoning a wrongdoer or canceling someone's debt, the offended party does not act in vengeance. Instead, the wronged one embraces the offender, putting aside the offense. Satisfaction for being wronged *is not* the means of forgiveness; satisfaction has nothing to do with forgiveness. For satisfaction, the offended person demands payment or punishment of the offender. But in forgiving someone, the offended person disengages from the offense for the sake of relationship.

Here we need to pause to ensure an understanding of how human forgiveness differs from God's. If someone offends me, my pride may be hurt. In other words, I am somehow changed because of the other's offense. Because of my hurt pride, my defenses rise, and I want satisfaction for my hurt. I don't want relationship with the offender until that satisfaction is met. However, if the offender apologizes, my rancor may ease because (1) I believe the person feels sorry (in other words, hurt in spirit) so that satisfaction (payment) is partly met, and (2) my pride is no longer offended by the attitude of the offender. So I can change back; I can forgive; I can allow relationship to be restored because I don't feel bad about that person any longer.

I've just described typical human forgiveness, but that is not what occurs in God's forgiveness, and we cannot imagine it occurring without harming our conception of God. As we've discussed, God acts in love for the purpose of love relationship. Perhaps the greatest fault of most atonement theories is imagining that an offense to God changes God (as it does us). But God, the infinitely immutable one, does not become indignant; he does not become remotely petulant; he does not become anything different from who he is. God is truth, goodness, and beauty, and he acts in love. And despite the malicious and pernicious doings of any human, our God will not shed an attitude of care to return evil for evil.

So how does divine forgiveness work? First, we must grasp this concept without qualification: God acts in love for the purpose of love relationship. No "except when" or "unless another does this" phrase can be tacked on. When God told us, "I AM" (Exodus 3:14; John 8:58), he meant it. He is not sometimes the God of infinite care and sometimes the God of violent indignation. So what happens to God when we spew offense at him? God still acts in love for the purpose of love relationship. He does not hold in his anger at offended pride until his frustration spills over. He also does not look for the right time and circumstance to allow his vengeance to return a hailstorm of fire and brimstone.

I've mentioned Matthew 23:37 a couple of times now. Remember that Hebrews 1:3 tells us Jesus radiates God's TGB by being its exact expression. Jesus cried out, "Jerusalem, Jerusalem, who kills the prophets and stones those who are sent to her. How often I wanted to gather your children together, as a hen gathers her chicks under her wings, but you were not willing!" He wasn't temporarily being nice until the boiling rage of his exasperation overflowed into violent retribution. He was acting in love for the purpose of love relationship. In that verse, Jesus recounted Jerusalem's sin and offense, and he met their attitude with a desire for their love.

But doesn't God want vengeance? In Romans 12:19, Paul quotes Isaiah 63:4: "It is written, Vengeance belongs to me; I will repay, says the Lord." But do you ever wonder why God tells us to leave vengeance to him? Perhaps God's vengeance doesn't look quite the same as what our vengeful hearts might express. In our chapter 8's treatment of God's wrath, we learned that

God responds to humans' rejecting his love by turning away. The absence of God—of the only TGB there is—results in the destruction and evil left in his absence. Vengeance means vindication from wrongs; it is a defense, an exoneration, a justification. God does exactly that—defends, exonerates, and justifies himself and his own—by turning away from the wrongdoer and turning toward those who embrace his love.

Let's continue reading past Jesus's rejected offer of love in Matthew 23:37. What will he do in the face of such rejection? In language similar to Paul's "delivering them over" (Romans 1:24, 26, 28), Matthew 23:38 reads, "See, your house is left to you desolate." Jesus, expressing the "entire fullness of God's nature" (Colossians 2:9), turns away.

God's forgiveness, then, requires no satisfaction for the offense. It requires no reparations. It requires only our turning away from the rejection and toward our God in faith and trust. And God's already open arms receive us in their embrace.

However, even secular psychologists will argue that merely letting go of vengeance does not always mean relationship is restored.[1] If some person wrongs me by lying or cheating, I may forgive, but an obstacle of distrust can remain for the future based on that person's character. And so it is that even if we sincerely plead for forgiveness from God and he does let go of vengeance, an obstacle would still remain to prevent completely restored relationship.

In 1 Corinthians 15:17, Paul declares that without atonement, an obstacle yet remains to keep us in the clutches of sin, estranged from God. The restoration process must include a means to remove that obstacle (the Redemption path of our chart). When we review those Old Testament forgiveness examples, we should not consider them to be fully developed reconciliation principles. God's progressive revelation throughout history teaches us about him in deliberately graduated steps. Those Old Testament illustrations were and are meant to teach forgiveness, but none of them individually holds a doctrinally complete theology of restoration. Each case provides an example of persons who had relationship with God, who sinned and thus withdrew from God (from his TGB), and who repented. Because of the repentance, God forgave; he cancelled the debt without requiring repayment. Those examples mirror the forgiveness pattern of the very first relationship: Adam and Eve's sins, their repentance and faith, and God's mercy in forgiving based on their repentance and faith. That process is the metanarrative for human reconciliation with God. But what we don't always see taught in those examples is the necessity for removing the imposing

---

1. "Forgiveness."

obstacle to restore full and everlasting love relationship. As the Bible's story unfolds, the emphasis grows on removing the obstacle—the curse on our physical essence—to complete forgiveness. Removing that obstacle happens only through the atonement of the cross.

Ignoring either of these restoration paths or falsely fusing them leads to many misinterpretations, misapplications, and misconceptions. For example, let's briefly look at the most commonly held atonement idea today: penal substitution (PS). The PS theory views Jesus as having paid the penalty of our sin on the cross, a satisfaction resulting in the removal of the debt and thus a restoration of our relationship with God. Our chart for restoration, however, reveals that PS breaks down regarding the means of forgiveness. PS does not view forgiveness as the pardoning or canceling of an unpaid debt; rather, it insists that the debt *must still be paid*. Death, that theory states, is the *payment* for sin. We mere humans cannot pay with our deaths to overcome death, so Jesus stepped in to pay with his death for us.

Two problems with this framing of the atonement immediately manifest themselves. First, if forgiveness really requires death (defined as *payment* for our sin), we would have to redefine forgiveness from "cancellation of an unpaid debt" to "payment of a debt." Imagine being told by a creditor, "Good news! I've decided to forgive your debt!" You say, "Wonderful! I no longer owe anything!" But the creditor replies, "Well, no, you still owe your debt. I'm just going to allow someone else to pay it." You would probably be confused, and rightly so, at the doubletalk. The creditor's conception of forgiveness makes no sense. Forgiveness, by definition, cannot mean the *cancellation* of an *unpaid* debt at the same time it also means the *required payment* of it, albeit by someone else.

Second, PS forgiveness actually degrades the justice of God, rather than satisfies it. Consider this question: if death is required as the *payment* for my sin guilt, and Jesus pays that sin guilt with his death, why does he receive his life back in resurrection? What is *just* about God's resurrecting Jesus? Note if *I* go to my physical death with my soul obligated for my sin, my spirit is *forever* obligated; I am forever separated from God. But when, as PS proponents see it, *that same sin guilt* is transferred from me to Jesus and Jesus physically dies, God decides to resurrect him. Why? Why is God justified in ignoring my sin debt placed on Jesus and raising him from the dead?

Let's pause here to be sure we understand the purpose for physical death. We have already defined spiritual death as God's forever separating from a person's spirit, which occurs because that person refuses to embrace life—relationship with God. If anyone refuses relationship with God, God ultimately and forever withdraws from that person. Since God, who is truth, goodness, and beauty, separates from that rejecting person, the person is left totally devoid of any TGB and is utterly destroyed.

But during this present age, as God is redeeming through drawing all people to himself (although not all will come), *physical* death occurs. For the non-Christian—the one who refuses to have relationship with God based on God's TGB—physical death marks the end of God's revealing and calling activity for that person. That end comes because God, in infinite knowledge of each image bearer, knows that no matter the circumstance or opportunity, that person will never desire God and forever refuse the love relationship God offers. Physical death, then, marks the end of God's revelation-response interaction with that person, and he or she exits earthly activity to await final judgment.

For the Christian, physical death means something different. For me as a believer, physical death means God has completed his interaction with and use of me on earth in this age in his efforts to draw and redeem others. Thus, the non-Christian differs from the Christian at physical death in that he or she dies with the guilt of sin charged against him or her, whereas the Christian (no matter which atonement theory applies) physically dies with the guilt of sin wiped away in forgiveness.

Now let's return to our previous question: what is *just* about God's resurrecting Jesus? As explained, the human who dies with the charge of sin guilt has only spiritual death before him or her—everlasting separation. Yet PS proponents argue that somehow it was different for Jesus. Although he took our sin upon himself to be charged with that sin guilt, God in this case ignored the rules and resurrected him anyway. Again, why? Where's the justice in that?

Of course, a first impulse might be to respond, "Well, Jesus is God. He has the power to raise himself from the dead!" But a major problem prevents our deeming that answer adequate. The PS proponent maintains that Jesus, with sin guilt on him, is acting as our representative. He became human to fulfill that requirement. So Jesus *the human* has sin obligation on him, and Jesus *the human* dies physically. What justification allows Jesus *the human* to rise from the dead with our sin obligation on him, when we *as humans* are doomed forever with our sin obligation on us? Arguing that Jesus rises by the power of his deity only adds to the confusion: why does he exercise that God power to raise himself but won't exercise that same God power to raise any other sinner? The point is that PS proponents cannot point to Jesus's sinlessness as a reason to rise from the dead. They have just argued that Jesus has taken our guilt. He is therefore, *with our guilt*, no longer sinless. You just can't have it both ways.

That Jesus became guilty of sin is a staple of PS theology. Martin Luther famously wrote these thoughts in his Galatians commentary:

> All the prophets of old said that Christ should be the greatest transgressor, murderer, adulterer, thief, rebel, and blasphemer, that ever was or could be on earth. When He took the sins of the whole world upon Himself, Christ was no longer an innocent person. He was a sinner burdened with the sins of a Paul who was a blasphemer; burdened with the sins of a Peter who denied Christ; burdened with the sins of a David who committed adultery and murder and gave the heathen occasion to laugh at the Lord. In short, Christ was charged with the sins of all men, that He should pay for them with His own blood.[2]

John Theodore Mueller, a noted Lutheran scholar agreed with Luther:

> The agony of being forsaken by God, Matt. 27, 46, was the endurance of divine wrath on account of the sins of men in His soul, just as if he Himself had committed the imputed transgressions.[3]

Theologian Wayne Grudem explains it like this:

> It was God the Father who put our sins on Christ. How could that be? In the same way in which Adam's sins were imputed to us, so God imputed our sins to Christ; that is, he thought of them as belonging to Christ, and, since God is the ultimate judge and definer of what really is in the universe, when God thought of our sins as belonging to Christ then in fact they actually did belong to Christ. This does not mean that God thought that Christ had himself committed the sins, or that Christ himself actually had a sinful nature, but rather that the guilt of our sins (that is, the liability to punishment) was thought of by God as belonging to Christ rather than to us.[4]

Some PS proponents do disagree with this characterization to argue a slightly different slant on Jesus's supposed guilt. Nevertheless, they've developed their own problems regarding sin's imputation, as shown in this example from John MacArthur:

> God the Father using the principle of imputation, treated Christ as if He were a sinner though He was not, and had Him die as

---

2. Luther, *Galatians*, 3:13.
3. Mueller, *Christian Dogmatics*, 294.
4. Grudem, *Systematic Theology*, 574.

a substitute to pay the penalty for the sins of those who believe in Him (cf. Is. 53:4–6; Gal. 3:10–13; 1 Pet. 2:24). On the cross, He did not become a sinner (as some suggest), but remained as holy as ever. He was treated as if He were guilty of all the sins ever committed by all who would ever believe, though He committed none. The wrath of God was exhausted on Him and the just requirement of God's law met for those for whom He died.[5]

MacArthur's view is held by only a minority of preachers and teachers because of the doublespeak inherent in applying the term "principle of imputation" to label transmission of sin without transmission of guilt. What of sin can be imputed to someone if not its guilt? Merriam-Webster informs us that *to impute* means *to attribute accusingly: lay the responsibility or blame.* Other definitions state it is *to reckon, consider, regard, impart, give,* and *charge someone with a wrongdoing or crime.* All those explications center on the transference of guilt! To say that Christ took our sin and God punished him for it means that God saw guilt in the one he was punishing. Without any guilt on Jesus, God would have punished him unjustly. MacArthur and like-minded PS proponents may sensibly regard it wrong to consider that Jesus could ever become guilty of sin, but the problem doesn't go away by arguing for an enigmatic but intrinsically illogical separation of sin from its guilt. Punishment is intended precisely for *guilt*—not for whatever remains in sin with the guilt removed. Therefore, regardless of these attempts to hide the "principle of imputation" within a cloud of mystery, these PS proponents incoherently imagine the transference of sin without a transference of guilt.

Thus, however we want to look at it, no justification exists for ignoring the justice of eternal death if someone physically dies with the obligation of sin upon that person. PS will just not work on this point.

Of course, the speciousness of the PS position on justice doesn't automatically make opposition easy. When anti-PS proponents point out the difficulties of PS (especially in regard to the meaning of forgiveness as the cancellation of a debt), they often fail to explicate any necessity at all for the cross. If Jesus wasn't paying the price of other people's sins, what did he in fact do? Does the cross actually have any necessary purpose? Often for those in opposition to PS, the cross becomes a watered-down symbol, as in the moral influence (mimetic) theories or even the governmental theory. Unfortunately, the Christus Victor idea fares no better because although its proponents insist that Christ defeated sin and death on the cross, they don't—or can't?—explain exactly how.

---

5. MacArthur, *One Perfect Life*, 513.

But if we're going to keep a good hold on God's entire forgiveness process, which includes the cross, we must consider what the cross actually does. And the view of Kinship Theology does indeed regard the cross as necessary: only by the cross can God remove that major obstacle to restored love relationship—the curse of human essence.

Let me offer an illustration. If a man with a tumor in his brain should attack me because the tumor was distorting his thinking, I would be wronged. If that person (during a period when the tumor was not influencing his behavior) begged forgiveness, I might be able to say, "Okay, I'll forgive you," but my willingness to forgive him would not by itself restore relationship. The tumor could still prompt the person at any moment to grab a knife to slice my heart out (and I really think that would pose a serious impediment to continued relationship). For relationship to be restored, the obstacle to the relationship would have to be removed. The tumor would have to come out.

Remember, the curse that infected Adam settled on his essence, physical creation. The curse is like a tumor—a black hole devoid of God—intent, as a cancer is, on infecting everything else around it. I think this view of the curse, or original sin, is helpful in indicating to us what the curse actually is. It is not just that we do wrong things and as a consequence owe a debt that someone has to pay, and Jesus our hero, steps up to pay the account and make everything right with our creditor God. The solution cannot simply be someone's taking punishment for a wrong incurred. The tumor is still there! The cancer will continue to eat. Furthermore, Jesus cannot solve the problems by having paid for the guilt of all future sin so that we're already forgiven for every evil the cancer adds to its growing blackness. No, for lasting relationship, we must be rescued from the tumor! Christ, the redeeming surgeon, must remove the festering mass. It is not just individual sin offense to God's honor (Anselm's satisfaction theory) or to his justice (the Reformers' PS) that keeps us from God. Rather, our very essence, infected and infectious, will not allow satisfactory relationship with God. A bile-filled tumor grows within us, and we must have it out!

Paul struggles with this condition in Romans 7. As the voice of the everyman—particularly one who recognizes the problem, finds it repulsive, and wants God's rescue—he realizes that the curse on his essence distorts everything. Read what follows here (Romans 7:14 to the chapter's end), while substituting the idea of a cancerous tumor for the word *sin*:

> For we know that the law is spiritual, but I am made out of flesh, *corrupted with this tumor of death*. For I do not understand what I am doing, because I do not practice what I want to do, but I do what I hate. And if I do what I do not want to do, I agree with

the law that it is good. So now I am no longer the one doing it, but it is *this tumor* living in me. For I know that nothing good lives in me, that is, in my [cursed] flesh. For the desire to do what is good is with me, but there is no ability to do it. For I do not do the good that I want to do, but I practice the evil *from this tumor's corrupting influence* that I do not want to do. Now if I do what I do not want, I am no longer the one doing it, but it is *this tumor* that lives in me. So I discover this principle: When I want to do what is good, *this corrupting tumor* is with me. For in my inner self I joyfully agree with God's law. But I see a different law in the parts of my [cursed] body, waging war against the law of my mind and taking me prisoner by *this tumor* in my body. What a wretched man I am! Who will rescue me from this *cancer-filled* dying body? I thank God through Jesus Christ our Lord! So then, with my mind I myself am a slave to the law of God, but with my *tumor-filled* flesh, to the law of sin.

God reveals himself to us (Romans 1:20). Because of our image-bearing qualities, we can recognize God and respond. But our response doesn't save us. We cannot overcome the curse of sin—the death of our essence that entraps our spirits and drags us to an eternity apart from God. But God through Christ rescued us. He came to defeat the curse, to remove the tumor, to free us from this death coil spun tightly about us. Through his rescuing, we are pardoned *and* restored. We are forgiven, *and* we are redeemed!

Redemption—as we have discussed and as evidenced all through the biblical record—rescues material possessions. Because of the curse on our essence, Jesus redeems by rescuing our physical essence from its curse. Forgiveness pardons wrongs in order to restore relationship. But since our wrongs are based on the obstacle of corrupted essence, which limits relationship, God doesn't stop at pardoning the wrongs; he also removes the obstacle so as to reach unobstructed love relationship. So redemption and forgiveness work hand in hand to accomplish God's restoration. In a sense, forgiveness powers redemption's rescue so as to remove the obstacle of sin's curse on our essence. By removing that obstacle, redemption provides the way for us to realize complete restoration.

Some may object, "But doesn't the Bible actually say Jesus *paid* for our sin?" Well, no, not in those words. When we hear a verse such as 1 Corinthians 6:20, telling us we have been bought with a price, we instinctively think of payment. Our restoration to relationship with God certainly did have a cost, which Jesus certainly did pay. But he did not pay for the guilt of individual sins; he paid for redemption. Think of it this way: I am in a log cabin out in the northern woods in the middle of winter. I want to ensure that I have a nice warm fire roaring in the fireplace that evening. So I spend the afternoon chopping wood. At the end of the day, with my fire crackling away, I sit back and think, "I paid for this evening with my afternoon of work, but it was all worth it." Now, I didn't really pay anybody for the evening. No transaction occurred in which an obligation I owed or a penalty I incurred was paid off. I used the expression just to explain a trade-off of sorts. I wanted that evening; I had a desire for that experience. And my desire motivated me to put into action the steps to realize my desire. Without that work, I could never have had that reward.

We can heartily embrace that understanding when considering restoration to God. The desire to forgive and redeem—to have relationship restored—motivated our God and our Savior to action. That action—the forgiveness canceling our debt and the redemption removing the curse—was the payment for us. Yes! Jesus paid it all. All to him I owe!

One other thing: we talk about the cross as having accomplished redemption. However, as mentioned before, that redemption has to do with our physical essence—our bodies. Our bodies in their current state will never realize their refinement from sin's curse until Christ's return. Therefore, Christ does not apply his accomplished redemption to us until his second advent. That raises the question of whether the cross was actually where Jesus accomplished redemption if he has yet to apply it.

The cross was the first step. The metaphor of Ruth depicted its purpose exactly: the cross qualified the Redeemer. In one sense, the scene in which Boaz secured the status of redeemer at the city gate images the cross and resurrection. Boaz became qualified, just as Jesus became qualified through his death and resurrection. Yet Jesus's act (unlike Boaz's) resulted in more than just qualification. In rising from the dead and taking back his flesh, Jesus filled it with life anew, turning it from corruption to incorruption so that his resurrected body became the firstfruits of redemption. Christ did effect actual redemption of a portion of created physical essence in his own resurrection. But full redemption will come at his return when Christ will cast out the corruption of the rest of physical creation, including our bodies. Then he will make all things new—new bodies, new heavens, new earth. What had been corrupt will be newly filled with that life of everlasting love relationship with God.

12

Justice & Mercy

The quality of mercy is not strain'd,
It droppeth, as the gentle rain from heaven
Upon the place beneath: it is twice bless'd;
It blesseth him that gives, and him that takes:
'Tis mightiest in the mightiest; it becomes
The thronèd monarch better than his crown;
His sceptre shows the force of temporal power,
The attribute to awe and majesty,
Wherein doth sit the dread and fear of kings;
But mercy is above this sceptred sway,
It is enthroned in the hearts of kings,
It is an attribute to God himself;
And earthly power doth then show likest God's
When mercy seasons justice.

—WILLIAM SHAKESPEARE, FROM *THE MERCHANT OF VENICE*, ACT IV, SCENE I

Does God pervert justice? Does the Almighty pervert what is right?

—JOB 8:3

> *He saved us—not by works of righteousness that we had done,*
> *but according to His mercy.*
>
> —Psalm 79:9a

In Romans, Paul explains the gospel—the *good news* that God, in covenant faithfulness and through Jesus, restored his creation, particularly his image bearers, to his originally intended purpose, which is everlasting love relationship. Relationship saturates that gospel message. God is the relational three-in-one. Jesus is the relational fullness of God and fullness of human. Christ restored embrace for his image bearers—multiple-in-one in relational reflection. And all elements coalesce for the relational love of the entire community, which rests on God's truth, goodness, and beauty.

Let's note the dependency within the multiple-in-one construct. We humans depend on our shared essence (our physical reality) to live and interact as humans. So also do God's persons thoroughly rely on their own shared essence (TGB) to live and function. We know that truth from God's having revealed it to us in creation and Scripture. In creating for relationship, God had to create image bearers—those who could recognize, accept, and then operate according to that same basis of his own function: his TGB. Only on that common bedrock could God's purpose of everlasting love relationship rest. Knowledge of God was no accident of creation nor was it given with arbitrary limits, just enough so God could demand slavish obedience as overlord. Rather, God made us to know him by giving us the ability to comprehend him and by revealing his love for his love relationship.

However, as we have discussed, his image bearers failed to depend on him for that relational basis. When they failed, God was left with a seemingly disastrous result. Being faithful to his Trinitarian Covenant of Operational Essence (which means always acting according to his TGB), he would have to forever separate from his image bearers. But separating would still leave him unrighteous—unfaithful to his Trinitarian Covenant of Creative Purpose (to create for everlasting love relationship). Of course, God had prepared for that. Chapter 9 discusses how God formed his restoration plan to bring about atonement and, therefore, remain faithful to both those Trinitarian covenants.

Certain aspects of God's restoration plan may still seem a puzzle. We do have a God of absolute justice. However, many of us may have unwittingly assigned to that term the distorted idea that wrongdoing always requires some kind of payment in order for justice to be served. That idea runs contrary to our last chapter's definition of forgiveness as the pardoning or canceling of an *unpaid* debt. God desires to forgive, and that desire is merciful

(Daniel 9:9). But in his desire to be forgiving, to be merciful, must God set his absolute justice aside? In other words, must he limit one of his infinite attributes to embrace another? The simple answer is no; God does not have to choose among his eternal, absolute, and infinite qualities to righteously engage with us. And, in fact, he could not eternally so limit himself and still, by definition, remain God. But we need to proceed carefully to find our way to that simple answer.

RELATIONSHIP BASIS: OBEDIENCE OR LOVE

We must begin with the purpose that I reviewed at the beginning of this chapter: for both creation and restoration, God's purpose was everlasting love relationship with his image bearers. Significantly, that starting purpose is also the clearest demarcation between Kinship Theology and Reformed Theology. Reformed Theology champions a master-servant relationship between God and us as the most basic and primary relationship. As Joel Beeke, President of Puritan Reformed Theological Seminary, puts it, "To be Reformed is to stress the comprehensive, sovereign, fatherly lordship of God over everything: every area of creation, every creature's endeavors, and every aspect of the believer's life."[1] He goes on: "We exist for one purpose: to give Him glory. We have only duties to God, no rights."[2] (Beeke 2016).

Like Reformed Theology, Kinship Theology proclaims God as our king and master and asserts that we owe him allegiance—the submission of our wills to absolute obedience. However, Kinship followers view the master-servant relationship as necessary only so we can realize that our vulnerabilities require reliance on God for our satisfaction and fulfillment. In other words, the reason God desires our obedience—in all we judge, act, think, and believe—is not concern for maintaining his lordship or to ensure regard for his status as the supreme commander and controller. Again, we readily acknowledge his supremacy! But *in his sovereignty*, his higher purpose, eclipsing the master-servant relationship, is the relationship which allows his love to shine. God is primarily a God of love rather than a God who demands obedience. God plainly tells us as much in Isaiah 1. He argues there that the merely dutiful presentation of worship activity—even though it seems to fulfill his very orders—disgusts him. Read this astounding passage:

---

1. Beeke, "Ultimate Concern."
2. Beeke, "Ultimate Concern."

What are all your sacrifices to Me?' asks the Lord. 'I have had enough of burnt offerings and rams and the fat of well-fed cattle; I have no desire for the blood of bulls, lambs, or male goats. When you come to appear before Me, who requires this from you—this trampling of My courts? Stop bringing useless offerings. Your incense is detestable to Me. New Moons and Sabbaths, and the calling of solemn assemblies—I cannot stand iniquity with a festival. I hate your New Moons and prescribed festivals. They have become a burden to Me; I am tired of putting up with them. When you lift up your hands in prayer, I will refuse to look at you; even if you offer countless prayers, I will not listen. Your hands are covered in blood. (Isaiah 1:11–15)

God argues that mere recognition of his authority means nothing. Let's be careful to note that. If love relationship is not the primary basis for worship, God views that worship as a burden and a waste, detestable and hateful. Judah had been slaughtering their animals, burning their incense, and participating in feasts and festivals all on the basis of duty—because their Lord and Commander had ordered them to do so. A god who cares only for recognition of him as supreme master should be satisfied with such an approach. But our God told them that simple compliance did not thrill him. The worship symbols were not pleasing when the worshippers had forgotten the very meaning of the images. Micah 6:8 clarifies: "Mankind, He has told you what is good and what it is the Lord requires of you: to act justly, to love faithfulness, and to walk humbly with your God." Relational activity based on God's truth, goodness, and beauty must be the *starting point* of our worship, not merely a side item to carry along as we perform our duty. And that is so because love and relationship are *who* God is. They are what he cares about, what motivates every aspect of his character and attributes, and what must shine at the forefront of our engagement.

The Reformed may point to Beeke's quotation and protest, "But look: the Reformed do stress the 'fatherly lordship of God.' Isn't that essentially the same as what you're saying?" No, it is not. Again, God's desire for love and relationship cannot be buried among the stiffer demands of rule and control. It must shine as primary. That is precisely the difference.

DOES GOD LIMIT HIS LOVE?

Of course, the Reformed would never argue that God does not love us or that we do not have a love relationship with God. I certainly don't want to imply that. Absolutely, most of the Reformed love God and believe he supremely loves us. Yet the subtle but important difference between Kinship Theology and Reformed Theology—the difference that aligns the trajectories of our understandings—regards the priority positioning of these two relationships—the master-servant relationship and the love relationship (which is frequently imaged in the Bible by the husband-wife relationship). The Reformed champion the master-servant relationship as the pinnacle bond of interaction with God, so it is easy to see why they understand marriage to be something of a master-subject dynamic. In Kinship Theology, however, the love (giving of self) relationship is the pinnacle—the ultimate purpose for creation and, subsequently, the ultimate purpose for redemption. This priority positioning alters one's perspective. If the primary purpose is love relationship, the scope of all activity must originate in that primary principle. Therefore, while some of our interaction with God may not relate to the master-servant relationship scenario, it surely must all relate to the love relationship. In Reformed thought, the opposite is advanced: our interaction with God must always find its way back to the master-servant relational purpose, not necessarily always relating to the love relationship.

I am insisting on this point not to speak badly about the Reformed. My bookshelves are filled with the writings of great Reformed scholars. Their ideas have helped the church of God flesh out crucial understanding of countless topics for hundreds of years. But this point of primary relational basis does color how we see God and his interactive purpose as he accomplishes his will. For example, all of us understand God as welcoming into his everlasting embrace those who by faith trust the gospel message. But there are some who do not by faith trust the gospel message. They will encounter everlasting destruction. Kinship Theology promotes the idea that God's infinite love extends the opportunity for salvation to everyone. Reformed Theology teaches that God's love extends salvation only to those he has enabled to have faith in him.

If the question (for both views) is "Why isn't everyone saved?" the answers will differ. The Kinship Theology proponent responds that although God provides revelation of who he is and an offer of relationship to all, unbelievers reject the offer based on their own selfish desire. The Reformed Theology proponent answers that God did not enable—through regeneration—unbelievers to turn to God in faithful desire. If love relationship is indeed foundational, the Reformed view should be faulted for suggesting God limits his love by enabling only some to have faith. However, if the Reformed are correct in elevating the master-servant relationship as primary, God would be just in not enabling everyone, since the starting point for an unbeliever is original failure in the master-servant relationship. By the failure, so the Reformed argue, God is just in separating from the person who broke the primary master-servant relationship, and he is under no obligation to extend love to that person.

The Reformed response appears to conclude that God may not be a God of infinite love. Infinite love implies love without limitation. God proves by regenerating *some* that it is possible for him to extend love to *all* who fail in the master-servant relationship, so the question must rightly shift for the Reformed from "Why isn't everyone saved?" to "Why does God limit his love in not saving everyone?" or "How can God be a God of infinite love yet not extend infinite love when he is able to do so?"

Noted Reformed author John Murray discusses this question in his book *Redemption: Accomplished and Applied*:

> It is necessary to underline this concept of sovereign love. Truly God is love. Love is not something adventitious; it is not something that God may choose to be or choose not to be. He *is* love, and that necessarily, inherently, and eternally.[3]

Well, good so far; we can all agree. But notice how he continues:

> Yet it belongs to the very essence of electing love to recognize that it is not inherently necessary to that love which God necessarily and eternally is that he should set such love as issues in redemption and adoption upon utterly undesirable and hell-deserving objects.

I find his statement baffling. It is decidedly at odds with what he previously stated. If God "is love, and that *necessarily, inherently,* and *eternally,*" love (who he *is*) would compel him to act in love if love were an available option. And we know it is an available option because God does so love in restoring many who are "utterly undesirable and hell-deserving objects" to fellowship through the life, death, and resurrection of Christ. How, then, can Murray deny that a God who necessarily *is* love necessarily *will* love? Murray's only escape from the illogic is in determining that love relationship is not God's chief relationship: God, therefore, can limit his love based on another, more highly prioritized purpose. That reasoning is supported in the writings of many others (e.g., Sam Storms, John Piper, Jonathan Edwards). Sam Storms puts it this way: "Thus, to say that love is sovereign is to say it is distinguishing. . . . Of this we may be certain: God was under no obligation to choose any. Were he to have chosen none, he would have remained perfectly just in doing so."[4] Storms underscores the Reformed foundation that the love relationship is not necessary. A higher relationship

---

3. Murray, *Redemption*, 10.
4. Storms, *Chosen for Life*, 183.

(e.g., that of master-slave) may limit the love relationship, and so this view places God's justice above his need for love.

In perhaps the most shocking statement about God's purported withholding of love, Jonathan Edwards excuses it by arguing that the existence of evil is actually necessary in order for God to be fully God:

> It is a proper and excellent thing for infinite glory to shine forth; and for the same reason, it is proper that the shining forth of God's glory should be complete; that is, that all parts of his glory should shine forth, that every beauty should be proportionably effulgent, that the beholder may have a proper notion of God.... If it were not right that God should decree and permit and punish sin, there could be no manifestation of God's justice in hatred of sin or in punishing it, ... or in showing any preference, in his providence, of godliness before it. ... So *evil is necessary* if the glory of God is to be perfectly and completely displayed (emphasis added).[5]

Evil is necessary?! That is the position of eastern mysticism, which calls for a yin-yang balance in all existence. John Piper writes much the same thing in defense of his notion that God limits his love.[6] In addition, Edwards's assertion is logically inconsistent. Edwards argues that God must withhold love from some in order for there to be a "manifestation of God's justice in hatred of sin or in punishing it." But the Reformed (including Edwards) categorically argue that in Jesus on the cross we see the "manifestation of God's justice in hatred of sin or in punishing it." So Edwards contradicts himself; according to him, Jesus has already provided that manifestation.

In contradistinction to this convoluted perspective, Kinship Theology argues that God's priority relationship matches his purpose for creation: everlasting love relationship among God and his image bearers. God does not limit his love. If some choose not to trust, it is not because of God's limiting the extension of his love; rather, it is the necessary impossibility of relationship without the shared basis of God's TGB that separates the unbeliever. If love is possible, God will act in love. But because of the nature of true love—that it cannot be coerced—God cannot enter into love relationship with someone who will not love. The basis for fellowship with God is God's truth, goodness, and beauty. God would cease to be God (of course, an impossibility) if he were not to operate according to that very essence. Therefore, it is not a choice for God to love just certain persons but in some respect limit his love for others. Rather, God consistently loves; it is

---

5. Edwards, *The Works*, 41.
6. Piper, *Does God Desire*.

the other party who may not reciprocate the love and thus end the possibility for love relationship.

But in insisting on the Kinship Theology view of infinite love, am I ignoring the absolute nature of God's justice? In other words, can the Reformed accuse me of saying God puts limits on his absolute justice just as I have charged them with supposing God puts limits on his infinite love? I want to approach that question by examining the quality of justice and its relationship to mercy.

MERCY AND JUSTICE

In Romans 12:1, Paul concludes that we're to present our bodies as living sacrifices in recognition of the mercies of God, which have been explained by Paul in the preceding chapters and sung of at the end of chapter 11. The Greek word (and its root) translated *mercies* means not only kindness but also compassion or compassionate pity—in other words, it involves the motivation for being kind. When we consider the reasons God redeemed, we find not only that through redemption God fulfilled his righteousness (his faithfulness to his covenant of creative purpose—Romans 1:17), but that he did so out of compassionate pity for us (Romans 5:8; 8:28; 8:31–39; and especially 9:23). While both these reasons exist distinctly, they are connected.

God established and committed to his Covenant of Creative Purpose for love—to create image bearers for everlasting *love* relationship. Therefore, when sin put that covenant commitment at risk, God resolved the problem for the sake of his faithfulness, but his faithfulness was based on his heart purpose—the desire for that everlasting love relationship. In that love motivation, his mercy shone clear. So let's follow that trail of God's compassion.

Compassion for the one estranged normally links back rather solidly to the reason for the estrangement. For humanity, that estrangement, of course, came in the garden. God had given a command for the purpose of growth through trust, and Eve and Adam disobeyed it: they ate the apple. The human race and all its physical essence in creation were plunged into sin and that required eternal separation from God. But doesn't this sound rather harsh—absolute, everlasting ruination for biting into a piece of fruit? When we read Matthew 13:50 about the wicked in hell, we could legitimately substitute Eve's name there, but we'd still have difficulty trying to justify the punishment as befitting the crime: "Throw [Eve] into the blazing furnace. In that place there will be weeping and gnashing of teeth! After all, she ate an apple!" (Okay, I added that last line in there for effect.)

To defend God's action (as if God needed defense), we need to call on his Covenant of Operational Essence—the requirement that God always act according to his perfect essence of TGB. We well know that absolute justice is incorporated in that TGB. Therefore, God must, we argue, be true to who he is by separating from even the smallest of sins. So, yes, we try to convince ourselves that Eve should be thrown into the fiery furnace for eating an apple because God must separate from every sinner, no matter how small his or her sin. We decide that outcome is unavoidable based on the fact that the absolute justice found in God's TGB must remain absolute.

But wait just a second. Isn't compassion also incorporated in that absolute TGB of God? What happened to *its* quality of absoluteness? When infinite compassion goes head-to-head with absolute justice, why do we consider justice's trumping infinite compassion as the "right" way for God to remain righteous? Did one of God's infinite qualities have to fall by the wayside? Are we somehow satisfied that the disregard of mercy in favor of justice makes everything okay? Thinking that way violently distorts our conception of God. Must we champion an image of God who no longer fits the very definition of God?

Let's back up to come at the question from another angle. Let's say a Hitler/Stalin-type person has been conducting his genocidal insanity for decades of his life. He is truly an evil person, disgustingly arrogant, without an ounce of kindness or compassion in his entire being. Imagine this person, after a lifetime of nonstop hate and horror, lying on his deathbed. Imagine music playing in his room in which a Bible verse happens to be sung. He hears it, and a sudden, Damascus-road light shines within his soul. He realizes his depravity and calls out to Christ: "I believe; I repent; rescue me, Lord!" Then he falls back, expelling his last breath.

Put that scene aside for a moment. Now imagine a young boy about ten or eleven years old. His parents are not Christians, but they are decent, honorable citizens, intent on raising their son to be of good moral character. The son is a particularly mild-mannered child, never giving his parents any trouble and actually interested in doing good. He is out one day on a city sidewalk and sees a little old lady attempting to cross a busy street. But the cars pay no attention to her. The boy rushes over to her, offers his help, and waves both arms to stop the stream of traffic. He escorts the lady safely across the street. She thanks him profusely, telling him what a kind and attentive boy he is. He smiles at her in appreciation, and then, turning to cross back, he steps into the street and is hit by a truck. He expels his last breath.

These two—the genocidal maniac and the ten-year-old boy—stand before the Great White Throne of God's judgment. Jesus looks at the man and says, "Your name is written on my very heart. Come, enter into the joy of your God!" Then he looks at the boy and says, "I never knew you!" as he casts him into the blazing Lake of Fire for all eternity.

We understand the Great White Throne scene to be the Bible's depiction of God's final justice for the world of sin. But how does it seem *just* for that child, based on his relatively few and minor sins, to receive eternal destruction while God receives the murderer of millions to his eternity of pleasure based on a last-minute cry of repentance? Of course, we can justify the redemption of the man: the forgiveness and redemptive death of Christ made that salvation possible. But what about the boy? Would we, standing around the throne while we viewed that heart-wrenching scene, not feel absolutely terrible for him? And if we felt that way—filled with compassion and pity, longing for mercy—wouldn't we wonder how our own compassion for this boy could exceed that of our *infinitely caring* God who at that moment was casting the boy to his eternal doom?

To make sense of the scene, we might try to stifle our repugnance and horror by reasoning that the indignity suffered by our glorious God demands that he fling the full fury of his wrath at even that little boy. But while the Bible does speak of sin's effrontery, that's not the real point at stake in this drama. We need to be asking ourselves if it's truly just, no matter how heinous the offense, for God to constrain his infinite compassion. Is not a permanent limitation on infiniteness a contradiction in terms? If God is defined by boundlessness, how can God remain God by eternally restraining his very essence—his mercy, his compassion, his love?

We need not become universalists to resolve this quandary. (Doing so would swing us from one extreme of the pendulum to the other, only to find there the same problem of limitation, but this time a limitation of justice.) Rather, I believe we need to adjust our perspective on this scene to achieve balance. I intentionally designed my Great White Throne setting with certain implied presumptions. But they are not presumptions that I believe our God would tolerate. We'll get to them in due time, but first we need to confirm our understanding of how God acts.

HOW GOD ACTS

We've covered at length God's two Trinitarian covenants: God operates according to his eternal, absolute, and infinite essence of TGB; and God created image bearers for everlasting love relationship. We've talked about how God could not put aside one covenant in favor of the other. To be righteous, he had to fulfill both. Thus, because sin eventuated in the curse, God devised his plan of restoration to ensure faithfulness to both covenants, which should clue us in as to how God acts. In other words, God does not limit or give up one portion of his essence to fulfill another. He will always embrace his absolute and infinite qualities. Put still another way, God will not deny any part of his essence (his being) in order to engage his existence (his activity). Thus, God will not engage his existence if the activity will destroy his essence.

God cannot cease to be God. That means God cannot cease to be absolutely just; *at the same time*, he cannot cease to be infinitely merciful. Both define God, and that brings us back around to this principle: God will always eternally act according to his complete, absolute, and infinite essence.

PERSONHOOD

We have talked before of the necessity of God's being one. God is defined as infinite, so two or more gods would necessarily limit each other. We also have discussed the necessity of God's being plural. If God is infinite TGB, and infinite TGB includes infinite communication (love), another necessary being must exist to communicate with. Therefore, the necessity of God's being both one and multiple gives philosophical sense to the Trinity—God is one in essence and three in Persons. But what exactly do we mean by *person*?

In the late 1700s (through the very early 1800s), a philosopher named Johann Gottlieb Fichte argued that God could not be a person. Fichte defined a person in contrast to a counterpart. In other words, the existence of a counterpart—another person—limits a person. Since God is *infinite*, he cannot be a person since a person, by very definition, is *limited* by a counterpart. While somewhat valid, the argument, of course, rests on Fichte's definition of a person, and it was with this definition that Georg Wilhelm Friedrich Hegel, another philosopher, found fault. Hegel argued that, contrary to Fichte's claim, a person is *not* defined by *contrast* to a counterpart. Rather, a person is defined by nature. And the relational nature of a person shows through the person's self-giving activity. In self-giving, the person finds himself or herself *in* the counterpart rather than separated from the counterpart. Self-giving, then, overcomes the contrast between person and counterpart. (Philosophy students may here recognize the thesis—antithesis—synthesis movement with which both Hegel and Fichte are credited.) Hegel concluded that the infinite God, through self-giving, represents *person* in its most perfect form.

Hegel's idea fits in perfectly with how Kinship Theology understands the Bible's revelation of God and his interaction. From a look at God's image bearers, we recognize that our one creator God must be person as well. Yet God cannot depend on his creation to be something beyond what he was in his perfection already. Therefore, if God was person prior to creation, the relational nature of that one God required him to have been multiple persons.

Further, the self-giving nature of a person requires that both mind and will be located in the persons of God rather than in the one essence of God. Those minds and wills can logically never conflict because they operate by their infinite essence. If infinite TGB motivates the will, two wills of the same infinite motivation and infinite resource could not harbor differing desires.

Putting together everything we've discussed about the nature of God, I would modify Hegel's definition of person for our purposes: a person is one who can comprehend TGB, desire that which will satisfy comprehended TGB, and interact according to that comprehended desire.

As Hegel explained, the relational, self-giving activity of persons is what puts those persons *in* each other. As we examine God's image bearers, we find Jesus praying for us, saying, "May they all be one, as You, Father, are *in* Me and I am *in* You. May they also be one *in* Us" (John 17:21). The sexual union within marriage illustrates this relationship of persons. In fact, it pictures all three relationships we've covered—the Trinitarian relationship, the relationship between God and humankind, and the relationship among humans. The act of sex—becoming one by being in the other—pictures the love relationship of multiple persons in one essence.

Finally, we come to the question of whether sin and death actually limit God's otherwise infinite compassion. The answer is an unequivocal no. It is correct that God cannot forgive to embrace in love all offenders, but *not* because his dignity has suffered. Rather, life and relationship require a non-limiting movement of one spirit into the other. God, being infinite, must move in relationship among all his creation. But the relationship, in order to be defined as love, must be uncoerced. Thus, if the other person limits involvement in the TGB of God by choice, relationship (life) cannot continue. God remains the infinite God, but death (separation) results for those who seek to limit God's involvement in them. Understanding that personal nature of God in relationship, we realize why death and separation are necessary—why they constitute the penalty of sin. God did not have to devise separation as a punishment; separation is the only possible conclusion for a person who will not give himself or herself to God.

Now we can see that my Great White Throne illustration didn't include all the pertinent facts. Our God of infinite compassion so designed and so implements the redemption plan through his infinite knowledge and involvement that every person who could possibly come to him will have opportunity as God coordinates all events to work out for good (Romans 8:28). God is patient with all, not wanting any to perish but all to come to repentance (2 Peter 3:9). Thus, the judgment scene in which I presumed the boy damned—a boy who wanted to do good and accidentally lost his life before he had an opportunity to hear about and accept Christ—is, in my estimation, an impossible scenario. God's revelation comes to all, and no one who would accept will miss that opportunity. That is what the Romans 8:28 promise entails.

BIBLICAL JUSTICE

As we work toward a conclusion regarding the embrace of both absolute justice and infinite mercy, we need also to ensure that our concept of justice is accurate. Most of us are familiar with an American justice system that simply assigns a penalty (punishment) to the guilty. With the payment of the penalty or punishment, we consider justice served. However, suffering a penalty for wrongdoing is only part of a fuller—a biblical—concept of justice. There are two Hebrew words that are often translated *just* or *justice*. One of these words we can think of as *primary justice* and the other as *rectifying justice*.[7]

Primary justice has to do with living justly. In other words, it is living based on God's essence of TGB. If I live faithful to our Covenant of Life with God, I am considered just. Acting in TGB, of course, means I do so in relation to others around me. Therefore, in one sense, others may see my relationship with God in my relationship with others. Acting in TGB means that when the hurting, the needy, and the weak cross my path, I will respond with my abilities to assist their vulnerabilities. Lacking that helpful attitude was often God's complaint against the Israelites as testified to by Old Testament prophets. God had harsh words for the Jewish leaders who did not treat the people on a basis of TGB.

Jesus acted in alignment with the TGB attitude throughout his earthly life. His conduct is what James meant by saying, "Pure and undefiled religion before our God and Father is this: to look after orphans and widows in their distress" (James 1:27a). James is not promoting some watered-down social gospel. As Christ sits on his judgment throne in Matthew 25 and separates the sheep from the goats, he *dispenses justice* by drawing a distinction between people based on whether they gave food to the hungry, drink to the thirsty, shelter to the homeless, clothing to the naked, care to the sick, and comfort to the suffering. Our helping the vulnerable is not simply a performance of random acts of kindness. Biblically, it is living justly. It is doing justice.

---

7. Keller, *Generous Justice*.

The second kind of justice is *rectifying justice*. When someone fails in doing primary justice, the need arises for rectifying justice. Rectifying justice makes the community right again; it returns the community to primary justice. It's imperative that we're clear on this: the goal of rectifying justice *is not punishment*. The goal is a return to primary justice. Separation is the penalty for those who fail in doing justice; the penalty removes the offender from the community of justice.

Simply hurting someone for an offense does not necessarily result in a return to primary justice. Therefore, simply hurting someone does not qualify as biblical justice. The primary concern is the community. If a person continues to act unjustly, the community forever separates from that person. On the other hand, if an offender repents and renews his commitment to the community so that the outcome is restored primary justice, we can declare that justice—*absolute justice*—was served, *even without the implementation of punishment*. Justice, therefore, is served not by the issuance of penalty or the meting out of punishment. Justice is served when the community is made right.

Jonah provides a notable example. Of course, the most memorable part of his story is his being swallowed whole by the great fish after he runs from God. But it's the reason for his running that's more important to the narrative. Jonah was no coward or villain intent on avoiding God because he despised God. Jonah believed God and knew him well. God had told him to preach to the Ninevites so they would repent of their evil. Jonah ran from that charge not because he was afraid of preaching to a wicked city that might attack and harm him. Rather, Jonah was afraid that his preaching would actually be successful, and that had him worried. He knew God's character. If Nineveh repented, the God of infinite mercy would surely be merciful to them, forgiving their evil. And that was exactly what Jonah wanted to avoid.

Jonah was probably not a particularly hateful person, wanting God's blessings only for himself and his people. There's more to the story. Nineveh was the greatest city of the old Assyrian empire. Even prior to its heyday as a world power, Nineveh had persecuted Israel. And a century later (during Manasseh's reign in Judah), Assyria evidenced extreme violence, dragging Judah's king off by hooks, binding him with chains, and torturing him. Artwork of the time depicts enemies of Assyria being skinned alive and having their tongues ripped out. Many Israelites died at the hands of the Assyrians and Ninevites. So in this case, Jonah was similar to a 20th century Jew whose family and people had been tortured by Nazi Germany. And now God wants that Jew to enter Hitler's high council to preach repentance? so that God *would forgive them?!* That was what had Jonah running.

After the great fish incident, Jonah did agree to call the Ninevites to repentance. But after doing so—and still hopeful the Ninevites would not repent—Jonah waited to see what would happen. Well, the Ninevites did repent, and God, true to himself, was indeed merciful. That made Jonah mad (Jonah 4:2), and he basically faulted God in saying, "See! I knew you were going to do this! You were gracious and merciful to them! That's exactly why I ran!"

The story teaches us a lot about Jonah and about how we are to interact with God. But the main point here is that God forgave when the Ninevites repented. God demanded no reparations from them to be given to Israel for previous cruelties and plundering. God simply forgave. And this event took place a century prior to Assyria's reengaging in its evil to again persecute Judah.

Here then is the question: did God act justly with Nineveh? If we answer, "No: they deserved judgment and punishment, which God failed to impose!" we know as little about justice as Jonah did. God was just in forgiving Nineveh, and God is just in forgiving—without reparation—all who come to him in repentance, desiring restored relationship. God is infinitely just because the goal of rectifying justice is to return the community to the activity of primary justice. If God accomplishes that goal—*even without punishment* (as in the instance of Nineveh's repentance)—justice is served.

No real conflict, then, remains between justice and mercy so that God cannot be merciful because he is required by justice to punish someone. God's work—his whole restoration plan—is to return his fallen image bearers to the primary justice of relationship with him. If God forgives the sinner who repents in faith, justice is served. If the sinner does not repent in faith, God separates to that sinner's destruction, and in that, justice is also served.

PART 4

Atonement—
Imaged & Accomplished

13

Son of God; Son of Man

As one apart, immune, alone,
Or featured for the shining ones,
And like to none that she has known
Of other women's other sons—
The firm fruition of her need,
He shines anointed; and he blurs
Her vision, till it seems indeed
A sacrilege to call him hers.

—EDWIN ARLINGTON ROBINSON, FROM "THE GIFT OF GOD"

I assure you: An hour is coming, and is now here,
when the dead will hear the voice of the Son of God,
and those who hear will live.

—JOHN 5:25

So Jesus said to them, "I assure you:
Unless you eat the flesh of the Son of Man and drink His blood,
you do not have life in yourselves."

—JOHN 6:53

The discussion of redeemer qualifications in chapter 10 mentioned the requisite kinsman connection. That relational intention highlights the ultimate redemption story of Christ's atonement, for the Bible tells us Jesus is both God and human. Nevertheless, in Jesus's qualification as kinsman redeemer, the full necessity for Jesus being both God and human may not yet be clear. The Boaz example in Ruth presented three requirements for the kinsman redeemer: (1) he had to be a close relative, (2) he had to be able to pay the price, and (3) he had to want to fulfill the obligation. Jesus's desire (qualification 3) and his ability to pay (qualification 2) both tie to his deity. But we needed Jesus to be *our* representative as well, and for that, he had to be our close relative—he had to be human.

JESUS—FULLY HUMAN

We have already dismissed representative notions tied to faulty atonement ideas. Jesus did not become our representative by taking the guilt for our sins on himself and undergoing their punishment. We needed the curse of our essence removed.

Hebrews 9 teaches us that our old Covenant of Life (characterized heavily by the Mosaic covenant) had to end and that the way lifelong covenants end is by death. That exact point is what drives our need for rescue! Our physical essence is under the curse of broken covenant. It has to be put to death. The only way Jesus could do that for us was to share in our physical essence—he had to become human. We are told he did indeed become human, particularly by joining in our oneness—the taking on of bodily essence (Romans 8:3), and by that he could suffer death for our sake.

Paul tells us in Romans 6 we who were baptized (immersed by the Spirit) into Christ Jesus, were baptized into his death. In other words, Paul contends we were buried with him into his death (Romans 6:4) and now consider our bodies dead (Romans 6:11a). Our sharing in his death is possible because Jesus shared in our physical essence so that it was his (our shared) physical essence that died in him. In resurrecting only *his* body, he reclaimed the firstfruits of our shared essence so that the full scope of our physical essence could, on his return, also be reclaimed.

When Paul talks about Christ as Redeemer, he emphasizes the death of Jesus's body (his physical essence) as our hope of the freedom to be gained for all our bodies (all physical essence):

> *1 Corinthians 15:20*
> But now Christ has been raised from the dead, the firstfruits of those who have fallen asleep.

1 Corinthians 15:22–23
For as in Adam all die, so also in Christ all will be made alive. But each in his own order: Christ, the firstfruits; afterward, at His coming, those who belong to Christ.

Romans 8:19–21
For the creation eagerly waits with anticipation for God's sons to be revealed. For the creation was subjected to futility—not willingly, but because of Him who subjected it—in the hope that the creation itself will also be set free from the bondage of corruption into the glorious freedom of God's children.

Romans 8:29
For those He foreknew He also predestined to be conformed to the image of His Son, so that He would be the firstborn among many brothers.

That "conformity to the image of His Son" in Romans 8:29 is not merely a sanctification process in which we try to live as Jesus did. The point about our imaging Christ occurs at the conclusion of Paul's description of restored creation's being like Christ in his resurrected body.

In the middle of that Romans 8 discussion, particularly in verses 26 and 27, Paul talks about the working of the Spirit in a passage I fear we often misread. Here are the two verses:

Romans 8:26
In the same way the Spirit also joins to help in our weakness, because we do not know what to pray for as we should, but the Spirit Himself intercedes for us with unspoken groanings.

Romans 8:27
And He who searches the hearts knows the Spirit's mind-set, because He intercedes for the saints according to the will of God.

Verse 26 tells us that the Holy Spirit helps in our weakness. He intercedes with unspoken groanings when we do not know for what or how to pray as we should. Verse 27 says that the heart-searcher (God) knows the Spirit's mindset because the Spirit is interceding for us according to the will of God. Okay, yes, so what's the problem?

I believe we often misunderstand Paul's meaning here, assuming Paul is saying that when our souls become so burdened for something that we don't know exactly how to pray, the Spirit comes alongside us in his groanings, praying (interceding) for us with God. But that mistaken idea makes that intercession necessary between us and God the Father. In other words, it is as though the Father is waiting to hear from us, but since we don't know how to pray so he can actually understand us, the Spirit (who somehow *does* understand what the Father can't) comes along to interpret our prayers because otherwise the Father would never have any idea what we were trying to say. Of course, that can't be true. I don't want to take away from the very real struggle we sometimes face in prayer or from the very real help that the Spirit provides. But in this case, we need to pay closer attention to the context of the verses.

All through chapter 8, Paul has been noting the conflict between our righteous spirits and our still corrupted flesh. Our corrupted flesh continues to influence us toward sin, while the Spirit renews the revelation of truth, goodness, and beauty to our spirits, assuring us we are God's children (Romans 8:16). So the specific subject with which Paul is grappling is the internal suffering caused by the conflict between righteous spirit and corrupt flesh. Throughout the chapter, Paul has also been trying to assure his readers that we will not be left in this state. He is telling us that just as Jesus—who had a righteous spirit which was "in flesh like ours under sin's domain" (8:3)—was resurrected from physical death, so will we also be resurrected to uncorrupted flesh. The metaphor Paul uses to describe this period of suffering and longing for that resurrection is a woman's groaning in labor pains. (The word translated *labor pains* is used only here in the New Testament but often in classical Greek for the idea of a woman's labor pains in delivery of a child.) In verse 22, Paul begins speaking of creation as groaning in this state, waiting for the birth of the new creation without sin. Verse 23 continues with our spirits also groaning in their current state, waiting for the birth or redemption of our bodies (that same new-creation hope). The hope for that birth, Paul says, is correctly labeled a hope because it is not yet realized. We must wait patiently for it (Romans 8:24–25).

Now we hit verse 26 where we are told that God the Spirit helps in our weakness. What weakness? Exactly the weakness Paul has been describing: the internal conflict between righteous spirit and corrupt flesh that has us groaning for the relief anticipated in the new birth of creation, our new bodies. We struggle in this conflict, not knowing always how to pray to manage it. Paul here provides his readers with assurance as he tells us that the Spirit "in the same way" (8:26a) groans with us. In other words, the Spirit, too, wants that redemption to be realized. So the Spirit's intercession is not between us and God, but between our righteous spirits and our flesh's corrupt influence; the Spirit helps us through this life manage the conflict between spirit and flesh as we "eagerly wait for [our hope] with patience" (8:25b).

Verse 27, then, provides *another* comforting assurance. Our God, who has not yet redeemed us from this conflict, is not acting differently from the Spirit, who is groaning with us. It is not as if the Spirit were on our side, while God—on the other side—is indifferent to our suffering. Rather, Paul is telling us in verse 27 that God, the heart searcher, *knows* (Greek—*has regard for*) the Spirit's *mindset* (*thoughts and purposes*). In other words, even though full redemption must wait, the whole Trinity—Father, Son, and Spirit—is united in a desire for our care. God the Father cares; God the Son cares; God the Spirit cares. They all care for the same thing in the same way. But the plan must continue until all is fulfilled—the plan that works all things "together for the good of those who love God: those who are called according to His purpose" (Romans 8:28).

The "for" at the beginning of verse 29 means Paul is telling us, "Here's how all things work together for good." Paul begins by referring to the foreknown. How God knows which persons will become believers ahead of time is not the point here. The point is that Paul is talking about the foreknown—those who will accept God's truth, goodness, and beauty in Christ when revealed to them. They are children of God, including the Roman Christians to whom Paul is writing. These foreknown—these justified by faith—are "predestined to be conformed to the image of His Son" (8:29a). What does it mean to be conformed to the image of God's Son? Keep in mind the context! Paul has been assuring believers that just as God raised Jesus, who had a righteous spirit, to life in uncorrupted flesh, so will he "also bring your mortal bodies to life through His Spirit who lives in you" (8:11). Paul repeats the point in verse 17, saying that if we are children, we are heirs, "so that we may also be glorified with Him." This conformity to the Son is the promise Paul has been assuring us about throughout: we will be raised incorruptible! We will forever be in glorious love relationship with our God. That is what God predestined for those who would be justified—a flesh and spirit uniting in sin-free union with God.

Thus, verse 29 is not a verse arguing who in the world will get to heaven. The group under consideration is not the world's population or all of created humankind. And the subject of discussion is not the destiny of heaven. Rather, Paul informs us that the people who would become Christians are predestined to have uncorrupted physical essence in resurrection just as the Son was resurrected in physical perfection.

Paul then concludes, in verse 30, the whole line of his argument from Romans chapter 3 on. God will complete his plan for these Christians, the ones who have been predestined to be conformed to the image of the Son. They may rest assured that the God who called them and justified them will indeed also glorify them. They are secure in him.

That's Paul's conclusion. Paul has completed his discussion of how Messiah's renewal of life (not the Law of the Mosaic Covenant) brings people into everlasting love relationship with God. He concludes this chapter, then, with a hymn of assurance. He begins by asking if God is for us, who can be against us? (Romans 8:31). The implied answer is no one. Paul emphasizes the point by drawing our attention to the fact that not only did God put to death our cursed essence, but he did so by allowing his only perfect relationship with humanity—the relationship with his Son—to be put to death. However, in the resurrection of Jesus's physical body, God will bring all who have spirit relationship with God into the full, incorruptible imaging and relationship that Jesus received in his resurrection.

In his next question, Paul wonders who can accuse us or condemn us (Romans 8:33–34). Again, the implied answer is no one. In his explanation, Paul hits on both aspects of our righteous condition: God has justified our spirits by faith so that we are beyond accusation and Christ's provision of the death requirement for sin-cursed flesh means we can no longer be condemned.

Paul then asks, "Who can separate us from the love of Christ?" (Romans 8:35). In answer, Paul recounts affliction, anguish, persecution, famine, nakedness,[1] and the sword. Yet, these dangers can and do cause physical death for Christians (Romans 8:36). The death of the body for Christians, though, does not hold the same horror as it does for non-Christians. While death of the body for non-Christians forever separates them from God, death of the body for Christians will not and cannot separate us from God. Our spirits are joined to Christ, whose body is redeemed. Even in our physical death, we are united with the resurrected, pure, incorruptible body of our Lord. Therefore, Paul concludes that nothing in the physical realm can keep us from losing our physical hope of resurrected, redeemed bodies to accompany our righteous spirits.

This hope of physical resurrection is made sure because Jesus was not only our redeemer but also our *kinsman* redeemer. He was of us. He was human as we are human. He had our same shared, cursed physical essence. And in that he represented us humans.

But he was more than that.

---

1. Nakedness here and in most other places in Scripture means being without protection. It is the shame of sin realized by Adam and Eve in the garden after they ate the fruit; they were no longer protected under the covenant of life with God. It is the same vulnerable state that Paul complains of in 2 Corinthians 11:27 and that John speaks of as ending through the protection of Christ in Revelation 3:18.

JESUS—FULLY GOD

Jesus had to be more. No human who ever lived, other than he, resisted the dominating influence of our corrupted essence, our flesh. No one else resisted because no one could. We humans with our limited spirits fail in the conflict. But Jesus was also fully God. He came to this world with perfect Spirit, the Spirit of God. Although he gave up, for a time, certain infinite expressions (or impressions) of his divine knowledge, he maintained his total trust in his own Godly essence—the absolute truth, goodness, and beauty held by the Father. By doing so—by trusting completely where Adam had failed—Jesus succeeded in proceeding through this earthly life remarkably (for humans) but understandably (for the divine) without sin, which means without conflict with the original Covenant of Life instituted for humankind.

No human spirit of creation could have lived that perfect life. But a perfect human life was necessary. Without it, the death of the body would have meant everlasting death for the spirit. But because Jesus was also God, he maintained his holiness in spirit (Acts 2:27)—*without any guilt of sin*—which those born of Adam could not do. Therefore, he qualified as redeemer because he could make the payment, and he will return to cleanse the body and resurrect it to new life.[2] God had determined that he himself would be the Messiah Savior. He told us he would (Isaiah 45:20–25), and he accomplished it through the coming of Jesus (John 1:1).

JESUS—SON OF GOD AND SON OF MAN

The birth of Jesus was also foretold to Mary with these words:

> The angel replied to her: "The Holy Spirit will come upon you, and the power of the Most High will overshadow you. Therefore, the holy One to be born will be called the Son of God." (Luke 1:35)

Notice that the angel's promise included the news that Jesus would be called "Son of God." Does that title speak to Jesus's deity? Well, yes, sort of. Jesus is also called Son of Man, and the two titles do, in a sense, denote his deity and humanity. But the predominant import of the titles is not simply the fully-man-and-fully-God hypostatic union. To be called "son of" means

---

2. Based on our atonement discussion, the return of Jesus must be a bodily return, unlike the preterists' claim. Since the bodily resurrection by Jesus was the purpose for the atonement, his bodily return will unite his resurrected firstfruits with the rest of creation in redemption.

there is (1) identification with or (2) likeness to whoever the person is called son of. The Aramaic *bar* in a name means *son of*. Therefore, when Jesus called Peter "Simon *Bar*jona" in Matthew 16:17 (KJV), he was identifying him as Simon, *son of* Jonah (Simon's father). In the same way, but in addition pointing out likeness, in Acts 13:6–10, Paul created a play on words by calling the false prophet *Bar*-Jesus (literally *son of Jesus*) "You son of the Devil!" to highlight his greater likeness to Satan than to the Lord Jesus.

But if, as we contend, Jesus is fully God (and fully human), why call him "son of" rather than simply "God" (or simply "man")? The reason is that Scripture is conveying a particular truth about the nature of Jesus. Consider, for instance, the reference to "son of man" in Daniel 7:13. At the beginning of Daniel 7, Daniel has a vision of four beasts which represent four kingdoms. The vision continues with a description of horns and a little, supplanting horn representing earthly kings. But then as Daniel watches, he sees "one like a son of man" coming with the clouds, an everlasting king figure. Why does Daniel call him "son of man"? The explanation is that Daniel recognizes him as something more than a mere man. Daniel sees a being coming on the clouds in glory, and although the image is supernatural and godlike, Daniel wants to let us know that this supernatural being *looks like* a human being.

That is the point Jesus is making when he refers to himself as Son of Man. For example, Jesus said, "Unless you eat the flesh of the Son of Man and drink his blood, you do not have life in yourselves" (John 6:53). He was telling the Jews that he recognized their claim to follow God. But Jesus was God, and in his full deity, Jesus was referencing his likeness to humans by calling himself Son of Man and saying they must accept him—God in the flesh—and his work as a man in order to have life. He is pointing at his humanity, but he does so from the perspective of his deity.

Likewise, the reverse is true. Jesus looked like a man, but he was and was recognized as more than a man; he was like God: "I have seen and testified that this is the *Son of God*" (John 1:34); "'Rabbi,' Nathaniel replied, 'You are the *Son of God*; you are the King of Israel!'" (John 1:49); "Truly I tell you, an hour is coming, and is now here, when the dead will hear the voice of the *Son of God*, and those who hear will live" (John 5:25).

I am not trying merely to clear up why Jesus sometimes calls himself Son of Man and why at other times he is referred to as Son of God. My point is that as we examine the references to Jesus as Son of God and Son of Man, we see aspects of both his God-like and his human-like attributes that qualify him as redeemer. Our God did become human-like so that he could represent us as he gave up his human life and could take it back again in holy victory. But this human was also like God, someone who could maintain a perfect dependence on God's truth, goodness, and beauty without being overwhelmed by the cursed flesh in which he was housed. Only this God-human Jesus could redeem humankind from the curse and bring those who in faith depend on God's essence for life into God's perfect and complete forgiveness.

14

False Ideas about Sacrifice

"Forward, the Light Brigade!"
Was there a man dismayed?
Not though the soldier knew
Someone had blundered.
Theirs not to make reply,
Theirs not to reason why,
Theirs but to do and die.
Into the valley of Death
Rode the six hundred.

—Alfred, Lord Tennyson, from "The Charge of the Light Brigade"

About three in the afternoon Jesus cried out with a loud voice,
"Elí, Elí, lemá sabachtháni?" that is,
"My God, my God, why have you abandoned me?"

—Matthew 27:46

In Romans 3, Paul introduces a word he uses only once in the New Testament: *propitiation*. Technically, it means *appeasement* or *conciliation*. I think we may appropriately understand it as simply *satisfaction*. It has everything to do with the atonement because it is by the atonement that God was satisfied (concerning the necessary requirements for restoring love relationship with us). But while the idea of *propitiation* is important for a proper understanding of the atonement, it is another term in the same verse (25) I want to look at more closely.

OLD TESTAMENT FLAVOR

In both verses 25 and 26, Paul's Jewish background comes into play. Paul is trying to fully convey the idea of God's righteousness revealed through Jesus. Paul begins verse 25 saying that God *presented* Jesus. Actually, the common Greek word for *presented* is something different, but Paul chooses here a word translated a bit more precisely as *put forth*, and his choice appears somewhat odd. If I were to say, "I'd like to put forth a gift for you," you'd understand my meaning but would probably wonder why I said it that way. Why didn't I just say, "I want to give you something," or even "I'd like to present you with something"? We wonder about Paul along the same lines in verse 25.

The word translated *presented* in the HCSB (or *set forth* in the KJV) is the Greek *protithemi*. The word is often used in the Septuagint, the Greek translation of the Old Testament that Paul used extensively. There, the word most often regards a *presented* sacrifice. Out of all the Old Testament presentations of offerings, the majority in which this word is used have to do with the presentation of the shewbread in the Holy Place. The shewbread is *put forth*, not simply presented. Therefore, we have a hint that Paul, here in Romans 3, may have chosen this word to tie Jesus's purpose to a discussion of shewbread sacrifice, with which the Jews would be familiar.

The term *propitiation* is also a term used in the Septuagint regarding the sacrificial and satisfaction process. The Greek word, translated here as *propitiation* (*hilasterion*), is also used in the Septuagint for the Hebrew *kapporeth*, the mercy seat, which is the lid to the top of the ark in the Holy of Holies. By his choice of uncommon words and phrasings, Paul is putting his readers in mind of the Old Testament sacrificial system. Of course, if Paul really wanted to draw minds to the sacrificial system, you'd think he would mention *blood* somewhere. And what do you know! Paul does tell us that Jesus was to be God's sacrificial mercy seat "through faith in His *blood*" (3:25). So this very Jewish, very sacrifice-oriented description, is complete. We can paraphrase the first part of verse 25, then, as "God put forth Jesus, whose sacrificial blood (in death) from his faithful life became the means of mercy."

THE RIGHTEOUSNESS OF FAITH

With that running start, we can view the rest of these two verses more clearly. Verse 25 tells us God put forth Jesus "to demonstrate his righteousness."

Verse 26 also begins with "to demonstrate his righteousness." In other words, these two verses offer two ways in which God demonstrated his righteousness by putting forth Jesus as the sacrifice.

The first way, in verse 25, starts out, "because in His restraint God passed over the sins previously committed." God did pass over sins throughout the 4,000 years recorded prior to Christ's atonement. Abraham sinned. Isaac sinned. Jacob sinned. Joseph sinned. David sinned. Daniel sinned. Isaiah sinned. Yet not a single one of these sinners did God banish to outer darkness. Rather, he passed over their sins to embrace them in fellowship: he counted the faith of Abraham as righteousness and equated the heart of David with his own. But how could God be thought *just* while ignoring their sin-cursed essence? The answer is that Jesus would come to be the necessary propitiation (that is, satisfaction). The sacrifice of Jesus demonstrated that God was not unrighteous in passing over their sin.

Verse 26 informs us of the second way God demonstrated his righteousness through Jesus: God put forth Jesus "so that He would be righteous and declare righteous the one who has faith in Jesus." English Bible translators are notorious for inserting words and changing prepositions to try to shape the passage to their private interpretations. Luckily, we have a more faithful translation in N. T. Wright's *The Kingdom New Testament*. There we read "that he himself is in the right, and that he declares to be in the right everyone who trusts in the faithfulness of Jesus."[1] Paul is emphasizing the faithfulness of Jesus in his sacrifice that accomplishes God's demonstration of righteousness for relationship with his image bearers.

By these two verses, Paul shows God's righteousness to both his Trinitarian covenants. By his sacrifice, Jesus proved God righteous in operating according to his essence of truth, goodness, and beauty. Also by his sacrifice, Jesus showed God to be righteous in ensuring his creative purpose—the everlasting love relationship with his image bearers. Thus, through God's sending Jesus to be sacrificed, God demonstrated that faith and faithfulness to God are the markers that declare one to belong to God. Paul can therefore conclude that we are justified, or "declared righteous by faith" (Romans 5:1).

FALSE IDEAS

I began this chapter with Paul's argument concerning Jesus's sacrifice. Our maintaining a hold on what God intended in sacrifice is crucial as we turn back to the Old Testament and consider the sacrificial structure

---

1. Wright, *The Kingdom*.

God implemented for Israel as well as the sacrificial thought of the pagan world of the time.

To the Old Testament world at large, and especially to those nations and peoples with whom Israel had most interaction, such as Egypt and the Canaanites, sacrifice had three primary purposes: (1) to appease a god whom the people thought they had angered, (2) to seek support from a god for a military victory or for security from an enemy, and (3) to buy favorable conditions from a god for such life-dependent activity as crop growing. Of course, from the more well-known myths of the Greek and Roman panoplies of deities, we find many other subdivided purposes, but the three I mentioned are at the categorical heads.

Because these three categorical reasons encompass so much of our knowledge of ancient gods and sacrificial activity, it is difficult to imagine other reasons God had for Israel's sacrificial worship, especially because of its relation to security and life-dependency. We can imagine the Israelites themselves, since they had been close to the practices of surrounding nations, confusing God-given sacrificial purpose with the purposes of these surrounding peoples. It is also not surprising that even today we misunderstand God's motives by projecting back some mistaken views about the sacrifice of Jesus. Here's the common line of thought:

1. Death is punishment for sin; persons sin; therefore, persons die.
2. God created the sacrificial system to illustrate that a substitute could pay the penalty for sin by dying.
3. Sacrifices, nevertheless, were only illustrations of substitutional payment because animals can't represent us and can't take away sin (Hebrews 10:4).
4. Jesus had to come as a human to be killed in our place because, although sinless, as human he could represent humans.
5. God imputed our sin to Jesus; that is, he made Jesus guilty of it so that he could punish him instead of us. Thus, Jesus suffered the penalty of sin (death) in our place.
6. Since Jesus paid the penalty for our sin, our sin is gone; we may now have fellowship with God.

While this line of thought is accepted by many Christians, I believe it contains gross errors that have swung us wide from the path of understanding true sacrificial purpose. Not only that, but its trajectory leads straight to Calvinism. If we conclude in point 6 that Jesus paid the penalty for *all* sins, how could God be just for requiring payment for these same sins from a

God-rejecting person? Did Jesus and that unbelieving sinner both pay for the same sin? As James A. Spurgeon (brother of Charles) said in a sermon on particular redemption, "Did he die for the sins of the whole world? Then justice cannot demand this again."[2]

However, while these six points do, in fact, lead logically to Calvinism's perspective of particular redemption, a problem arises. Jesus cannot qualify as a redeemer if he becomes guilty of sin, since redemption requires an unstained sacrifice (see chapter 12). Therefore, points 5 and 6 are problematic.

Another problem looms large regarding point 5: by what means could sin be imputed? For the penal-substitution theory to work, sin must be imputed from us to Jesus. How does that happen? By what means does sin travel from the sinner to another person and thus make that person responsible for it and required to pay for it? In other words, if I walk into the death-row section of some prison and tell the warden I wish to pay the penalty for someone set to be executed that day, by what justification could the warden agree? If the warden were actually to execute me, what court of law would not condemn that warden for *unjustly* putting me to death? There is no possible reason the warden could offer for believing the prisoner's guilt floated across the room to rest on me. I am simply not the guilty one.

Now the penal substitutionist (or simply someone who holds to the above six points) will object to my dismissal of this sacrificial reasoning. Of course, intricate designs are always woven to support eisegetical proofs. But should we be so insistent that this particular reasoning process must be defended? Why not instead simply assume we are mistaken on point 2? Perhaps the purpose of the sacrificial system was *not* to illustrate that a substitute could pay the penalty of sin for us.

As mentioned earlier, I believe we came to embrace this line of thought by projecting back a misunderstanding of the sacrifice of Jesus. One of the main contributors to our general misunderstanding is the cry of Jesus himself on the cross: "My God, My God, why have you forsaken Me?" (Matthew 27:46). Most Christians know that David groaned out that cry in Psalm 22. But many Christians seem not to want to bother examining the circumstances of David. We are too caught up in the horrifying, overwhelming scene of the cross. The sky has turned dark. The wind whips a chilling blast, as we hear those words of agony pouring out from Jesus's torn body and parched lips. "Where is God?" our souls wonder. Turning back to the Old Testament, we get no further than Habakkuk 1:13: "Your eyes are too pure to look on evil." We resign ourselves to the conclusion that God turned away from Jesus because of our sin imputed to his spirit. And thus Jesus died.

---

2. Spurgeon, "Particular Redemption."

But before he died, Jesus also cried out to God, "Father, into Your hands I entrust My spirit!" (Luke 23:46). If God had already turned aside, did this cry fall on deaf ears? Did Jesus believe God really wasn't listening anymore? Perhaps Jesus spoke a little louder at this point to get God's attention back. But if God's eyes were too pure to look on sin, would God have turned back to Jesus? *Could* God have turned back to accept that last cry from that sin-ladened sacrifice? The answer to all this confusion is simple: God never turned away. He was still there, still listening, still caring, still loving.

Looking back through the Gospels, we see that although the Pharisees wouldn't associate with sinners, Jesus—who was also God—did! Is it that Jesus could look on evil, although the Father could not? Was he not as pure in his spirit as the Father? But as we read through the Old Testament, we find God talking with Adam and Abraham and Moses. They were all sinners, condemned by their sin to an eternity of separation. Was God simply not all that pure at that point? How could God say of David, a sinner, "My faithful love will never leave him" (2 Samuel 7:15)?

This David, who was assured of God's continual presence, is the very one who wrote those words in Psalm 22:1: "My God, my God, why have You forsaken me?" Because of what God had said in 2 Samuel 7:15, and because of what David himself says later in the same Psalm, we know without doubt that God had *never* left David. To David, it might have seemed that God had left because God was the one who protected and secured him. But just as Job had to learn that God's silence doesn't mean he has left, so David learned it. Jesus shouted this Psalm from the cross, I believe, not because he thought God actually had left, but rather for the sake of those looking on. Their minds would immediately race to Psalm 22, not an unfamiliar Psalm to them). They would recall the Psalm's finish: "I will give praise in the great congregation because of You; I will fulfill my vows before those who fear You. . . . All the ends of the earth will remember and turn to the Lord. All the families of the nations will bow down before You for kingship belongs to the Lord. . . . They will come and tell a people yet to be born about His righteousness—what he has done." If God had not left David when David penned this Psalm, there is no reason to believe God had left Jesus, who followed David in quoting it. Jesus used this Psalm to draw the attention of those looking on—and us—to the rescue that God had promised in that same Psalm.

But what of Habakkuk's statement about God's eyes being too pure to look on evil? Remember that Habakkuk's discussion with God took place before the cross, before Habakkuk was washed clean of the same sin that stained those Assyrians he was complaining about. God was looking on Habakkuk in his sin *at the same time* Habakkuk was arguing that God could not possibly look at the sinful! Habakkuk's protest was occasioned by Judah's distress. Egypt, Assyria, and Babylon were in power plays for the world. Judah lay in the center of their triangle, trampled over by whichever army was on the move. The Jews were made vassals—spurned, scorned, and afflicted. Habakkuk could not stand it! He could not understand how God could allow this to happen to his people. Habakkuk fairly screams at the opening of the book: "How long, Lord, must I call for help and You do not listen!" In urging God to do something, Habakkuk reminds God of the evil of these nations, and in doing so, it is Habakkuk who informs God that God's eyes are too pure to look on evil. Habakkuk is trying to stir God up to destroy these nations. But God doesn't react to the goading. God tells Habakkuk that he has purpose for his forbearance, and Habakkuk should trust him: "The righteous one will live by his faith" (2:4b; also quoted by Paul in Romans 1:17). Therefore, it is not that God must shield his eyes from evil. He inserts himself purely into this evil world to ensure his will is done.

At the cross, God was not a whip-in-hand tormentor of Christ, nor had he left the scene. Those ideas—central to penal substitution—rest on the worldly, non-Christian idea of sacrifice as appeasement of a god's anger. But that was *not* what was happening at the cross. God's heart of love was breaking along with Christ's as the horror of sin lashed out its worst. This monstrous scene was necessary for love to win.

GOD'S DISPLEASURE IN SACRIFICE FOR THE WRONG REASONS

The confusion of conservative biblicists concerning the meaning of Jesus's sacrifice has also prompted some otherwise thoughtful Christians to dismiss anything they find difficult in the Old Testament (OT) as simply the false views of the OT ignorant. While it is true that OT followers of God, like Habakkuk, often failed to connect the dots, we must be very careful before dismissing the entire sacrificial scene out of hand. The God-breathed inclusion of the sacrificial system is meant to teach. Let's read through the following verses as background:

> *Psalm 40:6, 8*
> "You do not delight in sacrifice and offering; You open my ears to listen. You do not ask for a whole burnt offering or a sin offering. . . . I delight to do Your will, my God; Your instruction lives within me."

Hosea 6:6
"For I desire loyalty and not sacrifice, the knowledge of God rather than burnt offerings."

Jeremiah 6:20
"What use to Me is frankincense from Sheba or sweet cane from a distant land? Your burnt offerings are not acceptable; your sacrifices do not please Me."

Notice that these verses express a general theme: God's pleasure derives from his people's knowing him and following him, not from their merely performing sacrifices. Now, we could argue these verses show a contrast between what God wants and does not want (i.e., he wants people to delight in him and he doesn't want them to sacrifice to him). Consider the following passage:

Micah 6:6–8
"What should I bring before the Lord when I come to bow before God on high? Should I come before Him with burnt offerings, with year-old calves? Would the Lord be pleased with thousands of rams or with ten thousand streams of oil? Should I give my firstborn for my transgression, the child of my body for my own sin? Mankind, He has told you what is good and what it is the Lord requires of you: to act justly, to love faithfulness, and to walk humbly with your God."

These verses in Micah seem to spell out even more certainly that God doesn't want sacrifices; instead, he wants a committed life. And that interpretation has led some to think it was not God who commanded the sacrificial system at all but rather Moses and other presumed writers of the books of Law who thought up the idea in imitation of the Egyptian culture they had just left. Perhaps Moses conveyed it as coming from God to encourage them to follow their new God rather than cling to the gods they had become used to worshipping in Egypt. Could that be the reason for Jeremiah's apparently contradictory cry?

Jeremiah 7:21–23a
"This is what the Lord of Hosts, the God of Israel, says: 'Add your burnt offerings to your other sacrifices, and eat the meat yourselves, for when I brought your ancestors out of the land of Egypt, *I did not speak with them or command them concerning burnt offering and sacrifice.* However, I did give them this command: Obey Me, and then I will be your God, and you will be My people" (emphasis added).

I believe dismissing the entire sacrificial system as an attempt by Israel's leaders to satisfy the people's desire to be like other nations is wrong. I do believe sacrifices were instituted by God despite the loss of animal life. Of course, we must acknowledge that in many instances, they did not fulfill God's intentions. Once again, God's instituted sacrifices were not for any non-Christian purposes of appeasement, military security, or pay-off for blessing, which could have been Solomon's intent in his effusiveness. As Michael Hardin points out in the preface to the intriguing collection *Stricken by God?*, "And one thing this collision in the cross has produced is the demise of the power of sacrificial theories of atonement and justifications for actions that are *determined by the logic of violence*" (emphasis added).³ Notice Hardin doesn't, in this statement, simply reject sacrificial theories, but he does reject those "determined by the logic of violence."

A closer inspection of context in Jeremiah 7 reveals that what God is upset about is the Jews misunderstanding of *why* they were sacrificing. They had embraced the worldly categorical purposes and actually sacrificed to other gods as well. So God in effect is telling them that they might as well *add* those meaningless, rote sacrifices they supposedly performed for God to those other sacrifices they did for other gods, because they weren't impressing the true God by their sacrifices. God then told them precisely why they weren't impressing him: the Jews mistakenly presumed (as did the other nations) that the proper order was to sacrifice for a favor and then the god would grant the favor. But God points out that he did not ask for a sacrifice from the Israelites as a prerequisite for his freeing them from Egypt: "When I brought your ancestors out of the land of Egypt, I did not . . . command them concerning burnt offering and sacrifice." Rather, God asked first for obedience—for them to follow him and become his people. The sacrifices came later.

That idea leads us to the real, biblical purpose for sacrifice. It was not a trade-off or transaction to buy a favor from God. God's desire in Old Testament sacrifice was to illustrate redemption and forgiveness that result in relationship

---

3. Hardin, "Preface," 15.

15

The Day of the Atonement

To die, to sleep—
No more—and by a sleep to say we end
The heartache and the thousand natural shocks
That flesh is heir to—'tis a consummation
Devoutly to be wished. To die, to sleep—
To sleep, perchance to dream. Ay, there's the rub,
For in that sleep of death what dreams may come,
When we have shuffled off this mortal coil,
Must give us pause.

—WILLIAM SHAKESPEARE, FROM *HAMLET*, ACT III, SCENE I

He condemned sin in the flesh
by sending His own Son in flesh like ours
under sin's domain, and as a sin offering.

—ROMANS 8:3B

WHILE SOME OF THE potholes in traditional sacrificial thinking seem unavoidable, finding the right purpose for sacrifice should allow us to understand the system without flattening a tire. As we've seen, the Christian understanding of the atonement has suffered from the confusion of the world's faulty ideas. Christians, both progressive and conservative, have assimilated those faulty concepts of death-for-blessing. Some progressives shun the whole idea of sacrifice as a barbaric practice, whereas conservatives hold doggedly to the notion that sacrifice is substitutionary payment of a penalty to get back into the good graces of a God who is shunning them. But neither viewpoint is biblical. The sacrificial system simply was not set up as a means by which we might win God's favor, as if he were neutrally inclined toward relationship. But sacrifice does have a purpose of winning back, and it is necessary to God's deep interest in love relationship. Relationship must be the foundation on which we build our understanding of sacrifice to recognize how it signifies redemption for complete forgiveness.

The correct view of Old Testament sacrifice does include giving something up for the sake of some cause. The corruption in creation since the fall centers on image bearers' individual or selfish pursuits while ignoring a pursuit of relationship with God. Sacrifice entails giving up that selfish pursuit.

THE OLD TESTAMENT SACRIFICIAL SYSTEM

The Old Testament indicates five main offering (sacrifice) types: burnt, grain, peace, sin, and guilt. Let's examine those briefly.

Burnt offerings (covered in Leviticus 1:3–17 and again in 6:8–13) primarily atoned for sin in a general sense. The offeror brought an animal to the altar outside the holy place of the tabernacle. The offeror placed his or her hands on the head of the animal to identify with it and then killed it. The priest would take some of its blood and sprinkle it all over the altar. Then the priest would burn the sacrifice on the altar.

Grain offerings (Leviticus 2:1–16; 6:14–23) were presented to show devotion to God. The offeror would bring fine flour mixed with olive oil and salt, a preservative symbolizing the preserving, or permanent, aspect of the covenant, along with frankincense. The priest would take a handful of the flour mixed with oil and all the frankincense and burn that combination on the altar. The rest of the grain and oil, considered the holiest part of the offering, was to be eaten by the priest in the tabernacle courtyard.

Peace offerings (Leviticus 3:1–17; 7:11–21) showed satisfaction with God's activity. For example, an Israelite may have prayed about a distressing situation, and whatever the outcome the offeror would bring a peace offering to demonstrate contentment with God's interaction. The offeror would place his or her hands on the animal's head in identification with it and then kill the animal. The priests would sprinkle the blood all over the altar (as in the burnt offering). But only the fat of the animal—from the entrails, liver, kidneys, and tail—would be burned. The rest could be eaten by the priests or the offeror. This fat portion of the animal represented excess or abundance. Just as the Israelites were promised "the fat of the land" in Egypt (Genesis 45:18), the fat of the animal symbolized a return to God of the abundance he provided.

Sin offerings (Leviticus 4:1—5:13; 6:24–30) were intended to atone for unintentional sin. These unintentional sins were not really understood as sins when committed but recognized as sins later, for example, rashly vowing to do something that, upon thinking clearly or with full knowledge, the Israelite realized he shouldn't have. Again, the offeror placed hands on the animal's head for identification with the sacrifice and then killed the animal. The priests would sprinkle the blood on the horns of the altar and its base. The priests burned the fat on the altar, but the rest of the animal was taken outside the camp to be burned.

Guilt offerings (Leviticus 5:14—6:7; 7:1–10), also called trespass offerings or restitution offerings, made restitution for something wrong and harmful. The requirement was repayment through sacrifice or restoration to a person wronged, plus an extra 20%. The fat of the sacrifice was burned, and the priest could eat it within the tabernacle courtyard.

While all these offerings exhibit aspects of relationship, we are going to concentrate on the sin offering. It is the sin offering that we normally link to Christ's sacrifice on the cross. The sin offering is the predominant offering discussed in Leviticus 16, occurring on the Day of Atonement—the one day of the year specifically set aside to seek atonement for sin and to cleanse the tabernacle (the meeting place with God) for the uncleanness of the people.

SACRIFICES OF THE DAY OF ATONEMENT

For the sin offering on the Day of Atonement, two unblemished goats were presented to illustrate the atonement process for sin. One of the goats was killed according to the standard procedure: the high priest placed his hands on the goat's head, identifying it with Israel, and then slaughtered the animal, burning the fat on the altar and the rest of the body outside the camp. The high priest sprinkled the blood within the Holy of Holies. This one day of the year was the only time the high priest ever entered the Holy of Holies.

After this sacrifice, the high priest presented the second goat before the Lord. This time as he laid his hands on its head, he confessed the sins of the people over it, symbolically laying the sins on the goat's head. Now, this point is extremely important. If I subscribed to penal substitution, I would really expect God's next command to be to slaughter this goat. After all, if the penalty for sin is death, and the goat symbolically receives the sins of the people, it would seem the goat should die for those sins to relieve the people of their guilt. Isn't that the theory behind penal substitution? Isn't that what penal substitutionists believe happened at the cross—that Jesus had the sins of the world placed on him and then with his death paid the penalty for those sins?

But that is *not* what happened to this second goat. Instead, it was led away alive far into the wilderness, never to return. Again, this image is significant. The high priest's laying of hands on this second goat is the *only* time in the entire Old Testament presentation of the sacrificial system that sins were transferred to a sacrificial animal. And here at this one and only instance of transference, the animal *did not die*. The purpose of the transference was *not* payment for sin through death. The animal, rather, was led away alive; its permanent removal from Israel illustrated the forever removal of the people's sins.

This sending away is an image of forgiveness, not debt payment. It echoes David's cry in Psalm 103:12: "As far as the east is from the west, so far has He removed our transgressions from us." Note carefully that if God had wanted to show payment for sin, he could have had the high priest symbolically transfer sins to the first goat destined for death. But God did not do so. Instead, he specifically required a second goat to show the full scope of the atonement picture. He wanted to get across both ideas—forgiveness and redemption—without allowing them to be confused. Sin is sent away—that is, forgiven—with the second goat. It is the death of the first goat that symbolizes redemption. Let's go back to look at that more completely.

Recall what happens with the first goat. Its slaughter highlights the separation of blood from body, because the blood represents the life released from the body. Follow the action: the priest takes the lifeblood, which is not cursed or condemned, into the Holy of Holies—the place of communion with God. The body, cursed and condemned, is taken to be burned *outside the camp* and therefore removed from communion with God. The burning of the body shows it has no connection, because of its curse, with God. The body is not an offering given *to* God but rather something to be separated *from* God.

The blood, on the other hand, represents the unblemished animal's life, its spirit. The blood is accepted into the Holy of Holies itself, the meeting place with God, and it cleanses that meeting place. The blood symbolizes life and means relationship with God. Leviticus 17:11 tells us, "For the life of a creature is in the blood, and I have appointed it to you to make atonement on the altar for your lives, since it is *the lifeblood that makes atonement*" (emphasis added). I cannot stress enough the importance of that statement! Atonement is *not* accomplished by a penalty payment of death. Contrary to what penal substitutionists would have us believe, it is the pure spirit lifeblood that makes atonement.

But death does occur. What's the purpose of that sacrificial death if it's not a substitutionary penalty payment for sin? The separation of blood from body provides the answer. Let's recall from chapter 11 my distinction between forgiveness and redemption: forgiveness does not demand payment for sin; requiring payment, in fact, is the opposite of forgiveness. And the goal of forgiveness is restored relationship. But if an obstacle to relationship remains even after forgiveness, forgiveness cannot reach its goal. The obstacle must be removed. When it comes to our relationship with God, an obstacle does remain: the curse of physical creation. It is this body of death—the image bearers' physical essence—that must be rescued, refined, restored, redeemed. The removal of this obstacle is what we see pictured in the death of the sacrifice. When the sacrifice physically dies, the lifeblood (the spirit) separates from the cursed flesh. The lifeblood goes to God while the cursed flesh is removed outside the camp to be burned.

We are not Gnostics. The body—the flesh, the physical essence—is not by nature evil. It is evil only because of the curse placed on it at the fall, i.e., because of its identity as the image bearer's idol. If the curse can be removed, the physical essence—which is actually necessary for our existence—may be as pure as the forgiven person's spirit. And the death sacrifice illustrates that necessary removal of the curse. That which is cursed is burned up outside the camp. The renewal comes within the Holy of Holies itself.

Remember that the Holy of Holies is not God. Rather, it is the meeting place with God; it is the physical area for meeting with God. Consider these New Testament verses:

> *Matthew 1:23*
> See, the virgin will become pregnant and give birth to a son, and they will name Him Immanuel, which is translated "God is with us."

> *John 17:20–23*
> I pray not only for these, but also for those who believe in Me through their message. May they all be one, as You, Father, are in Me and I am in You. May they also be one in Us, so the world may believe You sent Me. I have given them the glory You have given Me. May they be one as We are one. I am in them and You are in Me. May they be made completely one, so the world may know You have sent Me and have loved them as You have loved Me.

Acts 17:24
The God who made the world and everything in it—He is Lord of heaven and earth and does not live in shrines made by hands.

1 Corinthians 3:16–17
Don't you yourselves know that you are God's sanctuary and that the Spirit of God lives in you? If anyone destroys God's sanctuary, God will destroy him; for God's sanctuary is holy, and that is what you are.

1 Corinthians 6:19–20
Don't you know that your body is a sanctuary of the Holy Spirit who is in you, whom you have from God? You are not your own, for you were bought at a price. Therefore glorify God in your body.

Ephesians 2:19–22
So then you are no longer foreigners and strangers, but fellow citizens with the saints, and members of God's household, built on the foundation of the apostles and prophets, with Christ Jesus Himself as the cornerstone. The whole building, being put together by Him, grows into a holy sanctuary in the Lord. You also are being built together for God's dwelling in the Spirit.

The New Testament makes abundantly clear that it is within believers, independently and collectively, that God meets with us. We, in our physical essence, are that new temple—the Holy of Holies to be purified with the lifeblood of Jesus. That idea is what the sprinkling of the blood in the Holy of Holies was meant to illustrate.

THE CLEANSING

So now let's take what we have learned from the Old Testament sacrificial process and move it forward into the ultimate sacrifice we find in Christ, because it is this Old Testament Day of Atonement picture that illustrates and should inform our understanding of the atonement of Christ. Jesus was born into this world as a human, which means he was born as an image bearer. All image bearers born since the fall have been born into the curse of our physical creation, and so was Jesus. Romans 8:3b verifies that fact: "[God] condemned sin in the flesh by sending His own Son in flesh *like ours under sin's domain*" (emphasis added).

But Jesus, although in flesh like ours, *did not* succumb in his spirit to the influence of the flesh. *He did not sin*, as all the rest of us have. He maintained his covenant-of-life obligation to God, depending on him and him alone for truth, goodness, and beauty—the necessary basis for relationship with God. He proved that dependence through his temptations by Satan. He proved it in his mission-minded attitude throughout his ministry. He proved it by the servant's heart he bore in feeding the thousands, healing the sick, washing his disciples' feet, and encouraging the weak in faith. He proved it by going to the cross, not following his will but the Father's. Because he was sinless and pure, there was no justification for his life to be taken from him. Yet he gave up his life by giving his body over to death.

Christ's voluntary death was illustrated in the Old Testament sacrificial system. His blood was shed, that is, separated from his cursed flesh, which was buried in a tomb outside the city walls. His lifeblood (pure spirit) was accepted by God as holy (Acts 2:27b). This acceptance explains why God never turned from Jesus. God never departed from the person—the mind, will, spirit—of Jesus. But Jesus did die, and death means separation. It means the turning away of God. Calvary pictures all of this. Jesus cried out from the cross, "Into your hands I commit my spirit." God was reaching out in love, holding, embracing, cradling the spirit of Christ at the same time he was turning from the sin-cursed flesh of Jesus's body. And just as on the Day of Atonement the blood of the sacrifice was taken into the Holy of Holies, so, too, did Christ's spirit return to his body, cleanse it from its corrupted curse, and resurrect it to new life (relationship with God).

Jesus had lived in perfect, sinless conformity to the Covenant of Life, his earthly life based completely on God's essence—his truth, goodness, and beauty. The spirit of Christ was pure as he went to the cross. He shed his blood in an imaging of his perfect spirit's release from the sin-cursed flesh. But because his spirit remained holy (Acts 2:31), it reasserted itself into the flesh and drove out the curse exactly as depicted with the pure animal's blood cleansing the temple. He was then ready to meet God. That is what the Old Testament's Day of Atonement sacrifice was meant to show us. It does involve violence and death. But Jesus was never separated from God, and God never struck out against Jesus. "Violence is no attribute of God."[1] All the violence of the atonement came from the evil apart from God, and all its love from the heart of God. Brad Jersak puts it: "While the Cross was a violent episode, we are not witnessing God's violence; the atonement is non-penal. Good Friday was not the outpouring of God's violence upon Christ to

---

1. Bunsen, *God in History*, 79.

assuage his own wrath. That day was God's 'No!' to wrath and 'Yes!' to love and forgiveness in the face of our violence and wrath."[2]

Christ's cleansing of his flesh, we are told, was the firstfruits of the resurrection of all those who are born in him (1 Corinthians 15:20). Thus, we who trust in God's salvation, who in faith look to live in relationship with God based on his truth, goodness, and beauty, die with Christ (Romans 6:4) and consider our bodies dead (Romans 6:11a). Our forgiven spirits are released from the cursed flesh (Romans 7:4) to take residence in his now pure flesh, being now "alive to God *in* Christ Jesus" (Romans 6:11b). And we look forward to the day of Christ's return when his purifying righteousness, which was given as firstfruits in the resurrection of his own body, will purify all physical creation and give us our new bodies, cleansed from curse, to unite with our forgiven spirits as pure and holy before our God.

FORGIVENESS WITHOUT PAYMENT

The treatment of the second goat shows the forgiveness of sin. That second goat upon which sins were placed was not scorned or punished. In fact, nothing was done to the goat. Instead of the goat's becoming guilty of and punished for sin, the goat carried the sin away into the wilderness: the departure symbolized the permanent removal of sin through forgiveness. The goat bore Israel's sin just as Jesus, Peter tells us, bore our sin (1 Peter 2:24). Just as the goat carried the sin away, so does Jesus carry our sin away—without becoming guilty of that sin or paying for that sin with death. It was the first goat in the Day of Atonement sacrifice that was killed; that goat pictured the separation of pure spirit (blood) from corrupted flesh (the rest of the animal that was to be burned outside the camp). The blood sprinkled to cleanse the Holy of Holies imaged the spirit of Jesus returning to the physical creation (his body) to cleanse it and resurrect it to life. That redemption is the atonement picture. Thus, the Day of Atonement sacrifice of the goats presents both aspects of Christ's atonement victory—forgiveness and redemption.

Once we understand this, many other Old Testament passages take on richer redemptive significance. Think of the teaching moment for Abraham. Facing God's command to sacrifice his son, Isaac, Abraham stood at the exact same decision crossroads that Adam faced: choose for God or choose for creation (earthly relationship). Abraham succeeded where Adam failed because he believed in God as the source of truth, goodness, and beauty, trusting that God would ensure relationship.

---

2. Jersak, "Nonviolent Identification," 19.

We also see similar aspects of the death-to-cursed-creation idea in Elijah's offering on Mount Carmel. God showed the importance of basing relationship on his essence and not human essence by burning up every physical aspect of that sacrifice—the wood, the stones, and the water that drenched it.

God's revelation of himself throughout history and throughout Scripture is a revelation of love. God created for relationship, and he rescued for relationship. God came in Jesus to remove the obstacle of a cursed essence that impeded restored relationship so that we might be both redeemed and forgiven, resting in faith on and in him.

16

The Bible's Emphasis on Blood

Who knows not Love, let him assay
And taste that juice, which on the cross a pike
Did set again abroach, then let him say
If ever he did taste the like.
Love is that liquor sweet and most divine,
Which my God feels as blood; but I, as wine.

—George Herbert, from "The Agony"

According to the law almost everything is purified with blood,
and without the shedding of blood there is no forgiveness.

—Hebrews 9:22

The previous chapter drew our attention to the separation of blood from the body in the sin sacrifice. That separation highlighted the two parts—essence and existence—of the image bearer. The essence is the physical self (all physical creation including the body), and the existence is the spirit (or person). Therefore, in the sacrificial separation, while the body links to physical essence, the blood plays the part of the spirit. In Christ, the one to whom the Old Testament sacrificial process pointed, his spirit separated from his body in his physical death on the cross, represented by the shedding of his blood. That spirit, because it was totally without sin guilt, returned to the body just as the blood of the sacrifice returned to a physical housing—the temple's Holy of Holies—and thereby cleansed it. In the same manner, as we by faith metaphorically die with Christ, we are assured of Jesus's cleansing at his second coming. He will give us new bodies, cleansed from sin, as he redeems all physical creation from its original curse.

God, in both the Old and the New Testaments, draws quite a bit of attention to blood and the shedding of blood. If blood is merely a symbolic tool pointing to the spirit, should it really receive so much notice? Or does that symbolic reference hold more import than we realize? Verses, such as Hebrews 9:22—"Without the shedding of blood there is no forgiveness"—suggest an inherent relationship between bloodshed and atonement. The question is whether shed blood was, in fact, necessary for atonement to take place.

My answer to that question is a qualified yes, so I have to explain what I mean. If the issue at stake is only whether the technical release of blood from its housing in Christ at his crucifixion *caused* atonement, then I'd answer no. But the biblical emphasis placed on the blood forces us to view even its symbolic purpose as essential in the revelation and working of God's whole restoration plan.

IMAGERY IN TERMS

Before we explore that idea further, we need to define a few terms. Blood, from any vantage point, definitely symbolizes life. We understand that from its internal function to supply continuing vitality to our bodies. But as we know, biblically speaking, life is more than continuing vitality. Life means relationship with God. From the very beginning, Scripture posits God as the source and sustainer of life. In the Genesis 2:7 formation of the *adam*, we are told God formed him from the ground and "breathed the breath of life into his nostrils, and the *adam* became a living being." When Moses called on the children of Israel to make a choice for God, he set up life and prosperity in opposition to death and destruction. The choosing for life meant that they were choosing for God (Deuteronomy 29:1–30:20). Further, throughout Scripture we see the choice for life entwined with relationship with God (Exodus 15:26; Proverbs 3:22; 4:13; 4:22; 6:23; 8:35; 10:17, 28; 19:23; 21:21; 22:4; Ecclesiastes 9:9–10). Without that life relationship with God, we plummet into our second term: death, which is separation from God.

Death, of course, has two aspects: spiritual and physical. Spiritual death is the everlasting separation of the created, image-bearing spirit from God. Physical death occasions two relationship separators. On the one hand, physical death separates the created, image-bearing spirit from its *relational activity with the rest of creation.* On the other hand, physical death separates the created, image-bearing spirit from *relational interaction with God* regarding the original Covenant of Life. Physical death is what Christ suffered on the cross to free us from the prison hold of our cursed essence.

The third term requiring definition is covenant. In Chapter 4 of this book, I altered the definition O. Palmer Robertson provided in his book *The Christ of the Covenants* from "a bond of blood sovereignly administered" to a *bond, or agreement, of persons for relationship*. My reasoning was that there was no blood involved in several Old Testament covenants, such as the original Covenant of Life with the *adam*, Isaac's covenant with the Philistine Abimelech (inaugurated in Genesis 26 with a meal instead of blood), and the Davidic covenant. Furthermore, the two trinitarian covenants—the covenant of operational essence and the covenant of creative purpose (also discussed in chapter 4)—had no sealing ceremony of blood.

I also took issue with Robertson's claim that a covenant is a bond "sovereignly administered." Again, the Isaac-Abimelech covenant in Genesis 26 does not mention God. Although God sovereignly oversees everything, we don't need to add that fact into the definitions of everything. We know that God is always present in every situation. Tacking on "sovereignly administered" carries no real point. The covenant is a bond, an agreement, and the purpose of any covenant is to define a relationship among persons.

That definition seems to fit well with the covenants we've discussed. The original Covenant of Life was an agreement among the persons of the Godhead and the persons of our created race for relationship. So, too, is the New Covenant of Life an agreement of relationship between the persons of the Godhead and the man Jesus, the Christ. God's whole restoration plan for humankind involves the movement from the original Covenant of Life to the New Covenant of Life. Movement from, or out of, a covenant occurs by death; thus Jesus, in moving out from the covenant in Adam, died. Remember that one of the definitions of physical death is the separation of spirit from its relational activity with the rest of creation, which occurred in Jesus's physical death. Movement to a new covenant, by the dead from the old covenant, can occur only with rebirth into life. The symbol of life, as I've mentioned, is blood. Thus, the born-again-into-life image was the sprinkling of blood in the Holy of Holies.

THE SHADOW AND THE TRUE

In regard to the new covenant, the Bible presents two perspectives: a shadow and the true form. The shadow is a teaching tool, imaged by the Law—the

Mosaic covenant, referred to in Hebrews as the old covenant. The true form is the new covenant actually realized by Christ's atonement work. Those terms, "shadow" and "form," are mentioned in Hebrews 10:1, and they put us in mind of Plato's discussion of shadow and form in his Allegory of the Cave. In the allegory, Plato describes a cave in which prisoners sit chained, facing one wall of the cave. (They have been chained there for their entire conscious existence.) They cannot move, and they cannot turn their heads to look behind them. At the opposite wall behind them, a huge fire continuously burns. Between the prisoners and the fire is a roadway across which people travel, and the people travelling the roadway, called puppeteers, hold up various items as they pass. The light from the fire behind creates shadows of the objects projected to the wall in front of the prisoners. Thus, if a puppeteer holds up a book, it is the shadow of the book against the wall that the prisoners see. The shadowy images on the wall are the prisoners' entire idea of reality, and yet those shadows are not the actual objects or forms. Plato relates our world in which we see objects to this world of shadows. The true forms exist in ideas alone—that which these objects, or shadows, represent.

My point, of course, is not to present all the ramifications of Plato's philosophy but rather to show how that shadow-and-form idea relates to what Hebrews says about the atonement. The Law and its sacrificial system, tabernacle, and high priest were shadows, the author tells us, of the actual form that was realized in the atonement of Christ. We are to see in the blood shed by the sacrificial animal, separated from its body, the perfect spirit of Jesus being separated in death from its cursed connection.

The first 10 verses of Hebrews 9 concentrate on the shadow imaging. They describe the tabernacle, the meeting place with God. Again, we need to recognize that the physical tabernacle, although an actual place of meeting with God, was in its grander sense to be understood as only a precursor, a shadow, of the intended meeting place with God envisioned in true form, the one of full spiritual significance—the perfected human essence.

Only the high priest could enter the Holy of Holies and only when carrying the blood of the sacrifice to be sprinkled within. The blood was from an unblemished animal, symbolizing the purity of the life. Its sprinkling cleansed the meeting place. Verse 9 insists that while the sprinkled blood effected its cleansing purpose, the cleansing was only symbolic; the animal blood could not actually cleanse the conscience. Thayer's lexicon mentions that the Greek translated here as conscience means "the soul as distinguishing between what is morally good and bad prompting to do the former and shun the latter."[1] However, we should understand the "good and bad" as

---

1. Thayer, *Lexicon*.

encompassing the entire gamut of TGB, so that perhaps a better definition is "the subconscious basis upon which a person relies for the understanding of truth, goodness, and beauty."

Continuing into verse 11 to verse 14, we learn about the true, or actual, form. Here the "more perfect tabernacle" is described. We should not picture this greater tabernacle as an actual building constructed in heaven since we understand that God is spirit and we worship him in spirit, not in a physical location. Jesus taught that truth to the Samaritan woman at the well, and Stephen also preached, "The Most High does not dwell in sanctuaries made with hands" (Acts 7:48). Jesus entered the Holy of Holies, not one of humankind's fashioning but of God's, which is resurrected creation—Jesus's own body. Christ, our high priest, entered it with his own blood. Notice verse 12: "He entered the most holy place once for all, not by the blood of goats and calves, but by His own blood, having obtained eternal redemption." That last phrase may be a bit misleading. It sounds as if Christ obtained eternal redemption, and then having obtained it, was able to enter the most holy place. But the obtaining of eternal inheritance happens *by* the entering into the most holy place. Remember that eternal redemption is the reclaiming of the physical (cf., Boaz's reclaiming of the land of Ruth and Naomi's family). That reclamation is imaged in the high priest's reclaiming the Holy of Holies, the meeting place of God with humans, with the sprinkling of blood. Just so, the true redemption occurred as Christ's perfect spirit returned to its physical body. A word-for-word translation of the Greek shows this idea more clearly. Instead of reading "having obtained eternal redemption," it reads that Christ entered the most holy place, "eternal redemption finding."

In Hebrews 9, verses 15 through 23a, we read of will and inheritance. Of course, the whole idea of gaining an inheritance is that something is willed to someone who benefits by it. A will, the author reminds us, cannot become actuated until a death has occurred. Our inheritance is eternal life. But this life must be actuated through the death of the one who gives us that inheritance. By virtue of his death, Jesus freed our indebted essence from the covenant obligation of the original Covenant of Life to which we were joined in Adam. He enabled us by our new birth in the New Covenant of Life to receive our inheritance from the one who died. All that is shown by the symbol of life—the blood. The author tells us that even the old (Mosaic) covenant was inaugurated with blood (Exodus 24:3–8) because the death of the animals showed the release of blood—that is, the life desiring relationship with God—from the cursed condition apart from God. That idea is also why Hebrews 9:22 tells us that "without the shedding of blood there is no forgiveness," or more literally, "no more release," the sending away of the curse. This separation, or release, must occur—a separation from the sin curse represented by the physical body to the rebirth of life in the cleansed physical body of new covenant with God. That, then, is the purpose of the blood: to show exactly that necessary release and restoration of life.

So, then, is the shedding of blood necessary? As I said initially, I believe the answer is yes. While it is indeed a symbol, it is not an arbitrarily chosen one. The whole picture of Jesus's crucifixion drove home the point of separation. Jesus began that day telling Pilate his kingdom was not of this world. In saying so, he was assuring the governor of the region that he intended no uprising to wrest the reins of the Palestine region from Rome. His kingdom was not the selfish lust for power to control others as was that of Rome and the other kingdoms of the world. And Rome sent the same message back: its kingdom wanted no part of Jesus, either. Crucifixion was not merely execution. Rome liquidated its undesirables "with the maximum degradation and humiliation. . . . It insisted, coldly and brutally, on the absolute sovereignty of Rome, and of Caesar."[2] The message was clear: Rome separated itself from Jesus. As much as the blood-from-body imagery showed separation of the spirit from physical essence, so did the fact of the crucifixion's separating Jesus (imaging life) from the world (imaging cursed flesh).

Like most Old Testament symbols, the blood has meaning in actuality that points toward its symbolism. Actual blood does maintain life in a human body. Thus, it is the perfect analogy to or symbol of that which gives our flesh its actual life—our spirits. Without the imagery of the blood, then, in the sacrificial system and especially in the sacrifice of Jesus's life, we lose an understanding of the whole story specifically revealed through that shed blood.

---

2. Wright, *Victory of God*, 543.

PART 5

Restoration—
Already & Beyond

17

The New Covenant of Life

Leaving off the curse of body,
His pure blood to cleanse—renew,
God's forgiveness here completing,
Death destroyed; life's cov'nant new!

—Dan Salter, from "Bread of Life!"

Come, everyone who is thirsty,
Come to the waters;
And you without money,
Come, buy, and eat!

—Isaiah 55:1

On the road to Emmaus, Jesus walked with two disciples, and "beginning with Moses and all the Prophets, He interpreted for them the things concerning Himself in all the Scriptures" (Luke 24:27). He must have drawn much of the discussion from Isaiah. In that book, we find the Messiah prophesied as the fulfillment of God's promises and collaboration with Israel. But in both the actual and the prophetic events of Isaiah, Israel is spoken of in multiple ways: as the physical offspring of Jacob (who had been renamed Israel), as the Messiah who would fulfill prophecy, and even as the Messiah's offspring—the ultimate rescued, remnant people who belong to God. Isaiah 52 brings together these ideas of Israel as nation, Messiah, and offspring to explain God's redeeming plan in bringing about Zion—God's forever dwelling with his image bearers in love relationship. This plan is the whole point of the Abrahamic covenant, and as such, it fulfills the atonement.

THE PROMISES THROUGH ABRAHAM

When we read of how it began, the Abrahamic covenant seems at times to be unrelated to our New Testament lives and God's overall purpose. The cut-up animals, the promises made to a long-ago prophet about a faraway land, and just the overall old-covenant flavor seem out of step with our New Covenant life. But God doesn't have multiple redemption plans for multiple ethnic peoples. He has only one plan, and in its individual features, the Abrahamic covenant establishes the significance of that one plan.

In Genesis 12, God told Abram, whose name meant "exalted father," that he would make of him a "great nation." In fact, although we don't yet have specific covenant language in that chapter, the major covenant blessings are promised: verse 1 calls Abram to a promised land, verse 2 gives Abram the promise of many offspring, and verse 3 specifies that all the peoples or nations of the earth will be blessed through Abram. The first and second promises—land and offspring—speak to the two aspects of humanity that would be redeemed and forgiven: the body (physical) and the person (spiritual).

In Genesis 15, where the covenant takes on a more formal tone, two of the major covenant blessings are repeated. In verse 5, God promises offspring as numerous as the stars, and in verse 7, God promises land. When Abram, apparently trying to make sure he has understood, asks for assurance, God conducts the formal covenant ceremony by having Abram split certain animals and lay them out on each side of a path. Normally, the two entering into covenant agreement pass along this path side by side, with the idea that they together promise their lives to the covenant. But in this particular situation, Abram just watches in his dream-like state as God alone (as a flame) walks the path, showing he alone will ensure the covenant purpose and blessings. God echoes that promise of land in verse 18.

Years later, and after the failed fulfillment scheme Abram tried through Hagar and Ishmael (chapter 16), God reconfirmed the covenant with Abram. In Genesis 17, God again promised offspring (verses 5–6) and land (verse 8). But this time, there is a significant difference. This time the promises move beyond Abram's merely gaining the land and offspring to God's describing these blessings as *everlasting* (verses 7–8).

At a later time, God once more repeats the blessing of offspring (Genesis 22:17a) and the blessing to the nations that would come through Abraham (22:18).

While at first glance this covenant seems rather straightforward, difficulties do arise. As I mentioned earlier, we know Israel is the name of the nation formed from Abraham's physical offspring. At other times, however, that same name is applied to the Messiah, the only true covenant keeper. Further still, Israel also becomes the collective name of the Messiah's own offspring of faith. Thus, when looking back at the promised blessings of the Abrahamic covenant, we may wonder at times exactly to which Israel God is making the promises.

In Genesis 12 and 15 when those first promises are made to Abraham for his seed, it appears that Abraham's seed is a collective for any and all his offspring. However, with just a little more consideration, we know this scenario cannot be true. The incident in chapter 16 with Hagar and the child produced by Abram—Ishmael—shows that God never intended in his promise to Abraham that his seed would be merely the fruit of his body. In fact, if we scoot up to Genesis 25, which recounts the end of Abraham's life, we note in verse 1 that Abraham had six sons besides Ishmael and Isaac. But it was to Isaac alone that the promise was given. Therefore, we find the covenant blessings originally discussed in Genesis 12 and 15 have a specific direction: they move out to only one of Abraham's sons, but from that one, they are directed to multiple that come from that one.

In Genesis 17 and 22 we find the blessings of covenant repeated, but this time with an *everlasting* connotation suggested. It is to these passages that Paul points in Galatians 3:16. Paul argues that the seed mentioned there is not plural but singular, referring to Christ. Now, seed may be written in the singular, but so are all collective nouns. How does Paul know this seed is specific to Christ, one person, rather than to the whole of Israel the nation? Paul is interpreting the Abrahamic promises in Genesis 17 and 22 differently from their original meaning in chapters 12 and 15 in the same way the Hebrews author interprets Christ's actual fulfillment of the Mosaic instructions of tabernacle and sacrifice. It is the deeper, symbolic fulfillment Paul has in mind.

Paul's intent is to say that just as Isaac alone among his brothers was the chosen seed from whom blessings would come, so is Jesus the singular seed from among the nation of Israel from whom God's forever kingdom community would come. In other words, the blessings of multiple offspring, land, and blessing from the one seed Isaac showed the everlasting blessings of forgiveness (to individual spirits), redemption (to physical essence), and love community from the one seed Jesus.

In Genesis 17, God changes Abram's name from Abram "exalted father" to Abraham "father of a multitude." Why the change, and why then? Back in chapter 12 when Abram was promised that a "great nation" would come from him, the name *Abraham* would have been just as fitting. But the difference in the promise of chapter 17 calls more specifically for the name change.

In Genesis 17:4, God says that Abraham will become "the father of many nations." This promise is certainly different from chapter 12 in which Abram was told he'd become the father of "*a* great nation." Israel was that great nation. Who, then, are the "*many* nations" of chapter 17? We may at first think of Ishmael, Abram's first son by Hagar, and Esau, Isaac's first son, both of whose offspring became great nations, yet they did not qualify to fulfill the promise (as shown in Genesis 17:20-21 and Malachi 1:2-3). So, while the one great nation came from Abraham's only son of promise, Isaac (whose only son of promise, Jacob, became father of that one great nation Israel), the many nations would come from that one *special* descendant of Abraham, Isaac, and Jacob—the Messiah. He would be the one to go on to bless the world and claim offspring from a *multitude* of nations. It is through the Messiah to the Messiah's offspring that we see fulfillment of the Genesis 17 promise that Abraham would be the father of *many* nations.

Thus, it is *not* Abraham's physical offspring—the Jews only—who will obtain these promises; rather these everlasting promises go to the Messiah's offspring. That realization is significant. It cancels out any presumption in our eschatology or ecclesiology that according to the Abrahamic covenant, God still must deliver some special promises to only the Jews. Rather, Genesis 17 tells us that all *everlasting* promises apply to the Messiah's offspring, his people—Jews *and* Gentiles—of faith.

But what about those earlier promises in Genesis 12 and 15 for Abram's physical offspring? Were they fulfilled? Did God keep his promises in those cases? The answer is yes. Take a look at these verses:

> *Joshua 21:43*
> So the Lord gave Israel all the land He had sworn to give their fathers, and they took possession of it and settled there."

> *Joshua 23:14*
> I am now going the way of all the earth, and you know with all your heart and all your soul that none of the good promises the Lord your God made to you has failed. Everything was fulfilled for you; not one promise has failed.

Deuteronomy 10:22
Your fathers went down to Egypt, 70 people in all, and now the Lord your God has made you as numerous as the stars of the sky.

1 Kings 4:20a
Judah and Israel were as numerous as the sand by the sea.

God's promises do not fail, and God's promises to Israel as a nation did not fail. But those fulfilled promises did not qualify Israel the nation to receive *everlasting* promises as a nation. God reserved those promises of everlasting fulfillment for his everlasting people—Messiah's offspring.[1] We see in the story of Israel the nation, therefore, the imaged story of God's full redemption plan for the whole world of faith—as Paul calls us, the Israel of God (Galatians 6:16). The connecting link throughout is the name Israel. We begin with Israel as the physical offspring of Abraham, Isaac, and Jacob—a nation of priests. We see Israel become the only true Israel—the true striver/worker with God—the Messiah Servant. Finally, we see Israel become the Messiah's offspring—all those who have faith in God as caregiver and in his rescue through Christ.

The story of Israel is the story of restoration. It is a story whose motif mimics the exile from Eden's garden to the end of exile in restored relationship with God. The nation of Israel was exiled (in judgment) in Egypt and Babylon. But the nation had its exodus (forgiveness and redemption) in its return back to the land (security, relationship, rest) of God. Jesus, the Messiah Servant, was exiled (in judgment) as he went to the cross. But his sin offering brought exodus from death in his redemptive resurrection to life. Finally, we, too, all the Messiah's offspring (Jews and Gentiles alike), experienced an exile from God under the curse of death. But that curse was overcome by Christ's atoning work so that our exodus results in fully received forgiveness as well as our redemption to come—life everlasting. Lamentations 4:22a (in a combination of NASB and Young's Literal Translation) presents the result perfectly: "Your iniquity has been completed, O daughter of Zion; He will exile you no longer."

---

1. Note that broadening the blessing recipients to all those of faith is not what is known as replacement theology. Replacement theology understands the promises and blessings originally given to the nation of Israel to be withdrawn and regifted to the church. According to what I'm defining as kinship theology, the church is not a replacement for Israel. Israel as a nation was never meant to be the everlasting kingdom of God. It was (as Hebrews explains) an image, a type, a shadow of what had been God's intent from the beginning—an everlasting love community of all his created image bearers (Jew and Gentile alike).

MADE PERFECT THROUGH SUFFERING

The Suffering Servant section of Isaiah (beginning in verse 13 of chapter 52 and continuing through the end of chapter 53) shows the fulfillment of God's redemption plan in Christ. In verse 13, God says, "See," to ask us to consider carefully. This word is often translated in other versions as *behold*. But it's not used here as a word of awe (as in *lo and behold!*). Here, it merely means *notice this*. God is wanting us to notice how the Servant proceeds through his work. Unlike Israel the nation, the Servant, who is Israel the Messiah, depends solely on God, his caregiver. The Gospels show us that Jesus did not say or do anything purely out of self-interest. He moved and spoke by God's leading, the attitude of right relationship with God. Following God's leading is not slavery because if God not only *performs* but *is* all virtue—all truth, goodness, and beauty—then we must follow truth, goodness, and beauty to have complete, joy-filled, perfect lives. We must follow God. So God urges us to notice the Servant's acting wisely—following God's leading. Because of that prudent attitude, the Servant will be raised, lifted up, and greatly exalted.

The first line of verse 14 begins a thought that is completed in the first line of verse 15. The rest of 14 is parenthetical, providing a description of just how the Servant was appalling. For the moment, let's skip over that portion to get the complete thought: "Just as many were appalled at [him], . . . so He will sprinkle many nations." The word *sprinkle* should remind us of the Aaronic priest's sprinkling the blood on the altar. The sprinkling action is startling (imagine yourself being sprinkled by blood, or anything for that matter). In fact, the Arabic root does mean "to startle." So not only are we appalled by the sight of the bloodied body of the Servant, but we are further horrified to an even greater degree as that blood of the Servant's body splatters us. In verse 15, kings shut their mouths in amazement. The sight had not been expected! The kings or nations of the world did not anticipate a criminal of lowly status from a lowly, inconsequential nation to affect the powerful nations of the world. They had not heard that this would happen. None of their wise men had predicted it. No one would have figured it.

Then we reach 53:1. Attention turns from these other nations to the nation of Israel. The Jews certainly *had* heard of this. Their prophets and their writings were full of God's rescue. Even this very book of Isaiah was giving them a detailed script. Yet the first cry of 53:1 is "Who has believed what we have heard?" The implication is that even though they knew God would rescue and God had revealed to them his nature of love, *no one believed* it was through this appalling Servant that God actually meant to claim victory!

What if the story had played out slightly differently? What if, in general, most of the incidents had taken place as we know them: Jesus was arrested by the temple guard in Gethsemane, he was taken to Caiaphas for the mock trial, he was marched at daybreak across Jerusalem to Pilate, Pilate asked Jesus where he was from, Jesus at first did not respond, and Pilate spoke of his authority to crucify. But then suppose something different happened. Suppose as Jesus was telling Pilate he would have no authority unless given it by God, Pilate flew into a rage at the presumed insolence of this peasant Jew and ordered the soldier standing near to run him through with his sword. Jesus crumpled to the floor, *spilling his blood as he died.* Would this death, from a soldier's stabbing him rather than that same soldier's nailing him to a cross, have accomplished God's atonement purpose?

Well, in that alternate scene, something is missing. Hebrews 2:9–10 reads:

> But we do see Jesus—made lower than the angels for a short time so that by God's grace He might taste death for everyone—crowned with glory and honor because of His suffering in death. For in bringing many sons to glory, it was entirely appropriate that God—all things exist for Him and through Him—should make the source of their salvation *perfect through sufferings.*

The author of Hebrews argues that sufferings were a part of the process. Why did the Servant have to suffer? We learn he was made perfect, or complete, through those sufferings. How or in what way did the sufferings make him complete?

We must remember that the mission of Jesus was to counter what occurred through Adam. Adam's time of testing was in being confronted with the possible loss of Eve, a trial he found intolerable and did not want to endure. In his time of testing, he chose to remove faith in God and place it in himself. That fault was the sin that flung Adam and all his descendants out from the Covenant of Life into death. Now Jesus, the second Adam, had to face his own time of testing, having to endure something he found almost intolerable, and it also regarded his physical essence.

We certainly remember the time of testing that started Christ's ministry. After forty days of Jesus's fasting in the wilderness, Satan came to tempt Jesus to remove faith from God and God's way in order to accomplish much the same goals but in Satan's proposed *better,* quicker way. Jesus, however, maintained faith in what his Father had told him to do.

At the end of his three-and-a-half-year ministry, Jesus again faced a period of intense testing—an even greater one. We are introduced to it in Gethsemane. Jesus prayed that the cup of suffering and death would be removed. But he based his request not on his own will (that of Jesus the man) but rather on God's. So just as at the beginning, he completed his ministry totally dependent on God and, therefore, sinless—never missing the mark. Jesus even told his disciples to watch so that they would also learn how to face temptation, with eyes of faith fixed on God.

Consider also that even as Jesus was spat upon, buffeted, and abused, he nevertheless remained God. He was not destitute, apart from the "ten thousand angels" he could have called. Since he was mindful of that advantage, the temptation surely intensified. At any time, he could have cried out for actual, certain relief to stop the torture. With each lash ripping flesh from his back, the thought of escape must have entered his mind. Every cut, every thorn jab, every pound of the hammer driving in the nails must have taken his mind to a fresh, raw point of temptation, but every time he answered, "Your will be done."

By this means, then, the source of salvation was made complete through sufferings. In his extreme temptation by the demands of his flesh, Jesus qualified to be redeemer by his *unfailing* dependence on God to become the unblemished offering for the sin of the world.

Isaiah 53 recounts the suffering of Israel in unique perspective. The chapter is divided into three sections. Each section provides a perspective based on a separate representation of Israel. Verses 2 through 6 show Israel the nation. Verses 7 through 9 picture Israel as the covenant-fulfilling Servant. Verses 10 through 12 highlight Israel as the offspring of the Messiah (as the purpose of God).

In each of the sections, the Israel perspective *wants* the Servant to suffer and die. We are told in verse 3 that Israel the nation despised the Servant and didn't value him. Certainly, we see that perspective in the Gospels. John 1:11 tells us, "He came to His own, and His own people did not receive Him." Although at times the people seem favorable to him when they expect to gain from him (miracles or leadership to overthrow Rome), they end up united in calling out, "Take Him away! Crucify Him!" (John 19:15).

Israel the Servant also wants to continue to the suffering and death conclusion of his earthly ministry. Isaiah 53:7 reads, "He was oppressed and afflicted, yet He did not open His mouth. Like a lamb led to the slaughter and like a sheep silent before her shearers, He did not open His mouth." Imagine Christ's surprise as he got up from prayer to meet Judas and the temple guard, his mind probably filled with faithful determination to confront the temptations about to be outpoured, and suddenly Peter rushes past him to take a swing at the servant of Caiaphas. With the same intensity Jesus had once told him, "Get behind me, Satan!" he called out to Peter, "Sheathe your sword! Am I not to drink the cup the Father has given Me?" (John 18:11). Israel the Servant is intent on the path to suffering and death.

Finally, in the third Israel perspective—that of Zion, the purpose of God—we encounter the same desire that the Servant should meet with suffering and death. Verse 10 tells us, "Yet the Lord was pleased to crush Him severely." Pleased? Why pleased? Did God take pleasure in the suffering of Jesus? We cannot misunderstand what is meant by the pleasure of God. The suffering itself was not pleasurable to him. God was pleased only because of what the suffering and death would accomplish. We learn what will be accomplished in the rest of verse 10: when the Servant becomes the restitution (or guilt or sin) offering, the promised blessings of offspring and resurrection follow, through which "the Lord's pleasure will be accomplished." As a result, God gives him "the many as a portion." That's we who believe! As we read in the chapter's closing, he "intercedes for the rebels"—again, us! By his suffering and death, we are rescued. In all three perspectives, then, suffering and death are the desired path.

COVENANT FULFILLMENT

Another element in this chapter regards fulfillment of purpose. For the nation, Isaiah uses a first-person plural pronoun to highlight the rescue for the Jews: "We are healed by His wounds" (53:5).

The Servant section presents an interesting counterpoint. In 53:9, the NASB translation best shows the intended meaning: "His grave was assigned with wicked men, Yet He was with a rich man in His death, Because He had done no violence, Nor was there any deceit in His mouth." The contrast between the wicked and the rich differentiates the before and after aspects of the suffering. As the Servant suffered and died, he was treated as a criminal, dying for sin. But on the other side of the death, with atonement made, Jesus's being placed in a rich man's grave indicates God's favor in his successful, faithful mission.

Finally, the Zion section shows the purpose accomplished for the world. Verse 12 reads, "I will give Him the many as a portion, and He will receive the mighty as spoil."

With the suffering over and the victory won, the triumph is complete. Isaiah 54 pictures the blessing realized from the accomplished mission of the Servant. The Servant came to the world not merely to suffer and be faithful but specifically to follow God faithfully to accomplish rescue. That rescuer, as God, came fulfilling the covenantal promise to Abraham. That rescuing Servant was, Paul tells us, a second Adam. The first Adam sinned, and based on the curse, all his children continued in his sin and its consequence. The second Adam came without sin so that all those reborn in him could take part in his covenant faithfulness. Therefore, when God speaks to the Servant in chapter 54, God is also speaking to those whom the Servant represents—Israel in its complete and truest sense—Christ *and* his offspring. Thus, those offspring God will no longer rebuke. That former rebuke is what we saw pictured in the crushing of the Servant on the cross. Christ did die for his offspring, and his death highlights the deaths of his offspring. Likewise, in the triumph, we see God's recognition of Christ and his offspring together.

Because the Servant came in fulfillment of the Abrahamic covenant, we should see the promised Abrahamic blessings fulfilled. Isaiah 54:1–3 shows us exactly that. But in keeping with the grander promise of Genesis 17 (everlasting benefits through the Messiah) over the possibly temporal expression in Genesis 15, these blessings of Isaiah 54 also go beyond the initial promise. God had promised offspring to Abraham. But the offspring of the Servant realized in 54:1 are "*more than* the children of the married woman" (emphasis added). The land, which is the location of God's presence and provision, must be enlarged (54:2). And not only are the nations blessed, but also the descendants of the Servant actually dispossess the nations (54:3). Thus, the Abrahamic covenant blessings not only come in with the Servant's victory but also go beyond the terms of the initial promise.

The Abrahamic covenant is completely fulfilled. But significantly, it is *not* fulfilled through the nation of Israel. The blessing to the physical lines of both Abraham and David terminate, while the spiritual blessings promised to them continue. Matthew emphasizes that point in his genealogy. He divides his lineage into three sets of 14 generations. The first follows the physical line from Abraham to David to capture the blessing. The second concludes with the deportation to Babylon that terminates the physical line of kings of Israel. And the third ends with a new king, but not until the break in physical lineage at Joseph, which highlights the virgin birth of the new Messiah King. Thus, God shows the promise to Abraham and to David fulfilled through the non-physical, faithful seed in Christ.

Although the Mosaic covenant faded through the fulfillment in Christ, God did not give up on the Jews. They, too, are invited as much as any other persons to become offspring of the Servant. In Romans, Paul speaks of the Jews' being grafted back into covenant relationship. Thus, we see the pattern of all Scripture: union—falling away—restoration. Isaiah 54:4–10 reminds us of this outline in the picture of the deserted wife. It is, in fact, the very metanarrative of the whole Bible. God's image bearers dwelled with him in the garden. They fell away. Through God's effort in the Servant, they are restored. Over and over we see God revealing this plan: Joseph, the favorite son, sold into slavery, is lifted up and restored; Daniel, the favored administrator, is sent to the lion's den, and miraculously restored; the Shulammite, caught up with the king, separated from her Shepherd Lover, is united with him again; Mary is pregnant, and Joseph will put her away, but God brings them back together. We even see Jesus in close communion with the Father, having his body torn away at the cross, only to be restored in resurrection. All those restorations bring victory and glory.

In the last part of Isaiah 54, we read about Jerusalem restored. Jerusalem was the place of the temple—the place where God met with humankind. But it had been ravaged, and the destruction pictures the fall in the garden. But God intervenes through the Servant to realize his purpose of everlasting love relationship with his image bearers. And we read of fulfilled Jerusalem—realized restoration—as being adorned in sapphires and rubies. This New Jerusalem receives its righteousness (faithfulness to the covenant) from God (54:17b).

The struggle occurred in Isaiah 53. The victory was celebrated in Isaiah 54. With the opening of Isaiah 55, a sense of settled life in victory emerges. The chapter begins with an invitation for the thirsty to come drink. The invitation ought to remind us of the very last chapter in our Bibles. In Revelation 22:17, the one who is thirsty is invited to come. In fact, we find quite a few similarities.

> *Isaiah 54:1-3* promises offspring who will dispossess the nations; they will enlarge the site of their tent.
> *Revelation 20:11—21:1* also shows the people recorded in the book of life, while others are dispossessed of the book of life; the offspring realize the new heaven and new earth.
>
> *Isaiah 54:4-10* promises they will forget the shame of their youth; they will no longer remember.
> *Revelation 21:2-8* also promises that he will wipe away every tear; the previous things have passed away.
>
> *Isaiah 54:11-17* speaks of the New Jerusalem.
> *Revelation 21:9-27* speaks of the New Jerusalem.
>
> *Isaiah 55:1* calls out to everyone who is thirsty to come!
> *Revelation 22:17* echoes by saying the one who is thirsty should come.

18

New Covenant Living through This Age

Let knowledge grow from more to more,
But more of reverence in us dwell;
That mind and soul, according well,
May make one music as before.

—Alfred, Lord Tennyson, from "In Memoriam A.H.H"

"And let the peace of the Messiah,
to which you were also called in one body,
control your hearts. Be thankful."

—Colossians 3:15

As discussed in chapter 4, Kinship Theology understands that God purposed creation for everlasting love relationship. However, before he even formed the world, God knew the probability that sin would intrude. He knew that not because God sits outside time and views the past and future as if all rested in an ever-present now. (I can't even imagine such an incoherent construct, and I don't believe its proponents can, either.) Rather, he knew it because our God is infinite in knowledge. While any future to the present has not yet occurred, God may certainly know *infinitely* well the realm of possibilities as well as the creation he would make—including predispositions, tendencies, and influencing factors. Therefore, God could know (and as infinite, he *would* know) right well that newly created image bearers, uncoerced to love and yet to learn, would likely fail in relationship and require rescue and restoration, especially since these creatures would have to look past their own essence to rest on God's for relationship.

God's restoration plan involved redemption from the curse of sin in which our physical creation was otherwise hopelessly entangled. Because of that redemption, all persons who by faith give themselves to God and his revealed essence of truth, goodness, and beauty (revealed ultimately in Christ) will find that originally purposed everlasting love relationship.

Yet sometimes we don't feel rescued. This still-cursed essence intimidates, delivering blows and slinging darts that bruise and prick as we struggle through our lives often burdened in sorrow. It is not merely persons who have rejected God and cling to their own evil who cause this struggle for believers. We each struggle within our own skin in personal battles against the still-cursed dominant influence of our physical essence.

THE FACT OF SUFFERING

Verses 25 and 26 of Isaiah 10 urge the faithful remnant not only to be patient in suffering, but also to do so while enduring the consequences of God's withdrawal from the unfaithful majority of Judah and Israel. We learn from passages such as these that not every good or every bad that happens to us is a response to our individual actions. Isaiah offers a prime example: the children of Israel suffered for years as slaves in Egypt before God, in his perfect timing, rescued them. Israel—and we—have to be patient for purposes of trust, justice, and glory.

Suffering has characterized the church to some degree from its apostolic inception to our time. We may wonder why we who have given ourselves to God, believing in Christ's redeeming, atoning work, must still suffer. Are we somehow partially paying for sins of the past—or present?

Acts 14:22 tells us that Paul's missionary group revisited their converts, "strengthening the disciples by encouraging them to continue in the faith and by telling them, 'It is necessary to pass through many troubles on our way into the kingdom of God.'" Apparently, the suffering is not accidental but expected. Philippians 1:29 reads, "For it has been given to you on Christ's behalf not only to believe in Him, but also to suffer for Him." Is Paul telling the Philippians that only they will suffer, or is the statement meant for all Bible readers and believers? Evidently, the instruction is to a broader group than just the Philippians since the Acts passage said basically the same thing to the Christians of Lystra, Iconium, and Antioch.

First Thessalonians 2:14 and 3:2–5 include others in the suffering:

> For you, brothers, became imitators of God's churches in Christ Jesus that are in Judea, since you have also suffered the same things from people of your own country, just as they did from the Jews.
>
> And we sent Timothy, our brother and God's coworker in the gospel of Christ, to strengthen and encourage you concerning your faith, so that no one will be shaken by these persecutions. For you yourselves know that we are appointed to this. In fact, when we were with you, we told you previously that we were going to suffer persecution, and as you know, it happened. For this reason, when I could no longer stand it, I also sent him to find out about your faith, fearing that the tempter had tempted you and that our labor might be for nothing.

Paul tells the Thessalonians that they should expect suffering, and then he follows up by pointing out that they, too, had suffered. The "we" in these verses could be referring to Paul and his party or to Paul and the Thessalonians together.

To confirm even further our expectation of suffering, Paul states in 2 Timothy 3:12–13, "In fact, all those who want to live a godly life in Christ Jesus will be persecuted. Evil people and impostors will become worse, deceiving and being deceived."

The church, then, was universally persecuted in apostolic times, and did, in fact, expect to be persecuted, relying on Paul's claim that they were "appointed" to suffering in no uncertain terms. We know also from history that both church persecution and other normal kinds of suffering have continued unabated until now. But when will it all end?

Let's take a look (again) at Romans 8:16–25. The passage begins, "For I consider that the sufferings of this present time are not worth comparing with the glory that is going to be revealed to us." Paul contrasts present suffering with future glory. Verse 17 continues: "For the creation eagerly waits with anticipation for God's sons to be revealed." Why does Paul speak of *creation's* waiting? What does creation's waiting have to do with *our* suffering? We examine Romans 8 carefully in chapter 13 of this book. We found that Paul provides a strong contrast between *flesh* (body or the physical) and *spirit*. His explication of the contrast actually begins in chapter 7, where Paul discusses the agonizing influence of the flesh (cursed physical essence) on the spirit, which yearns for truth, goodness, and beauty.

Chapter 8 explains that Christ condemned sin in the flesh through his redemptive atonement. Paul calls his flesh dead, but his spirit is alive in the righteousness (covenant faithfulness) received by the forgiveness of God. Then, in verse 11, Paul argues that just as Christ was raised from the dead, we, too, whose spirits have been forgiven, will have our mortal bodies come back to life—that is, they will be cleansed in resurrection. Thus, verse 17 says, "We suffer with Him so that we may also be glorified with Him." In other words, our suffering is in this corrupt, dead physical body of flesh, so that when our cleansed/resurrected bodies are realized, we will be glorified with Christ, who is the firstfruits of the resurrection.

This flow of thought follows closely what we have discussed so far regarding the atonement. Christ's redemption of cursed physical creation (our bodies—our essence), accomplished at the cross, was realized for Jesus as the firstfruits at his resurrection. But it will be realized for us when Christ returns and claims all physical creation in redemption.

Now, with this background, we go back to our passage in Romans 8:16–25. By following Paul's argument, we no longer find it odd that Paul suddenly speaks of creation as *waiting*. This *creation* is the corrupted physical world of which our bodies are composed. The point of verse 19, then, is that since the creation (the physical world) links to our bodies, our bodies (physical essence) are what wait. Surely, this realization should come as no surprise. The source material God used to make the *adam* was this earth, and we know our bodies are made up of physical matter and energy. Our bodies of this physical creation share not just composition but also the curse of sin that Paul discusses. Verse 20 says just that: all physical creation (the world and our bodies) is under that same curse of sin (ref. Gen 3:17: "The ground is cursed because of you"). Paul continues, describing how the whole earth is groaning (8:22) and how we are groaning (8:23—reflecting Paul's struggle of chapter 7). So why does Paul say in 8:19 that creation eagerly waits for God's sons to be revealed? It is exactly because the resurrection of our physical bodies is linked to creation. Since all creation is our physical essence, all—bodies and earth—will be resurrected together at Christ's return.

At Christ's coming both our resurrection (new bodies) and that of all the rest (new heavens, new earth) will occur. Notice that in verse 18, Paul contrasts present suffering with the glory to be revealed. He has discussed at length that suffering will cease *at the time of the resurrection!* So we find that the New Testament does teach that suffering will continue through this present age. It will be at the resurrection—at the coming of Christ—that suffering ceases and everlasting, uninterrupted, and perfect peace and joy begin.

Romans 8 is not an isolated passage giving us this perspective. Paul tells us in 2 Corinthians 4:7–18 the same thing. He begins there saying that our treasure (our spirit, which has been made alive) exists in clay jars (corrupted, dead flesh). Through several verses, Paul explains the experience of continued suffering because of the sinful physical world's cursed corruption. Then Paul provides the same resurrection example as in Romans 8, starting in verse 14. He says just as Jesus, the firstfruits, was raised physically from the dead, so also will our physical bodies be raised from the dead to end this suffering and to experience the eternal weight of glory. Paul ends the passage by saying that we do not focus on the temporary (these corrupted bodies of death), but we rather rest on what is unseen and eternal. Our hope is not in this corrupted flesh and world. Our hope is in resurrection!

Finally, Revelation 21 begins telling us about "a new heaven and new earth, for the first heaven and the first earth had passed away" (verse 1). This scene is after Christ's return—after the resurrection of our bodies and all physical creation. It is in the following verses, especially verse 4, that we learn *finally* tears are wiped away; death no longer exists; grief, crying, and pain no longer exist. Prior to this point of Christ's triumph-of-atonement return, there had been no golden age of absence of suffering, as post-millennialists surmise. Suffering continues until we reach the resurrection of creation. We experience an end to suffering only when "the previous things have passed away."

THE NECESSITY OF SUFFERING

The above passages indicate not only the fact of suffering but also hint that this suffering is necessary. If the perfect (new heaven, new earth) has no suffering and that is our hope, why would God require the road to our ultimate triumph to necessarily include suffering? Let's begin by looking at a couple of passages. First, Acts 5:40–41 tells us that John and Peter were flogged for preaching Christ. However, they left the Sanhedrin "rejoicing that they were counted worthy to be dishonored on behalf of the Name." Keep that in mind as we move back to Romans 8 but this time to verses 36 and 37. There we find Paul saying that in our suffering we are "more than victorious." Also, in 2 Corinthians 12:5–10, Paul talks about his thorn being necessary to keep him from exalting himself. Further, he says that power is perfected in weakness. He concludes by saying when he is weak, then he is strong.

Why should these weaknesses and this suffering be viewed as triumph in this life? As we link our first point to this, we recognize that the corruptible flesh will be with us constantly until the resurrection. Therefore, since we live in this amalgamation of cleansed spirit and sinful flesh, embracing suffering does indeed help us subdue the flesh. We observe that persecutions tend to draw the church closer to God, whereas times of ease tend to ease the church away from God. That's why the Bible tells us that tribulation works patience and then hope (Romans 5:3–5).

So we should not be discouraged when we suffer. We should not wish suffering away while we still live in this corrupted world in these corrupted bodies. Paul implies that ease and pleasure within this corruption tend to move us away from God precisely because it feeds the idolizing of our corrupted flesh. It is in suffering that we may triumph in our dependence on Christ. This state, though, will not exist in heaven. There is nothing inherently good about suffering that draws us close to God so that heaven will need to include suffering. Suffering is necessary now only because we remain within this cursed flesh. Once it is cleansed at Jesus's return—a return that concludes the redemption and atonement—suffering will *not* be necessary for our continual, full, and mindful embrace of God.

WRATH OF GOD

We began our section on suffering by noting the suffering of the remnant in Isaiah 10. We found that they were suffering not simply because of cursed-flesh existence but because God had also simultaneously withdrawn to a degree from the unfaithful of Judah and Israel. How does the wrath of God, which we normally understand as resulting in death, interweave itself in the current fabric of our lives? We covered the wrath of God in chapter 8 of this book, but a few more points need to be made.

To gain insight into the wrath of God, let's look first at how God shows his love. Throughout the Old and the New Testaments, God speaks of relationship as the demonstration of his love. In passages too numerous to list exhaustively, God tells Israel that he will dwell or live or walk among them. (Here are a few examples: Exodus 29:45, Leviticus 26:12, Isaiah 12:6, Zephaniah 3:15, and Zechariah 2:10–11.) God's dwelling with his image bearers begins its everlasting fulfillment in Matthew 1:23, where Matthew clarifies the birth of Jesus as the birth of *Immanuel*, which means *God with us*. At the end of God's Word, we read in Revelation 21:3 that indeed God's dwelling is with humanity. We learn in James 4:8 that if we draw near to God, he will draw near to us. Thus, *God with us*—coming to us, turning toward us, living with us—speaks of God's love and favor and the dissemination of his glory—his truth, goodness, and beauty—to us. In this expression, our God loves, and indeed, we say God *is* love (I John 4:8) because we recognize the gift of himself to us in relationship.

But would it be right to say God *is* wrath as we do God *is* love? After all, God does express wrath, too. As we discussed in chapter 8, a little logic should dismiss this characterization. In chapter 1, we considered God in his existence before the world began. God—being God alone—existed in a love community of the Trinity, but he did not engage in wrath. It was not a necessary characteristic that he had to display. It came about only in reaction to his creation's turning away from his essence of truth, goodness, and beauty. God, therefore, is not, in his essence, wrath as he is love.

How, then, does God express wrath that is not part of himself? He does so (again, as we discussed in chapter 8) by doing the exact opposite of what he does to express love. He expresses love by turning toward the ones he would love. A change occurs for those who are loved: since God *is* truth, goodness, and beauty, those he turns toward experience that truth, goodness, and beauty when—*and only when*—God turns toward them. The opposite of love is turning away. As God turns away, his truth, goodness, and beauty necessarily turn away as well from the one not loved (i.e., the one who ultimately refuses or rejects God's love relationship). Think of it this way: the opposite of light is dark. But how do we define dark? We define it as the absence of light. Just so, the wrath of God is defined as the absence of his love. With its removal, the one who loses it—suddenly devoid of it—realizes a dreadful consequence. All that is left is the horrible—pain, ache, frustration, agony, despair, loneliness—and every evil imaginable.

Thus, we read how God judges. He took his faithful love away from Saul (2 Samuel 7:15). We read in Romans 1 that he *gave over* those who turned from him. The idea of *giving them over,* or *delivering them over*, is a letting go—the release of those persons, as it were, into the hands of another. How does God intend us to act toward evil? We are his image bearers; we image him. So we are instructed as well to turn away from those who *embrace* evil—not just *do* evil; we all *do* evil, and God doesn't turn from us at every sin. But God turns from those who *embrace* evil—and by that example, we should as well (I Corinthians 5:13, Ephesians 4:31, Psalm 101:7).

Is that it, then? Is that how God responds to evil? Doesn't the Bible say explicitly that God *acts* in hostility toward evildoers? Acting with hostility doesn't sound like simply turning away. While it's true that *turning away* sounds rather mild to us, it is only because our turning away doesn't carry with it the enormous effect it does when God turns away. God's turning away is an action that yields immeasurable horrific consequence, because TGB exist only with him.

Notice how the Bible marries the two ideas of God's acting in furious hostility with his turning away. Leviticus 26:23–24 reads, "If in spite of these things [which were incidents of God's discipline] you do not accept My discipline, but act with *hostility toward Me*, then I will act with *hostility toward you."* God says if the Israelites *act* a certain way toward him, he will *act* in the same way toward them. God calls their action *hostility* toward him. What did they do in this instance that God characterized as hostility toward him? They *turned* from him. They went off to worship other gods. They did not listen to him. So God promised he would perform the same *hostile action* toward them, which must mean that he would *turn from them*. In his turning away, terrible consequences ensue.

Here, of course, we have to understand the balance God endures throughout this age for the ultimate benefit of his everlasting-love-relationship purpose. God turns aside from people to a certain degree without abruptly leaving this world to utter ruin. He does that for the sake of us who already are his followers and for those who will still come to him as life continues. But there are those from whom God turns in this life, who by that action lose their lives to physical death. God's ultimate turning away is described for us in Revelation 21. That turning occurs as part of the final redemption of creation, fulfilling the atonement and restoration plan. The turning aside is described in the horrific terms of the lake of fire.

Unfortunately, the many wrong-headed attempts to understand the future, and the subsequent bizarre treatments of Revelation that construct fantastic storylines of future chaos and evil, have distracted us from recognizing the significant horror occurring right now. The three aspects of humankind's cursed essence that have plagued us since the fall include (1) our never-ending yearning for satisfaction in truth, goodness, and beauty apart from God, (2) our belief that satisfaction in truth, goodness, and beauty can come from our own essence—the physicality of creation itself, and (3) the false absolutes (imaginings) we develop ourselves that we come to believe *are* truth, goodness, and beauty. These three distortions are the essence of what sin and evil mean. And these three, in fact, are what John writes about as the beasts and image of the beast in chapter 13 of Revelation. We do wrong to imagine the beast as some future, single world leader, opposed to God and ruling over us, who will someday lead an army of demons and demon-controlled persons to battle against us. No, the *beast* is alive and well right now in this age, attacking the hearts and souls of all humanity through this cursed essence of ours.

REVELATION: SHOWPIECE OF THIS AGE

The entire book of Revelation, from the time John is called through the door of Heaven in the first verse of chapter 4 to the last chapter, is filled with vivid imagery that describes the period from the first advent of Christ through his coming again. We read of the sun's being darkened and colored horses coming forth; we see a serpent, a prostitute, a beast from the sea, 10 horns on a beast's head, a lake of fire, and a new heaven and earth. But in all this representation, nothing should compel us to leave the support of the rest of Scripture. We should not translate the language of the symbolic into a literal future fantasy world where evil is somehow worse than our darkened hearts and cursed state has ever been. The Old Testament is filled with the same kind of imagery. We see the same prophetic darkening of the sun in Joel, horses coming forth in Zechariah, a serpent in Genesis, a prostitute in Hosea, beasts from the sea in Psalms, 10 horns of a beast in Daniel, and a lake of fire and new heaven and earth in Isaiah. If we hold closely to the teachings of the rest of Scripture, both Old and New Testaments, our understanding of Revelation can return from the swirling phantasm of comic books to a sensible coalescence of the entire redemption story.

Redemption is the key subject matter of the book, held together by the scroll images of chapters 5, 10, and 20. That framework leads us from the need for a Redeemer, through redemption accomplished, and on to inheritance in the redemption won. Still, the largest section of this book focuses on the environment of evil, especially in the era from redemption's accomplishment at atonement won to redemption's fully realized victory in eradicating sin at the second coming. It is for us living in this evil era that the book of Revelation was written.

This book is not meant merely to satisfy some degree of curiosity about what's going on in this age and what's to be expected. The pages pour out encouragement and hope for our struggle in this life. The human-focused, those spurred on by a host of spiritual evil, react violently to God as he gathers the Godly minded through this age. The encouragement given is necessary, because those Godly minded, living here and now, can be overwhelmed in spirit. "Here is the story," God declares. "Victory is assured. Meaning is wrapped up in redemption. Hold fast. Continue on. The suffering will be short-lived. The glory of love relationship for all eternity will be ours. But hold fast." That encouragement is the purpose of this apocalyptic book's telling the redemption story.

To balance that framework, which began in the prologue, we need to jump all the way to the end of the book to view the epilogue. The epilogue contains most of the elements of the prologue, paralleling the thought and giving greater assurance of both the purpose for the book and the actual confidence we may have in God because of it. The epilogue begins in 22:6 and runs to the end.

The first thing we notice is that the message pattern is the same. God speaks to and through Jesus who is the Word—faithful and true. We even see this exact same reference from 22:6 back in 19:11 as Christ comes from heaven on a white horse and is called Faithful and True. The words come to the angel who, in turn, presents them to John, who writes them for the benefit of all God's people.

In the epilogue, John begins to bow before the angel, but the angel quickly redirects his gaze. The angel proclaims that the words—the message—are not his but God's. It is to God as the true and good and beautiful one, that all worship must be directed. Note that John's action is not treated as an effrontery to the lofty sensibilities of a God who is offended if worship is not directed to him. The point is that God *is* truth, goodness, and beauty. All our lives and rejoicing—our faith, hope, and love—have that essence of God as our purpose, goal, and blessing. We were created to have relationship with him filled with truth, goodness, and beauty that can come only from him. So we rejoice in that, and like John, we worship God for who he is.

We also note that God's message delivered through *his* (God's—22:6) angel is the same message John receives from Jesus through *his* (Jesus's—22:16) angel, an equivalence showing indeed that Jesus is God. Yet this fact does not negate the importance of his humanity. He is, as we're told in verse 16, the root (Creator, Giver of life) of David as well as the offspring (fulfilled human king promise—Romans 15:12) of David.

Revelation 22:17 continues with the connection that we sense in this epilogue. God is to be worshipped as the only one deserving of worship for who he is—all truth, goodness, and beauty. But we must not forget the emphasis of Scripture: we were created to joy in everlasting love relationship with him. We were not created to cry out how scummy we are, hiding under rocks so that we can make sure God gets all the glory. We must remember that glory is the manifestation of God's truth, goodness, and beauty. We cannot glorify God well while hiding under a rock. We were made to dance in his presence and before all creation.

We see that idea clearly in verse 17 as God not only extends the call but also wants and expects us to join in with him, pursuing the kingdom in pure delight. Yes, the Spirit says come, but the bride says come as well. *We* are the bride. God gives us the message to take to others. We join with God in the happy pursuit of his kingdom.

Here in the epilogue, we are also struck with the urgency of the message. Again, we read that these things (including and especially the extending of this time of trouble) will take place, but they will take place quickly. Endure! We are also urged to understand that this message is not some concern about the future. The time is near (22:10); it is at hand; it is now. Notice the contrast in the angel's instruction not to seal this book with the instruction for Daniel and his prophecy (Daniel 12:4). Daniel was to seal up his prophecy because it was intended for a later time. John's revelation prophecy is for now, and so it remains unsealed.

Jesus is coming! Blessed are those whose robes are washed clean, made righteous (faithful to the covenant) through the faithfulness of Jesus. Outside this group—this kingdom—are those not righteous, not faithful to the covenant. Six descriptors identify this outside group (22:15). They are liars, murderers, dogs, idolaters, sorcerers, and the sexually immoral. Notice that these six categories (all referenced as abominations in the Old Testament and lined up in this sequence) are those things that directly attack the image of God in his truth, goodness, beauty, faith, hope, and love.

For those inside the kingdom, blessing overflows: the blessing of the Bright Morning Star (22:16), the blessing of the water of life (22:17b), the blessing of God's deliverance (22:20), and the blessing of God's grace (22:21).

Revelation summarizes for us the glory of God's full redemption story from estrangement from God (chapter 4) through atoning victory (chapter 10) to everlasting love relationship (chapter 22). Along the way, during the great portion of the gathering of this age, evil swirls about us, attempting to harm God's community and build itself up (chapters 13–19). Christ warns of this battle and encourages firm trust in him (chapters 2 and 3).

This story is not only that of Revelation: it is the story of the entire Bible, summarized in Revelation as a full recap of God's plan. Jesus told his disciples that he no longer called them slaves because a slave does not know what his master is doing (John 15:15). He called them friends because he made known to them everything he heard from the Father. So now we who have this complete story from God through the revelation of Jesus, who have believed it and hope in it, are embraced as friends of God and will be so forever.

19

The End of the Age & the Finishing of the Atonement

And he who disregards the news, and doth his day of grace abuse,
Shall find the worm that never dies, as in the burning lake his sighs
To all eternity, shall be—"There was provision made for me:
I might have been in heaven above, but I despised God's mighty love."

—William Blane, from "The Atonement"

"And anyone not found written in the book of life
Was thrown into the lake of fire."

—Revelation 20:15

Wouldn't it be wonderful if every person ever born were to enter God's everlasting community of love? Wasn't that the point of creation? Wouldn't a God of infinite love work toward that end? Despite the Calvinists' claim that God is better glorified by destroying some people, I would agree that, yes, not only would the prospect be wonderful, but our God of infinite love would certainly desire it. He actually tells us that in the biblical record and through his revelation. But sadly, it will not turn out that way. The problem is not that God is not loving enough or that the period of choice is too short—cut off either by physical death or by Christ's return. In fact, the impossibility of everyone's ending up reconciled to God has nothing to do with his love or the opportunity he gives. The fault lies with the creature, not the Creator. So why is it that not everyone will be saved?

CALVINISM'S SHIFTING SAND

Let's begin by dismissing the false reasons, the most egregious of which is that God simply chooses only a subset of humanity to belong to his kingdom and thereby ensures that not all will be saved. We discussed this point briefly in chapter 8 and a little more in chapter 12, but the idea is so rampantly and cavalierly held today that a little more wrestling with it is warranted. Huge numbers of Reformed scholars agree that God simply chooses not to save, and many of them undeniably possess great intellect and wisdom. Some of the most prolific and astute from whose writing I have benefited are Arthur Pink, R. C. Sproul, G. K. Beale, and Gordon Clark. No one, I think, has ever made the claim that any of these men were not deep thinkers and absolutely sincere in their desire to handle God's Word correctly. My point is not to attack the intellectual credentials of Calvinists. However, even while admiring the intellect of others, I must be careful—as all Christians *must*—to understand God as well as *I* am able. My father (in my opinion, another intellectual giant) never stood over me forcing me to memorize positions he held so that I would be the better for it. He realized the impossibility of my becoming a better thinker by simply drilling someone else's views into my mind. He stressed that I should know not only *what* I believe but also *why* I believe it, and the why, in regard to theology, speaks past a mound of knowledge we may store up to burrow deeply into the heart of our relationship with God.

Because there are so many who hold the Calvinistic position of a limited atonement (or, as they may prefer, particular redemption—which admittedly has a subtle yet significant difference), and since I don't want to be accused of creating a straw man (an attack almost everyone flings against almost everyone else of differing opinion), I am going to narrow the focus of my arguments to the theological position of John Piper, pastor, author, and noted Reformed thinker, and in particular, with a couple of paragraphs from his short book on the subject called *Does God Desire All to Be Saved?*[1] Under the heading "What Keeps God from Saving Whom He Desires to Save?" he asks, "What are we to say of the fact that God desires something that in fact does not happen?" He then follows with these two paragraphs:

1. Piper, *Does God Desire*.

> God wills not to save all, even though he "desires" that all be saved, because there is something else that he wills or desires more, which would be lost if he exerted his sovereign power to save all.... [B]oth the Reformed and the Arminians affirm two wills in God when they ponder deeply over 1 Timothy 2:4.... Both can say that God wills for all to be saved. And when queried *why* all are not saved, both the Reformed and the Arminians answer the same: because God is committed to something even more valuable than saving all.
>
> The difference between the Reformed and the Arminians lies not in whether there are two wills in God, but in what they say this higher commitment is. What does God will more than saving all? The answer the Arminians give is that human self-determination and the possible resulting love relationship with God are more valuable than saving all people by sovereign, efficacious grace. The answer the Reformed give is that the greater value is the manifestation of the full range of God's glory in wrath and mercy (Rom 9:22–23) and the humbling of man so that he enjoys giving all credit to God for his salvation (1 Cor 1:29).

Perhaps if you have tucked away all that has been said in this book so far, you notice immediately the most glaring problem with Piper's claim. Notice he has treated "being saved" as something different from the "possible love relationship." Piper says that, for the Arminian, God limits *salvation* to only those who will have a *possible love relationship* with him, as if salvation is a state that is different from having a love relationship with God. Salvation, Piper must therefore presume, is merely the saving from destruction that God could apply irrespective of whether the people saved would actually desire a love relationship. That mistake is one embraced as well by some Arminians, but it cannot live in a Kinship Theology environment.

Note carefully the point being championed throughout this book: the entering into love relationship with God *is* what is meant by being saved. This idea is crucial in defining salvation. It is not merely that God holds out a prize of escaping the horrors of hell as a payoff to those who meet the condition of love relationship with him so as to receive the prize. It is rather that the embrace of God cannot—*cannot*—occur with those who choose not to enter into love relationship with God. Piper misses this point entirely (as do most Calvinists). The whole creative purpose of human existence is for love relationship with God. By definition, God cannot force—coerce—love and have it remain love. So God never throttles back on his desire for all to be saved, that is, come into this love relationship. He remains the God of *infinite* love, something Calvinists cannot claim if they actually understand what *infinite* means. It is the fatal choice of humans who reject him that causes the ultimately eternal separation. It is not just that God *won't* embrace those who will not engage in love relationship; it is that he *cannot* embrace them and remain God—a God whose essence necessarily is truth, goodness, and beauty. There is no *choice* in the matter whether to save or not to save, as if God could embrace a relationship with a creature that was not a love relationship. God doesn't choose not to save because he'd rather have love (as Piper implies). Salvation *is* the love embrace of God for which he calls out longingly, lovingly, *consistently* to all. The only reason a love relationship fails to eventuate is not that God pulls the reins to limit his infinite love. Rather, it is that the unregenerate person refuses to give of himself or herself, which is part of the definition of love.

As discussed in chapters 8 and 18, the wrath of God is real and terrifying. But it is not the violent eruption from a heart of hate. It is the turning away of God from rejecters when there is no longer hope. Piper's claim—that God chooses to withdraw love because he has an innate desire to show wrath—is not an apples-to-apples comparison to Kinship theology. Piper fails to demonstrate a rationale for the monstrous thought that God's will to show anger is greater than the expression of his infinite love.

Wrath is not an innate attribute of God's essence, even what we may call righteous wrath. As we did in chapter 1, in hoping to understand who our God is, we need to imagine who he is apart from all else—before the world and its fall and even Satan's rebellion. When there was nothing else, was wrath part of God's character, demanding to be expressed as his love was? It is a gross misunderstanding to think that God had to create sin because he needed to show how much he hated it. If that were the case, it is an equally gross misunderstanding to think God can't go on in love without selecting by default certain ones to be crushed in a necessary demonstration of his rage.

Again, as mentioned in chapter 12 in reference to Jonathan Edwards, even if Piper were right about the necessity of God's showing off his anger (and I cannot emphasize enough that Piper is *not* right in holding that incoherent concept), God had, according to Piper, *already shown* the fullness of his wrath. On Piper's website, desiringgod.org, an article states, "There, at Golgotha, our Savior drained God's cup of burning anger down to the dregs. God poured out his wrath, full strength, undiluted, onto his Son."[2] Note the seriousness of this inconsistency. Piper argues that God chooses not to save because he must have the opportunity to manifest his wrath. Yet, according to Piper, God already did manifest his wrath at Calvary. If the manifestation

---

2. Lee, "The Cup."

of wrath at Calvary *fully* satisfied God's wrath for all chosen to be saved (as Piper asserts), why didn't that display include the wrath against all humans ever and thus satisfactorily fulfill Piper's claim that God needed to display his wrath?

Simply put, if the wrath was already completely and fully demonstrated on Jesus, why does Piper continue to argue that God cannot choose all to be saved because he still needs to manifest his wrath *again* on others? Was the demonstration of wrath on Jesus, described on Piper's website as "full strength, undiluted," not enough? What, then, makes it enough? The shifting sand of this foundation for why God was right in choosing only some to save is not something on which to build a theology.

UNIVERSALISM'S QUICKSAND

Universalism is a nice thought, but unfortunately its hope can't be sustained, either. Universalism, the idea that everyone ever born will at some point become an eternal child of God, depends on one of two scenarios. One scenario is for God simply to make it happen. But, of course, as we've argued several times now, God's forcing it to happen is just as impossible in the world of universalism as it is for Calvinism. Creation's purpose was and is for everlasting love relationship, and true love, by definition, cannot be coerced. If God would force the situation (either for universalism's entirety or for Calvinism's subset), he might well end up with everlasting relationship, but it would not be a relationship of love. No amount of semantic juggling can alter the definition of love away from including the free giving of self. Controlling minds is simply not within the scope of God's idea of love as it is for a brainwashing kidnapper.

The abduction of women by men is an abominable evil. The attempt of these men, craving love, to twist by force the minds of their captives toward loving devotion is also repulsive, *even if they succeed*. What possible praise could we then have for our God if he resorted to such a practice to ensure development of his own love community? Even if the kidnapped, brainwashed believer would be unaware of the coercion imposed, God would still know, and thus he would be at odds with his nature of operating only in truth, goodness, and beauty.

The other, more prevalent solution for universalists is that opportunity in this life does not end all opportunity. Could it be that the chance to appreciate and accept God's gift continues after the grave—after physical death? The Bible seems to argue against that. Of the numerous passages that speak of hell's destruction, perhaps the one picture that illustrates best the finality of opportunity for salvation is the parable of the rich man and Lazarus found in Luke 16:19–31. The story depicts a rich man and a beggar who die. The beggar goes to Abraham's bosom, a place of comfort and hope. The rich man goes to a place of torment. A few features in the parable seem to indicate that a second chance at salvation is not plausible:

1. *No change despite desire*—The rich man longs for the comfort of the saved, crying out to Abraham for relief, yet no change to his suffering is provided.

2. *Impossibility of crossing to blessing*—The rich man is told that a great chasm exists between Abraham's bosom and the hell in which the rich man is located so that "those who want to pass over from here to you cannot; neither can those from there cross over to us." The crossing over from hell to God is unachievable.

3. *Warning required during life*—In his concern for his brothers, the rich man appears to realize he himself has no more chance. He wants Lazarus to go back to the physically alive to warn his brothers before they reach this same dreadful place. The need for warning before they get there confirms the fact that no change can take place after they arrive.

Of course, universalists lump this parable in with similar passages as merely stories and instances of urging the living to be saved, not as God's arguments against the notion that people can subsequently be saved. However, I think a more reasonable reaction to this parable along with other verses warning that people are appointed "to die once—and after this, judgment" is that there is no longer any hope for a change of heart.

As mentioned in the early chapters of this book (chapters 2, 4, 5, 6), life, in ultimate and lasting form, is not mere animation but a *relationship* with God. Death is the opposite—ultimate and lasting *separation* from God. Further, we noted in the chapters of Part 2 that an aspect of the brokenness of the fall was reversing the role humans in their spirits had originally held: dominance over their physical essence devolved to a role of subservience to that now-cursed essence.

Therefore, a person's physical death means something more than his or her spirit's merely moving on to another opportunity. It is the conclusion of the opportunity to control with his or her mind the operation of the body—his or her allotted portion of shared physical essence. With the end of that opportunity, the guilty spirit has no wherewithal to influence his or her cursed flesh for God. In death, the guilty spirit, now completely dominated by the cursed physical essence, merely awaits the judgment.

This meaning of physical death helps us understand even more the glorious victory Jesus won at the cross. His spirit was not guilty. He never allowed the cursed physical to influence the activity of his spirit in life. He was led always and only by God. Therefore, at his physical death, when his spirit separated from his allotted portion of cursed physical essence, he was able—on the basis of the purity (sinlessness) of his spirit—to return to that body, to seize control, to drive out the curse, and to bring the whole of his being—body and spirit—to God. Only Christ could do that, and he could do that only by the perfection of his spirit—something that no other human ever was or could be. The point of conquering death at the cross and resurrection is precisely that physical death could not be conquered by any other human in any other way.

We who now claim Christ are deemed saved because we have in this life regarded these bodies of ours dead (Romans 8:10) and consider ourselves to be in Christ—in his redeemed body. That is our assurance of salvation from judgment—the fact that our forgiven spirits unite with Christ's resurrected body as whole beings of purity to stand before God now. The opportunity, then, for life, for relationship with God, must occur prior to the loss of spirit control—that forever unification with the curse that ensues at physical death.

THE GOODNESS OF GOD

"Then the One seated on the throne said, 'Look! I am making everything new'" (Revelation 21:5). The return of Jesus marks the dawn of the new creation. It is new because the curse is removed. It is the culmination of the redemption story—God through Christ taking back the physical essence of his image bearers that had been imprisoned in separation from God. When will that day occur?

Christians long for the day. We cry out with John, "Amen! Come, Lord Jesus!" (Revelation 22:20b). But that day begins with a heaviness. In 2 Thessalonians 1:7–10, Paul tells us that the day of revelation of the Lord Jesus includes vengeance by Christ "on those who don't know God and on those who don't obey the gospel of our Lord Jesus. These will pay the penalty of eternal destruction from the Lord's presence and from His glorious strength." So our call for Christ to come quickly is a call also to hasten the approach of that destruction. Still, "the sufferings of this present time are not worth comparing with the glory that is going to be revealed to us" (Romans 8:18). Even creation itself—the physical essence we've talked so much about through this book—"eagerly waits with anticipation for God's sons to be revealed." Why not get on with it? For what is God waiting?

The infinite heart of God waits, I believe, for all those who could possibly come to him. While the future has not yet occurred, God does know his creation infinitely well. God knows the minds and hearts of all those living. He knows their sorrows, their likes, their loves, their inclinations, what excites them, what repulses them, to what they are attracted, and to what they pass by in indifference. And he knows those things to an infinite degree. While there remains even one person here in this world who has not yet embraced God's presentation of his truth, goodness, and beauty—but God, in his infinite, intimate knowledge of possibilities for that person, knows that he or she may still—I believe God will wait for that person, working in the condition of this world to bring about the opportunity for reconciliation.

The downward spiral of sin, however, in this cursed existence is powerful. It has held the hearts of the selfishly unmoved for centuries. Despite the postmillennialists' desperate hope, that the world will eventually walk away from sin, Jesus pronounced, "Lawlessness will multiply, the love of many will grow cold" (Matthew 24:12). And so, God waits. He waits until there is no one, based on his knowledge of possibilities, who will respond to him. He will wait until he sees "that man's wickedness [is] widespread on the earth and that *every* scheme his mind [thinks is] nothing but evil all the time" (Genesis 6:5). Then the end will come.

The story of Noah images the end times. It explains for us God's motivation for not having redeemed all creation the moment Jesus rose in uncorrupted flesh. The waiting then and ever since has been because God is not willing for any to perish. Just as in Noah's time, when Noah alone stood righteous in the Genesis 5 line of image bearers who called on God, God will wait for all those who will come to him to stand before him, forgiven in faith. Then Christ will return to redeem the rest of physical creation of which his body had been the firstfruits (1 Corinthians 15:20). That will mark the atonement's end.

20

Heaven!

And that with everlasting peace,
Joy, and felicity,
From this time forth they shall increase
Unto eternity.

—John Bunyan, from "Of Heaven"

"Night will no longer exist,
and people will not need lamplight or sunlight,
because the Lord God will give them light.
And they will reign forever and ever."

—Revelation 22:5

Heaven! The word sparks hope, but perhaps sometimes for the wrong reasons. To some, heaven simply means escape—*I've made a mess of my life here; a redo where nothing could go wrong would be great!* Or perhaps, we imagine, along with the revivalist songs, that "this world is not our home, we're just a passing through." But is our treasure laid up somewhere beyond the blue? Or is our treasure something richer, deeper, and, perhaps, a little closer to home?

In discussing the end of the atonement implementation in the last chapter, I necessarily spoke of an ending that would come about precisely because, for those left on earth, there would be no more potential embracers of God's offer of love relationship. That is a decidedly sad point for those rejecters. For this reason, postmillennialists have attempted to characterize amillennialism as a doctrine of pessimism.[1] I favor an amillennial approach, and therefore, I disagree with the postmillennialists who call my understanding pessimistic while they think of theirs as optimistic. I think they misunderstand by about 180 degrees.

Briefly, the postmillennialists call "golden" the hope that our present age will eventually see a vast majority of those living on earth at the time having become Christians. Yet despite the glories the Bible speaks of (and amillennialists hope for) in redemption—such as a new heaven and new earth, the absence of evil, the immediate in-the-flesh presence of Christ, tears wiped away, and the fully realized love relationship of God's community—postmillennialists include *none of that* in what they characterize as their optimistic golden-age hope. Their *optimism* is realized in a period that still contains death, cursed physical essence, unbelievers, and, therefore, the continuing fallen nature of humanity. Conversely, amillennialism's hope is fixed on the return of our Lord with his unending truth, goodness, and beauty in a community of fully realized love relationship without a whisper still of evil in us or around us, which is the so-called "pessimism" I am thrillingly optimistic about!

In opposition to the postmillennialists' attempts to belittle the glories of the amillennialists' hope stands the most optimistic expression of hope there is: God will not limit his love! His arms of embrace continue reaching out as long as there exists the possibility for any potential recipient to come running. That is good news! That is the success of the gospel and the Spirit who absolutely will save all—*ALL*—who will come to God. As C. S. Lewis says, "Joy is the serious business of heaven."[2] Not one less person in this scenario comes to Christ than in the hoped-for all-at-once numbers of postmillennialism.

---

1. Amillennialism, postmillennialism, and premillennialism (along with further breakdowns) are doctrines of eschatology regarding the return of Christ in association with the millennium (1000 years) mentioned in Revelation 20 (and recognized without the term in Ezekiel, Isaiah, and elsewhere). Premillennialists believe Christ returns in a Rapture event after which he reigns for 1000 years on this earth prior to the redemption of creation and transformation to the state of new heaven and new earth. Postmillennialism calls for an inexact number of years (though figuratively projected as 1000 in the Bible) that occurs before Christ returns at the end of the current age. It is characterized by an increasing percentage of the population's becoming saved until almost all are saved. Christ will then return in this "golden age" to a world that is almost entirely Christian. Amillennialism also sees the 1000 years mentioned in the Bible as figurative but representing the entirety of the current age between the advents of Christ. Christ's return in judgment and reward will mark the end of this age, and the redemptive transformation into new heaven and new earth will immediately take place.

2. Lewis, *Letters*, 93.

WHAT OF THE LOST?

What, then, happens to unbelievers as atonement finishes when Christ comes back to redeem all physical creation? I have mentioned that physical creation is the one essence that we all share as humans. That one essence was cursed at the fall. All physical creation was under that curse, and all physical creation groans (Romans 8) in this age, waiting for the redemption to be brought by Christ. But when Christ does return and redeems *all* physical creation, what does that mean for the rejecters—those who will not give themselves to love relationship with God?

Remember, to be human means to be a multiple-in-one being of body and personhood (physical and spirit). Without that union, the idea of being human is lost. So, when we say that Christ will, at his return, redeem all physical creation, that means no bit of unredeemed physical essence is left for those humans who would not, in the minds and wills of their spirits, embrace God. Thus, expelled from physical creation, their very identification as humans is lost. Spirits alone, wrenched from physical essence connection, are the remains—the ashes, if you will, of these former image bearers. C. S. Lewis puts it this way:

> In all our experience, however, the destruction of one thing means the emergence of something else. Burn a log, and you have gases, heat, and ash. To have been a log means now being those three things. If soul can be destroyed, must there not be a state *having been* a human soul? And is not that, perhaps, the state which is equally well described as torment, destruction, and privation?[3]

Lewis equates the destruction the Bible speaks of for lost image bearers as the end of their humanity—the end of their beings as humans. He does so, however (as we can see even in the brief portion quoted above), while still defending the continuation of whatever that burned-up, ashed soul looks like, albeit not human. While I have tremendous respect for Lewis as a thinker, I think his reasoning stopped a bit too early on this point.

He begins his statement about continued essence with the phrase "In all our experience." However, all our experience has been with the hand of God actively engaged in his creation, supporting his creation. Ultimate death, as I have repeated several times now, is total separation from God. In our apologetic reasoning, Christians often say that God is the only independent being. All else, being or non-being, is dependent on him for its very existence. If God withdraws—turns away, lets go, gives over—*completely*,

---

3. Lewis, *Problem of Pain*, 125.

existence is not conceivable. How that actually happens—the spirit's departing from physical essence to become . . . nothing—is impossible to say. How that is illustrated, however, is found in our last book of the canon.

> Then the sea gave up its dead, and Death and Hades gave up their dead; all were judged according to their works. Death and Hades were thrown into the lake of fire. This is the second death, the lake of fire. And anyone not found written in the book of life was thrown into the lake of fire. (Revelation 20:13–15).

The lake of fire—that second (final) death—is the complete loss of God's outstretched arm of truth, goodness, and beauty. It is a horrible, terrifying scene, but it does contain an overriding sense of completion. In this scene, all rejection—opposition, sin itself—is gone forever. The finality of completion is shown in that Death, too, is cast into this fire. If death means separation from God, and Death itself becomes separated from God, it logically means that there exists nothing that remains in any kind of condition separated from God. When the Bible cries out that Death is no more, it means there is nothing separated anymore. It is not merely in a concealed hole just outside the boundaries of God's realm; rather, it is summarily gone.

So, then, our eternal state is not one of mourning and grief or any lingering sadness for perpetually tormented rejecters, kept alive by God's sustaining hand solely for the purpose of torture. Again, an image like that could have nothing to do with a God of truth, goodness, and beauty who is necessarily and always infinite love.

WILL EARTH BE OUR HOME?

That state of eternal bliss could not be this world, could it? We seem to sing that song with fervor: "This world is not my home!" A surface reading of the Bible surely seems to indicate as much. The world is a bad place—"You adulterous people! Don't you know that friendship with the world is hostility toward God? So whoever wants to be the friend of the world becomes the enemy of God" (James 4:4); and "For everything in the world—the lust of the flesh, the lust of the eyes, and the pride in one's possessions—is not from the Father, but is from the world" (1 John 2:16). Even Jesus wanted to disassociate himself from it: "'You are from below,' he told them, 'I am from above. You are of this world; I am not of this world'" (John 8:23), and "'My kingdom is not of this world'" (John 18:36).

So we wait to leave because "we do not have an enduring city here; instead, we seek the one to come" (Hebrews 13:14). "Our citizenship is in heaven, and we eagerly wait for a Savior from there, the Lord Jesus Christ" (Philippians 3:20). That certainly makes sense if "the heavens will pass away with a loud noise, the elements will burn and be dissolved, and the earth and the works on it will be disclosed [or, burned]" (2 Peter 3:10). God will fashion for us "a new heaven and a new earth; for the first heaven and the first earth had passed away" (Revelation 21:1).

When we read these passages with our eyes fixed only on cosmic disruption, we lose sight of the greater story revealed throughout the Bible. This world and all physical existence was cursed, cursed by human sin that originated in our father Adam, who idolized the physical over God. He lost our dominion so that this cursed physical essence calls and pulls and tempts toward sin. We were slaves to this sin until Jesus in his atonement added to our forgiveness his resurrected physical essence; in clinging to the redemption of his body, we have hope for the earth's redemption that includes our new bodies. But note that *redemption* is our hope, not a discarding or destruction of what is here to create something new. It is this world "set free from the bondage to decay" (Romans 8:21). Though the current condition of physical creation is cursed and something to be resisted because of its pull toward sin, it is nevertheless this world that will undergo the refining fire Peter imagines, which will transform it to newness of life (relationship with God) by the redeeming power of Christ. "God's plan is not to abandon this world, the world which he said at its beginning was 'very good.' Rather, he intends to remake it. And when he does he will raise all his people to new bodily life to live in it. That is the promise of the Christian gospel."[4]

Heaven is not a physical place. God is spirit; his existence is not confined to physical location. While the Bible talks much about the physical as it describes God with anthropomorphisms in scenes of throne room (Revelation 4–5) and city (Revelation 21), it does so to help us in conceiving it. But heaven is not to be confused with a *place* where God lives so that, when we die, we will join him *there*. Heaven, rather, is the presence of God. When the Christian dies, we may say that he or she goes to heaven, but we must realize that it is only in the sense that the spirit goes to be with Christ and with God.

We, however, are humans, and as human, we by definition have a physical essence. For Christians who die, their physical essence is found in Christ, an exchange already transacted at conversion as we consider ourselves "dead to sin but alive to God in Christ Jesus" (Romans 6:11). Christ's resurrected physical body is the only portion of creation's physical essence already transformed into newness of life—that is, without the curse and

---

4. Wright, *Simply Christian*, 219.

with God). When Christ returns, he will complete the redemption process, transforming all creation from cursed existence apart from God to newness of life without curse and in the embrace of God.

Therefore, we shouldn't expect to be living in some alternate reality—a different quasi-spirit place for eternity to come. And we certainly won't be strumming harps while sitting on clouds (despite the imagery of Revelation 15:2). Physical reality will change only as much as the curse is lifted. I don't mean by that to sound as if it won't change very much. Certainly, without sin's curse, it will be radically changed. However, we will still have rocks and trees and sky and sea. Physical reality will remain as the essence we humans share as we individually conduct our everlasting lives of love communion with God and each other.

COULD SIN HAPPEN AGAIN?

The Bible's statements about our eternal state seem sure:

1. No more sadness—"He will wipe away every tear from their eyes" (Revelation 21:4).
2. No more pain—"Pain will exist no longer" (Revelation 21:4).
3. Life with God—"I will give the victor the right to eat from the tree of life" (Revelation 2:7). This right was denied to Adam and Eve following the fall, but not to us alive through Christ.
4. No separation from God—"The victor will never be harmed by the second death" (Revelation 2:11).

But since this book has from the start been asking *how* questions concerning the atonement, we can't stop now at the end. *How*, then, will it be possible never to depart from God? How do we know we will never sin again as Adam did, choosing creation over God? Over and over, part of the argument of this book was that God does not coerce; God does not force himself on us. What is there, then, to stop us from wanting our particular *Eves* (whatever physical-essence idols we may lay our faith and hope desires on) so much that we choose again physical essence over God's truth, goodness, and beauty?

First, let me make clear that I agree with both the Bible's above statements of fact and the firmness of its dogmatic stand. Those statements are not presented in Scripture as either mere desire or with qualification. The victors will not need to keep striving to keep the reward; the passages depict them as having won and receiving the trophies for the accomplishment.

The first step toward understanding the confidence Scripture projects in this regard is to recognize that our heavenly state and humanity's original Edenic state are not equal. After being formed from the ground and receiving God's breath of life, the *adam* was introduced not merely to a new world but to a newly cognizant existence. The simplest of knowable things—ideas as well as objects—must have bombarded and amazed the *adam*. Even the ability to *communicate* with God might have had to be learned, although I wonder at whether some innate creative help had been given him for that purpose. The point is that full knowledge of relationship and love were as yet mere whispers in Adam's and Eve's hearts and minds at their beginning. So, too, must have been their knowledge of God—who he was to the universe and who he was to them in particular. We, who are armed with the revelatory gift of our millennia of experiential knowledge with God, will move into our new heaven and earth more confident than Adam and Eve in that awareness. Even more, we have had a relational interchange through Christ in which the Holy Spirit of God actually dwells within us, testifying to our spirits that we are his children (Romans 8:16).

We must also remember that God designed the human spirit with a desire for truth, goodness, and beauty. Adam and Eve had barely begun learning to recognize the truth, goodness, and beauty surrounding them when they made their false choices. We, who will enter our eternity with full revelatory knowledge of God's TGB, will constantly see and recognize its unending and abounding flow as we live our eternal lives in our love community, imaged for us as the river flowing from the throne of God at the start of Revelation 22. It is then not coercion but constant, full satisfaction for that for which our spirits long that keeps us. The infinite flow will never end, and we will therefore never experience want. That never-ending experience was God's purpose in engaging in this Covenant of Life with us from the beginning of creation.

CONCLUSION

So the record will be complete. Creation's purpose will be fulfilled. Did God know from before creation that his image bearers would fall? Certainly, God knew it could happen, and certainly, God, in his infinite character of love, was prepared for love to win. The atonement plan, merging God's heart of mercy with his justice of operating in truth, goodness, and beauty, accomplished both forgiveness for the guilt of the spirit and redemption for the cursed physical essence so that we, who come to God believing in him, through Christ live in his glory forever!

Appendix

Kinship Theology

KINSHIP THEOLOGY IS THE theological view that God interacts with his creation always and only on the basis of love relationship. While the Bible insists God is love, we should not conclude a different God based on passages of his wrath. With love relationship as his basis, God embraces those committed to his essence and turns away from those rejecting relationship. His truth, goodness, and beauty abound in his embrace, but their absence when he turns away leaves destruction in their wake.

KT'S SEVEN FOUNDATIONAL PRINCIPLES:

#1: **God** (*Theism*): God is the one eternal, infinite, self-conscious being. He exists as one essence of truth, goodness, and beauty in three persons, functioning according to his essence in faith, hope, and love, with love as his principal attribute.

#2: **Creation** (*Anthropology*): Creation is God's conception and formation of all that is not God. Creation is divided into (1) the heavenly host (angelic beings) and (2) image-bearing beings along with all the physical reality supporting them. God created for the purpose of everlasting love relationship with his image bearers.

#3: **The Fall** (*Hamartiology*): When pressed to decide, Adam chose relationship with physical creation rather than relationship with God because he thought it would better satisfy his own passion for truth, goodness, and beauty. By his choice, Adam fell from covenant relationship with God both by (1) lading his spirit with the guilt of that sin and (2) causing his essence, physical creation, to be cursed. God had given Adam and Eve possession and rulership of physical creation. By his choice, Adam reversed roles, positioning physical creation as his god, leading to the curse and his own spirit's subjection to that cursed flesh.

#4: **Atonement** (*Christology*): To restore his image bearers to their created purpose in love relationship, God planned his atonement. Restoration requires forgiveness, the removal of the two-part obstruction to resumed relationship. God removes the first part—individual guilt of sinful activity—by his own mercy extended in grace to those who desire relationship with him based on his essence. God will remove the second part—the curse of human essence—at Christ's return when Jesus applies the redemption he won in death and resurrection (and of which he is firstfruits) to all physical creation, resulting in new bodies, new heavens, and new earth. Jesus accomplished redemption by first becoming human, an individual spirit entwined with a body of the shared and cursed human physical essence. Unlike all other humans, Jesus's spirit never succumbed to the evil influence of the flesh. Therefore, without guilt of sin, Jesus put his cursed body to physical death in fulfillment of its curse. His guiltless spirit, being holy and undefiled, reclaimed (redeemed) his body from its separation in death, bringing it cleansed to life (renewed and sinless relationship with God). At his return, Jesus will bring all physical essence to that same renewed life with God.

#5: **Salvation** (*Soteriology*): God elects to restore image bearers on the basis of faith (also called *faith electionism*). God offers mercy and redemption to the world of sinful humans to restore his love relationship; however, since love relationship is the only possible result of salvation, God absolves (forgives guilt and redeems from the curse) only those who desire that relationship.

Placing trust in God as Savior means believing he alone is the source of truth, goodness, and beauty; he alone can rescue from curse-induced death; and he alone provides hope of everlasting life through the love relationship based on his essence. God has provided to everyone the necessary revelation of who he is so that everyone may believe, rendering everyone without excuse (Romans 1:18–20). Without faith, it is impossible to receive salvation because without faith, it is impossible to please God (Hebrews 11:6). No such thing as "coerced love" exists; love by definition is a free giving of self. Thus, image bearers must believe as condition for God's reconciliation. Yet God's salvation is his through and through. From the initial revelation of himself, to his atonement made possible, to his application to the believer, God provides salvation.

#6: Last Things (*Eschatology*): The restoration result necessarily includes full redemption—the application of Christ's victory removing the curse and thus restoring all physical creation to its original and intended place. In this redemption, Christians realize their hope (Romans 8:23b–24a). Because all physical essence is restored together, the judgment of the wicked, the gaining of our new bodies, and the start of the new heavens and earth must all occur together immediately at the coming of Christ (Titus 2:13).

#7: Community (*Ecclesiology*): The kingdom of the world presumes authority and hierarchy to control behavior. Image bearers of Christ's kingdom express in love (John 13:34) God's truth, goodness, and beauty held as a matter of the heart (Jeremiah 31:33). The restored community strengthens each other in relationship. We uphold the oneness of our essence by submitting selfish desire in favor of the good of the whole. We reciprocally apply our respective God-given abilities for the benefit of our individual vulnerabilities. By doing so, we knit our lives in fulfillment, satisfaction, and joy.

Bibliography

Anstey, Martin. *The Romance of Bible Chronology.* Vol. 2, *Chronological Tables.* New York: Marshall Brothers, 1913.
Beale, G. K. *A New Testament Biblical Theology: The Unfolding of the Old Testament in the New.* Grand Rapids, MI: Baker Academic, 2011.
Beeke, Joel. "The Calvinist's Ultimate Concern." Ligonier Ministries. June 27, 2016. https://www.ligonier.org/blog/calvinists-ultimate-concern/.
Bishop, Robert C. et al. *Understanding Scientific Theories of Origins: Cosmology, Geology, and Biology in Christian Perspective.* Downers Grove, IL: InterVarsity, 2018.
Boyd, Gregory A. *Cross Vision: How the Crucifixion of Jesus Makes Sense of Old Testament Violence.* Minneapolis, MN: Fortress, 2017.
Bunsen, Christian Karl Josias. *God in History.* Vol. 3. Translated by Susanna Winkworth. London: Longmans, Green, and Co., 1870.
Calvin, John. *Institutes of the Christian Religion.* Translated by Henry Beveridge. Peabody, MA: Hendrickson, 2008.
———. "Quotes from John Calvin." Accessed July 23, 2020. http://www.angelfire.com/ok5/quatsch7/Calvinquote.html.
"Council of Trent," University of Oregon. Accessed April 30, 2020. https://pages.uoregon.edu/sshoemak/323/texts/Trent%20on%20Justification.htm.
Edwards, Jonathan. "Sinners in the Hands of an Angry God." Accessed June 20, 2020. http://www.jonathan-edwards.org/Sinners.pdf
———. *The Works of Jonathan Edwards: Volume II–IV* (Revised). Edited by Anthony Uyl. Revised and Corrected by Edward Hickman. Carlisle, PA: The Banner of Truth Trust, 1834.
Enns, Peter. 2012. *The Evolution of Adam: What the Bible Does and Doesn't Say about Human Origins.* Grand Rapids, MI: Brazos, 2012.
———. "A Thought about Easter and the Bizarre Christian Faith. Pete Enns. Accessed May 11, 2020. https://peteenns.com/a-thought-about-easter-and-the-bizarre-christian-faith/.
Erickson, Millard J. *Christian Theology,* 2nd ed. Grand Rapids, MI: Baker, 1998.
"Forgiveness." Psychology Today. Accessed May 18, 2020. https://www.psychologytoday.com/us/basics/forgiveness.
Grudem, Wayne. *Systematic Theology: An Introduction to Biblical Doctrine.* Grand Rapids, MI: Zondervan, 1994.

Hardin, Michael. "Out of the Fog: New Horizons for Atonement Theory." In *Stricken by God?*, edited by Brad Jersak and Michael Hardin, 54–76. Grand Rapids, MI: William B. Eerdmans, 2007.

———. "Preface." *Stricken by God?*, edited by Brad Jersak and Michael Hardin, –. Grand Rapids, MI: William B. Eerdmans, 2007.

Jefford, Clayton N., ed. *The Epistle to Diognetus (with the Fragment of Quadratus): Introduction, Text, and Commentary.* Oxford, U.K.: Oxford University Press, 2013.

Jersak, Brad. "Nonviolent Identification and the Victory of Christ." In *Stricken by God?*, edited by Brad Jersak and Michael Hardin, 18–53. Grand Rapids, MI: William B. Eerdmans, 2007.

Keller, Timothy. *Generous Justice: How God's Grace Makes Us Just.* New York: Riverhead, 2010.

Lee, Steven. "The Cup Consumed for Us." Desiring God. April 7, 2014. https://www.desiringgod.org/articles/the-cup-consumed-for-us/.

Lewis, C. S. *The Four Loves.* London: Geoffrey Bles, 1960.

———. *Letters to Malcolm: Chiefly on Prayer.* San Diego: Harvest, 1964.

———. *Mere Christianity.* New York: HarperCollins, 2001.

———. *The Problem of Pain.* New York: Macmillan, 1962.

Luther, Martin. *Commentary on the Epistle to the Galatians.* 1535. http://www.gutenberg.org/files/1549/1549-h/1549-h.htm.

MacArthur, John. *One Perfect Life: The Complete Story of the Lord Jesus.* Nashville, TN: Thomas Nelson, 2012.

McKnight, Scot. *The Hum of Angels.* Colorado Springs: Waterbrook, 2017.

Moreland, J. P., and Kai Nielsen. *Does God Exist: The Great Debate.* Nashville, TN: Thomas Nelson, 1990.

Mueller, John Theodore. *Christian Dogmatics.* St. Louis: Concordia, 1938. https://archive.org/stream/Mueller/Mueller_djvu.txt.

Murray, John. *Redemption Accomplished and Applied.* Grand Rapids, MI: William B. Eerdmans, 1955.

Perkins, Pheme. "The Letter to the Ephesians: Introduction, Commentary, and Reflections." In *The New Interpreter's Bible Commentary*, 10. Nashville, TN: Abingdon, 2015.

Piper, John. *Does God Desire All to Be Saved.* Wheaton, IL: Crossway, 2013.

———. "Rebuilding Some Basics of Bethlehem: The Centrality of the Glory of God." Desiring God. November 4, 2009. http://www.desiringgod.org/articles/rebuilding-some-basics-of-bethlehem-the-centrality-of-the-glory-of-god.

Pitchford, Nathan. "Is Penal substitution Biblical." OpenAirOutreach.com. March 17, 2008. https://openairoutreach.proboards.com/thread/3558/penal-substitution-biblical

Reymond, Robert L. *A New Systematic Theology of the Christian Faith.* Nashville, TN: Thomas Nelson, 1998.

Robertson, O. Palmer. *The Christ of the Covenants.* Phillipsburg, NJ: Presbyterian and Reformed, 1980.

Sproul, R. C. *The Holiness of God.* Carol Stream, IL: Tyndale House, 2000.

Spurgeon, James A. 1861. "Particular Redemption." Spurgeon Gems. 1861. http://www.spurgeongems.org/tulip-3-jas.pdf.

Stewart, James Stuart. 2012. *Man in Christ.* New York: Harper & Row.

Storms, Sam. 2007. Chosen for Life: The Case for Divine Election. Wheaton, IL: Crossway.

Thayer, Joseph H. *Thayer's Greek Lexicon*. Blue Letter Bible. Accessed May 23, 2020. https://www.blueletterbible.org/lang/Lexicon/Lexicon.cfm?strongs=G4893&t=KJV.
Wright, N. T. *Jesus and the Victory of God*. Minneapolis, MN: Fortress, 1996.
———. *The Kingdom New Testament*. New York: Harper-Collins, 2011.
———. *The Resurrection of the Son of God*. Minneapolis, MN: Fortress, 2003.
———. *Simply Christian: Why Christianity Makes Sense*. New York: Harper-Collins, 2006.

www.ingramcontent.com/pod-product-compliance
Lightning Source LLC
Chambersburg PA
CBHW062024220426
43662CB00010B/1467